T0208261

HEALTH THROUGH THE PSALMS

TO DO GOD'S WILL

MAUREEN GREER

authorHOUSE®

AuthorHouse™
1663 Liberty Drive
Bloomington, IN 47403
www.authorhouse.com
Phone: 833-262-8899

Published by AuthorHouse 02/22/2024

ISBN: 979-8-8230-0188-5 (sc)
ISBN: 979-8-8230-0187-8 (hc)
ISBN: 979-8-8230-0189-2 (e)

Library of Congress Control Number: 2023903534

Print information available on the last page.

The information, ideas, and suggestions in this book are not intended as a substitute for professional medical advice. Before following any suggestions contained in this book, you should consult your personal physician. Neither the author nor the publisher shall be liable or responsible for any loss or damage allegedly arising as a consequence of your use or application of any information or suggestions in this book.

This book is printed on acid-free paper.

Scripture quotations marked KJV are from the Holy Bible, King James Version (Authorized Version). First published in 1611. Quoted from the KJV Classic Reference Bible, Copyright © 1983 by The Zondervan Corporation.

DEDICATION

To

My Husband Dana

A man of integrity who has lived and worked diligently to provide peace and safety for his family because he knows that a good name is to be chosen rather than great riches.

To Our Children

Reese
Who knocked me over at his birth with the
overwhelm of love; I am still recovering.
Your strength will never match our love for you.
Always know that God's love and strength
are far greater than yours or ours.

Gracie
Who gave me the freshness of gratitude with her
health scare at age 3 and now brings more delight and
accountability to me than I could ever have imagined.
Remember, a kindhearted woman gains respect.

MaryClare
Who, at her birth, provided the first real experience for me
to be freed from the oppression of fear, never to return. You
are a constant source of encouragement and wisdom.
Do not grow weary in your well-doing.

Paul

Who possesses humility even greater than his strength while
he encourages anyone and everyone along the way.
Never forget that humility is your friend.

Magdalene

Who has given me experiences that none of the
others could have. Your insight even as a youngster
has brought challenge, clarity and comfort.
The future pages you write will be a treasure.

Mollie

Who is the ultimate image of peace and love. God has given
me the highest and most honored position as your mother
and yet I did absolutely nothing to deserve or earn it.
Without words, your life speaks volumes.

To Grandma and Grandpa Hart, my parents,
Who diligently tended to their farm, fields and
family and now at age 89 and 92
enjoy their own Pasture of Peace
together.

CONTENTS

DYNAMO Health and Wellness
Better Brain and Body

Health through the Psalms
Twelve-Week Program

INTRODUCTION TO MY PASSION

Hello, everyone! Welcome to my twelve-week Health through the Psalms program. I am so glad that you have decided to join me and that you are ready to let God's Word help you in your health. I am passionately diligent to promote better brain, body, and beliefs in anyone while using scripture and sound health guidance. None of this is medical advice, but rather it is my effort to do good, to seek peace, and to pursue it by using scripture and providing information to you so that you might be encouraged to see how the brain, body, and beliefs affect our overall health and how these are uniquely connected in all individuals.

God calls all of us and knows us by name. He created us. He knows the number of hairs on our head. He loves us and has given everything for life to us. He sent His Son to us, to save us, to teach us, to carry our burdens, and to be our source of peace. He never intends for us to live in a state of oppression, of condemnation, of hopelessness, or of constant stress. His plan for us is peace through Him, because of Him, and for Him. This is the path of righteousness He has for us, for our complete being. This is for each individual in their brain, body, and beliefs. This is for the entire church body. This is for the world.

Yes, this path of righteousness is for everyone, but it must be present in us, His people, if we are going to be a light to the world. If we are depressed or oppressed, if we are ungrateful or selfish, if we are fighting or arguing, if we are tired or unmotivated, if we are unhealthy or unholy, how can we do His will? How can we fulfill the good works that He has prepared in advance for us to do if we never progress out of unhealthy or less than optimum conditions to be able to share, with compassion and understanding, both the truth of His love as well as what we have learned through and from the trials we have faced? In fact, if we have any stress or challenge that causes any part of our brain, body, or beliefs to be ill, we are not in a position to lead others, but rather we are in a position to be led.

I am not at all saying that our hardships, whether they be illness in our bodies, mental challenges, or spiritual setbacks, are going to prevent God from using us. Not at all. In fact, He might very well use us more during the lowest points of our lives. His strength is made perfect in our weakness. However, I don't think He wants us to dwell there. God wants us to have freedom. He wants us to have joy and satisfaction in Him. He wants to bring us to a spacious place to freely enjoy Him and others and to be able to embrace, encourage, challenge, and help others. Ultimately, He wants us to do His will, and loving Him and others is His will. However, even if He chooses to keep us in certain places despite our yearnings to be set free from them, we are assured that His peace will guard us. Storms do not need to destroy us unless God chooses to use them to give us final deliverance to Him.

This is why I so desire to bring this material to you. Calling it *material* is actually far from what it is. What follows is my deepest yearning and learning from a place of craving God's satisfaction, wisdom, peace, joy, acceptance, strength, and guidance, from a place of feelings of rejection, sadness, fear, concern, anxiety, struggle, and the desire to control and fix, and ultimately from a place of realizing how God's Word is related to health in my own brain, body, and beliefs. It represents years of research and personal study both for myself and my family, stemming from the realization that the world, the medical community, the food industry, the social guidance, and even many of the church leaders have been too overwhelmed to address or connect, not to mention to adequately help. This has prevented the church from offering trusted individuals to walk alongside those looking to them for guidance. It has prevented doctors from truly giving their clients what they need, and it has prevented the proper training of all practitioners. The principle is the connection of the brain to the body to the beliefs, or the connection of the body to the brain to the beliefs, or the connection of the beliefs to the brain to the body. All three matter.

Many individuals rely on just one thing or one person or one idea as the solution to their problem or dilemma. Just as our bodies need all of the parts to work together for the whole, and our church body needs all the members with different gifts to fulfill God's plan, we also need more than one aspect to influence our overall health. I believe the easiest way to say this is that we need to look at the brain, the body, and the beliefs of our entire person to tackle everything, whether it be fatigue, sickness, depression, poor relationships, financial concerns, poor job opportunities, family dilemmas, or even the celebration of a baby's birth. We must nourish all three areas of our complete person because these are all related in every individual, and they affect one another uniquely. They all matter.

It is my strong opinion and belief—based on knowledge, research, scriptural study, and personal experience—that we cannot expect to have optimum health if we are not nourishing ourselves the way God intended. You might think I am talking about food. Well, at times, yes, I am definitely referring to food, and I will continue to without stopping. However, I propose to address the nourishment of other facets of our person, which include nourishing relationships, nourishing habits, nourishing mindsets, nourishing teachings on God's Word, nourishing reading, and all other kinds of nourishing inputs that come our way. Food is not the only nourishment we get, and while we usually nourish our own selves, our environment, unbeknownst to us, might nourish us without our cognitive awareness. The environment of what we see, hear, smell, feel, and touch certainly nourishes our complete being, but is this nourishment always beneficial for us, or is it harming us? These are the types of ideas I want to encourage you to analyze as we spend the next twelve weeks together. Please do not feel lectured to or judged; these are the questions I ask myself, sometimes with unwillingness to behave according to what I know would be good for me. When I refuse the wisdom of healthy choices, I weaken myself, I weaken my family, and I weaken the whole church. Think about that for a minute. If I am not at my personal optimum level of health in my brain, body, and beliefs, the whole church is affected. I judge myself here. I do not judge you, but I most adamantly want to encourage you. I yearn to awaken you to the same ideas and truths that challenge me and continue to keep my desire for God and His will, both for myself and everyone.

Think about what health really is and what health challenges any of us could have. Consider difficulties like poor sleep, undisciplined behavior, lack of forgiveness, addiction, financial irresponsibility, social oppression, or even fear. How are these related to each other? How are they related to your spiritual health? How are they related to what you think about? How are they related to what you hear and see? How are they related to the people who influence you? How are they related to your nourishment? In fact, how are they related to the inner workings of your own self that affect all of you? After all, how can you expect to sleep well if you are ingesting stimulating food and drink right before bed? How can you expect to be kind and patient with others if you have blood sugar spikes related to your intake of sugar and then experience a plummet that would make any of us "hangry" or rude or stressed? How can you have good relationships if you have never truly forgiven and decided to let things go but instead remember what that person did in the past?

We cannot truly have peace if something is awry. God wants us to have peace, and this peace comes from Him. However, we are able to influence His work in our lives by our choices. While it is the human condition that we cannot walk perfectly and that we will make mistakes, both willingly and unwillingly, God still commands us to follow Him, to obey Him, to learn of Him, to walk with Him, to love Him, and of course, to love others. We are not free to deviate from these principles. So I challenge you a bit further. If you have not given your Lord, the Almighty, the King of the Universe, the Author of your life, your heavenly Father, your Defender, your Stronghold, your Peace, and your Greatest Joy, the attention that is due Him, your own heart might be condemning you. I posit that this causes stress and a lack of peace, which affects every part of you—brain, body, and beliefs. In fact, this could be the cause of poor sleep, of stress eating, of disordered thinking, of chaos in your home, of your child's ability to learn, or even of your job performance. Everything matters. What we do in one area of our lives and how we behave is an indication of what we will do and how we will behave in other areas, or might do or be more tempted to do. Remember what Jesus said, "A little leaven leavens the whole lump." Only you can judge yourself, no one else can, but God knows all, and yet He forgives all; He redeems all. He has unfailing love for all.

Let's just look at one of my favorite psalms, which is actually not one of the twelve that are in this twelve-week program. Please read Psalm 34 with me:

Psalm 34

1   I will extol the Lord at all times; his praise will always be on my lips.
2   I will glory in the Lord; let the afflicted hear and rejoice.
3   Glorify the Lord with me; let us exalt his name together.
4   I sought the Lord, and he answered me; he delivered me from all my fears.
5   Those who look to him are radiant; their faces are never covered with shame.
6   This poor man called, and the Lord heard him; he saved him out of all his troubles.
7   The angel of the Lord encamps around those who fear him, and he delivers them.
8   Taste and see that the Lord is good; blessed is the one who takes refuge in him.
9   Fear the Lord, you his holy people, for those who fear him lack nothing.
10 The lions may grow weak and hungry, but those who seek the Lord lack no good thing.
11 Come, my children, listen to me; I will teach you the fear of the Lord.
12 Whoever of you loves life and desires to see many good days.
13 Keep your tongue from evil and your lips from telling lies.

14 Turn from evil and do good; seek peace and pursue it.

15 The eyes of the Lord are on the righteous, and his ears are attentive to their cry,

16 But the face of the Lord is against those who do evil, to blot out their name from the earth.

17 The righteous cry out, and the Lord hears them; he delivers them from all their troubles.

18 The Lord is close to the broken-hearted and saves those who are crushed in spirit.

19 The righteous person may have many troubles, but the Lord delivers him from them all;

20 He protects all his bones, not one of them will be broken.

21 Evil will slay the wicked; the foes of the righteous will be condemned.

22 The Lord will rescue his servants; no one who takes refuge in him will be condemned.

How absolutely beautiful and encouraging is God's Word! I love it. I delight in it. I treasure it. It nourishes me so much, and how passionately I desire this for *you*, for our church, and for the whole world. Just reading this psalm makes me feel better. I don't even want to take a sip of my coffee right now, and I really like my coffee (just gotta remember, not too much—moderation!). I feel hopeful. I feel happier. I feel loving and forgiving. I feel like God can use me right now. I feel so encouraged. Reader, please don't despair if you are not having this response. You must remember that I, without any hesitation, know and believe that God's Word is my salvation; it is my guide; it is my strength. I do not want to go through the day without it, but this is because I have developed a taste for it. I have nourished myself with it so much that it is my food and my counselor. It keeps me company, and it keeps me comforted. Without it, I feel deprived, ill-nurtured, hungry, anxious, unfulfilled, wanting, negative, and much more. I yearn for satisfaction, and I will not have satisfaction without God and His Word. I need Him. I need His love. I need His Word.

I have past experiences, challenges, struggles, and hardships, both good and bad, as well as joys and opportunities that have brought me to this point. While the specifics of these are not the point of my twelve-week program, I do emphasize that without them, I would not be who I am, nor would I have the understanding, compassion, or willingness to delve into these concepts that I present to you. At this point in my life, I have a passionate desire to share and to help, and so I often express that "I am passionately diligent to help people get a better, brain, body, and belief using God's Word as their foundation for health." It is not at all medical advice. It is my effort to pass on what has been given to me. It is my effort to emphasize the principles we see in Psalm 34, principles such as those that indicate that God is close to us and will deliver us, principles such as those that call us to action to turn from evil and do good, principles that give us full assurance that God is good and is close to us.

I guess you could say that Psalm 34, while it gives us great hope and relief from trouble while we look to, trust, and wait for God, is the source for my passion. Verse 34:14 sums up my passion best: "Turn from evil and do good; seek peace and pursue it."

Read this again with your mouth!

"Turn from evil; seek peace and pursue it."

This has become the foundational verse for my personal ministry to help people using my background as a teacher, a nurse, a functional nutrition counselor, a health coach, and as a Christian who knows that we cannot leave God out of the picture. Of course, not everyone wants to hear God's Word or even believes it matters concerning the specifics of their health, but I do. I know that the truth of God's Word is what sets us free. Believing God's Word and meditating on it day and night by our minds and hearts is the avenue to be connected to God while we continue to go to Him and pour our hearts out to Him. Without God, we cannot have peace. We need His peace to stay healthy. Without it, we are not truly healthy.

After delving into much personal study on the knowledge I possess from my own medical and nursing training, along with nutritional training, I have come to realize that much of what I intuitively knew is actually correct, but our current system does not treat health accordingly. Our current medical system deals with the problems of poor health, including disease, chronic illness, mental illness, cancer, and genetic anomalies, but it does not have the time to fully explain what people need to know along with what they can do to prevent poor health and to improve it. Thankfully, we do have many voices out there who are waking us up and who are challenging the current system, but unfortunately, many of our loved ones, our coworkers, our brothers and sisters in Christ, and most people do not realize that their doctors are only prescribing medication and addressing their concerns with protocols that were part of their training. This is not their fault, but many doctors are realizing that their clients are not getting better but rather worse. Thus, we are beginning to see a gradual shift to addressing illness and poor health with the same principles I am attempting to bring to you.

However, most of these very knowledgeable practitioners are not addressing the spiritual component of our overall health. Again, this is no fault of theirs. They are only able to do so much. Doctors do not have time to study scripture as it pertains to their clients, and many do not believe in the scriptures. Pastors, having their hands full with serious ministry, do not have time to study health. Finally, therapists are usually trained to focus on their clients without considering this overwhelming information. All of these individuals may be highly qualified but just don't have the time and energy to walk with the weary and deal with every component of their health. Be assured, this is what I want to do here. I want to bridge the gap between all three of these professions and walk beside you. This is only to help what they, the professionals, are already trying to address with you. Again, I am trying to bridge this gap between them so that you are served in a way that leads to improvement with the goal of doing God's will with vigor.

I believe that if you have any health concerns, such as despair, lack of sleep, fatigue, fear, or even the need for applause or overachievement, God's Word is necessary along with a good look at your nourishment and habits to bring you to a place to realize the causes and effects of your particular situation. Only God truly knows what is troubling you, and this is all between you and God, but I zealously want to point you to Him. If I don't point you to the Lord, I have failed. All of the knowledge and experience pales in comparison to what God knows and what He is able to do, and with this, I now ask that you commit to twelve weeks to look at many issues and receive information both from God's Word and from the knowledge that our frail humanity has obtained. Twelve weeks, twelve psalms, and twelve prayers with numerous action steps and plenty of information about your brain, body, and beliefs to see how these are uniquely connected in every individual, who God has so fearfully and wonderfully created. Join me.

INTRODUCTORY LESSON

GOD'S LAW AND YOUR LAW OF HEALTH

Dear reader, welcome to my twelve-week Health through the Psalms program. I am so glad you have decided to join me and that you are ready to let God's Word help you in your health. I am passionately diligent to promote better brain, body, and beliefs in anyone using scripture and sound health guidance. None of this is medical advice, but rather, it is my effort to do good, to seek peace, and to pursue it by using scripture and providing information to you so that you might be encouraged to see how the brain, body, and beliefs affect our health and how these are uniquely connected in all individuals.

Today is the introductory lesson of my twelve-week Health through the Psalms program using the psalms to influence our decisions for a healthier life in general. Before we begin, I want to remind you of what you know is true. God cares about you. He understands you. He created you. He knows your innermost being, and He has invited you and me to pour our hearts out to Him, to go to Him for help, to rely on Him for strength and peace in our brains and in our bodies. Please remember this as we go through the next twelve weeks.

Today's focus will be on Psalm 1, which is foundational in giving us direction on a major point—the law of the Lord and how it is to be part of our everyday focus, both morning and night. Let's read it together now.

Psalm 1

1   Blessed is the man who does not walk in step with the wicked or stand in the way that sinners take or sit in the company of mockers,

2   But whose delight is in the law of the Lord, and who meditates on His law day and night.

3   That person is like a tree planted by streams of water, which yields its fruit in season and whose leaf does not wither—whatever he does prospers.

4   Not so the wicked! They are like chaff that the wind blows away

5   Therefore the wicked will not stand in the judgment, nor sinners in the assembly of the righteous.

6   For the Lord watches over the way of the righteous, but the way of the wicked leads to destruction.

As you can see, Psalm 1 emphasizes that we are to meditate on God's Word day and night, and the person who does this will be like a tree planted by rivers of water, and this tree bears fruit. When you envision this, you probably think of a very strong, healthy tree, one that will not easily be toppled or blown over, one that will not wither and probably one that has endured many years of assaults and growth.

The correlation I want you to think of is this: God's Word is absolutely necessary to guide us in our spiritual walk. It leads us; it nourishes us; it helps us to see what we should do in such a way that most of the time we do not even need to question what the right choice is. In fact, much of the time, we don't even need to make a decision because the decision to be made is already a habit of our lives. No question exists about what to do. The law of the Lord is necessary to achieve spiritual health. We need this truth as the foundation for our spiritual health, which impacts our physical and mental health.

So consider this analogy. The law of the Lord is a mandatory foundation for spiritual health; we need the law of the Lord to guide us so that we will be strong and prosperous and have fruitful lives. We are to meditate on this day and night. This guides and helps us to know and do God's will. Likewise, we need a law of health as a foundation to guide us, not just for physical health but for relationship health, financial health, occupational health, sleep health, family health, and mental health. These are all related to our overall health, and they affect us greatly, and they affect each other.

Of course, this won't be the same for everyone. Everyone is unique—different ages, different needs, different physiological responses to different inputs, different lifestyles, different financial options, and different relationships. What is good and healthy or necessary for one individual might be detrimental to another (eggs and tomatoes are two examples; they both are healthy options but not for everyone). What is necessary for one individual might not be necessary for another. For example, a body builder needs more protein than someone who does only aerobic exercise or who is of lesser weight. Water intake is another example. Someone who works in the sun all day and sweats needs more water than someone who works in air-conditioning. Depending on the daily responsibilities of certain individuals, more emotional rest may be necessary for replenishment than for someone who doesn't have as many emotional demands of others. Sleep, stress, nutritional needs, genetic makeup, lifestyle, financial situations, relationships, occupational demands—these present different needs and challenges to each individual.

So this is what I want you to do: develop your own personal law of health. This does not mean that you are going to develop a plan that will allow you to do whatever you feel like doing without considering others, but rather, the purpose is to develop the guidelines that you know you need to follow to be truly healthy, or at least to move in that direction. I am talking about soundness of mind here, with wisdom and acceptance for what you know is good for your overall health—health of your body, your family, your finances, your relationships, your job. This is different for everyone. Think about what you need to tackle right now. Why are you looking at this? Is it your physical health that needs attention? Your mental health (which is actually very related to your physical health and affects your body)? Your financial health? Only you can ascertain this. Accept what is going on, realize how it is affecting you, and care for yourself by making decisions to promote improvement.

Brain	Body	Beliefs

This is what you will do. Take out your journal (or just a sheet of paper). At the top of the paper, please write the title—*My Law of Health* or *My Law of Physical Health* or *Financial Health* or *Relationship Health*—whatever area you are focusing on at this time. Believe me, by focusing on one aspect of your life, you will soon realize how everything is connected. Some individuals may decide to work on their financial health and will soon discover that fewer arguments exist in the home because the finances are better managed. Maybe you struggle with relationships but soon experience improvement in them because you started to get adequate rest. Possibly, your energy level increased, and you are able to keep a tidier home because you simply started to drink more water and ate less sugar, and these actions boosted your energy. Or maybe you were able to finally stop smoking because you learned to manage stress more by exercising or eating a healthier diet. Only you can ponder and admit what you need at this time.

My Law of Health

Brain	Body	Beliefs
I will think about how good I will look and feel when I exercise. I will envision this.	I will begin walking for thirty minutes each day. I will begin using dumbbells to work on resistance training. I will start eating two more servings of healthy fruits and vegetables. I will quit snacking after 7:00 p.m.	I will go to the Lord each day and ask Him to give me the strength and perseverance to follow through on this goal. I will listen to my Bible or a Bible teaching while I walk.

On your sheet of paper, please make three columns. Above each column, write our three focus areas for health—*Brain, Body,* and *Beliefs.* In each column, come up with your own personal "commandment" to address your law of health, no matter what area you are choosing to focus on. For instance, if you are trying to get more physically fit, in the brain column, you could write, "I will think about how I will look and feel when I exercise." You could also envision how you will look and feel without doing this. Avoiding a negative outcome is a very driving motivator. In the body column, you could write, "I will begin walking for thirty minutes each day," or "I will begin using dumbbells," or "I will start eating two more servings of healthy fruits and vegetables a day and quit snacking after 7:00 p.m." In the beliefs column, you could write, "I will go to the Lord each day and ask Him to give me the strength and perseverance to follow through on this goal" or "I will listen to my Bible or a Bible teaching while I walk."

Only you can decide what needs to be addressed in your life right now. Currently, I need to limit my snacking after supper. I struggle with snacking as I clean up the kitchen and get things prepared for the next day. Afterward, I feel too full and uncomfortable, and this sometimes affects my sleep (and brain health, I must mention—this is another important topic). Furthermore, I do not want to be controlled by my cravings or desires; I want to be able to say no to myself so that nothing masters me. Because of this scenario, the following three commands could be in my columns:

Brain: Think about how good you will feel if you don't go to bed with too much in your stomach, as well as how much better you might sleep.

Body: Physically remove yourself from the kitchen and put tempting items away first before cleaning up the kitchen and getting things ready for the next day.

Beliefs: Quote Bible verses that strengthen and remind me of the importance of denying myself and things that I want while I am in the kitchen. A good one for this is 1 Corinthians 6:12: "All things are permissible for me, but not all things are beneficial. All things are permissible for me, but I will be mastered by nothing."

Of course, I have the freedom to snack when I want; there is no law against it, but evaluating if it is good for me is wise. I realize that eating too close to bedtime impairs my sleep and makes me feel uncomfortable. So even though it is permissible, it is not beneficial, and the fact that I am having a hard time controlling this indicates that it has mastery over me rather than my having mastery over it. Later, we will discuss the physiological reason of why snacking too close to bedtime impairs sleep and just isn't optimum for our bodies and brains.

At this time, I want to help you to develop more foundational ground by challenging you to ask yourself a series of questions. Please write the following questions down, ponder them, and then write answers to the questions. Revisit the information; analyze your answers; be honest. The truth sets us free. God has a path of righteousness for all of us—for you. Believe this; it is true. This path is full of green pastures, but it also takes us through the valley of the shadow of death; it takes us through enemy territory, areas where we are surrounded by enemies, and temptations are formidable enemies. This sounds brutal, but the path that God has for us always leads to peace and promises a cup that runs over; it promises that goodness and mercy will follow us all the days of our lives, not just when we feel strong or when we have succeeded or when life is easy. His goodness and mercy indeed are with you through every struggle you encounter, and the law of the Lord is the foundation for your strength and guidance.

Let's do this together. Your first step is to ask yourself the following questions:

Question #1: "What do I want to achieve or gain?" And why? What is your big MOFA—motivational factor?

Or put another way, we could ask, "What do I want to see in my life in ninety days?" This will be different for everyone. One of you might want to lose twelve pounds. Someone else might want to get peace in their relationships. Another might want to pay off credit card debt, quit smoking, quit gossiping, eat more healthily, exercise consistently, start going to church, attend a Bible study, be a more faithful employee by arriving on time and not using work time on social media or other personal activities. Maybe you want to quit complaining. The goals are quite various and unique to each of us.

It is very important to state your goal in a specific, concrete manner and to be realistic with what your goal is. If your goal is beyond your reach, you are setting yourself up for failure; however, if it is too easy, you might not be stretching yourself enough. It must be achievable or attainable yet challenging enough to provide the opportunity for growth and improvement. It also should be concrete, and you should be able to measure it. For instance, stating, "I want to eat more healthy foods," is not concrete. Instead, state the goal like this: "I want to eat two more servings of vegetables a day than I do now"; or "I want to start strength training three days a week using ten-pound dumbbells along with my cardio workout on the other days"; or "I will walk two miles five days a week"; or, for financial health, "I want to pay down my credit card balance by $500 by the end of the twelve weeks." Having the goal timed is also important. This way, you are able to assess that you have reached it or have made progress toward the goal. Our time here is twelve weeks.

But even more important for you to realize is why you want this. I know several stories of people's eyes being opened as they finally admitted or realized why they were after something; it had nothing to do with what they thought was the reason for what they wanted. One example is a gal who wanted a PhD. When her coach invited her to answer the why questions with honesty, she was able to get to the why underneath the why, and then she came to understand that the real truth was that she wanted a PhD so that she could write a book, which would then cause her father to finally accept her for doing something academic. She was the only one in her family who was not a top-notch scholar, and she was the least educated. She felt unacceptable to her father. After she realized this, she was able to see that it really wasn't even true that she wasn't accepted by her father. She had put this false expectation on herself. She also realized that she did not want a PhD and was quite happy in her occupation.

I know of many situations where a person's behavior is embedded in a very misunderstood why or in poor reasoning. For instance, a workaholic may appear to be providing for their family and feel the need to work as much as they do; however, many situations of this nature really stem from a fear of failure. The individual has more money than needed, the family is quite financially stable, yet the providers are driven by the big why of fear. Knowing this could enable the individual to pull back and enjoy life.

Consider your big why. Do you want to lose weight so that you look more beautiful? This could be vanity, or it could bring the outcome that you get off of medication, or it could mean that you are able to move more easily and decrease joint pain. Or it could mean that you could wear a bunch of clothes in your closet and won't have to go out and buy more. This would improve your financial health also. What is your big MOFA? Be honest. Try to realize, understand, and be honest about why you really want something and why you are going after it.

I coached two women who simply wanted to lose weight so that their joints would not hurt so badly, but their real goal, their real *big why*, was that they wanted to be able to pick up their grandchildren from the floor. They also wanted to be able to sit on the floor and play with them. Their big MOFA was not about looks or health markers; they simply wanted to ensure that they would have healthy relationships with their beautiful grandchildren. It was about love and experiencing what God intends for families.

Another word about your goal. Be advised that your goal should be specific and measurable. It should also be attainable and realistic. Again, make sure your goal is not too difficult but not too easy either. Finally, acknowledge it in a way so that you will know that you have attained it.

Question #2: "How long have I wanted this?"

Think about this. Is this just a flippant desire that you had not even considered but now thought of because someone asked you the question, or is this a goal you have had for years and have kept putting off due to a lack of clarity, commitment, or no support? Have you avoided it due to fear or embarrassment? Have you avoided it due to disobedience or the belief that it isn't possible? Be honest about how long you have wanted this and try to understand why you have not achieved it yet. Again, this is different for everyone.

Question #3: "What will having this do for me?"

What will you really gain from having this? Will you gain more peace, more friends, more time, more financial stability? Will you gain better physical health, better relationships, better reputation, better coping skills? Will having this open up other doors of opportunity? Will it unlock a stifling situation and bring improvement? Think of the personal gain this will mean for you in your complete person—in your brain, body, and beliefs.

Question #4: Who else will benefit from this?

Will you be the only one who will benefit from having this? Who else might benefit from the change that you will finally achieve? Your family? Your employer? Your church? Your neighborhood? How would it be good for them? Possibly, it could spark change or improvement in many people. You might spur on a chain of events that could bring about a huge impact on many people both near and far away, an impact that might bring much good to many others.

Question #5: "What has worked for me in this past?"

Maybe this is not the first time you have tried to tackle your particular issue. In truth, you may have succeeded in accomplishing this goal or others in the past, but this time you are having a bit more trouble due to your age, your environment, different demands of life, or various other reasons. Consider what has worked in the past. It could work again. If it isn't working, consider why it might not be working; analyze the situation. What is standing in the way of a strategy that worked before? Is it a person, a schedule, a new habit that negatively impacts you, your family stressors? Only you can determine your situation. By the way, family stressors are not necessarily bad. Most of family life is very stressful, but that stems from the demands and the relationships that make your life full and vibrant. We still need to identify and manage these, however. Happy times can be stressful. Too much fun can be stressful. Being pregnant is stressful. Stress can look good sometimes. We will talk more about stress during our twelve weeks.

Question #6: "What needs to go to achieve this goal?"

We have somewhat touched on this already, but consider what you answered earlier about what is standing in the way as well as what might be preventing your success this time as compared to another time of success in your life. Sometimes we need to get rid of things that are distracting us from accomplishing our goals or that are preventing us from living life to the fullest. Let's call this clearing the clutter. Sometimes actual items are standing in your way—like too much clutter in your pantry, in your fridge, in your email, in your schedule, in your social life. Clear the clutter. What needs to leave your pantry or fridge so that you avoid temptation? What is in your schedule that is making life too busy so that you can't do what you need to do to achieve your goal? Maybe just taking one thing out of your schedule allows more time for you to exercise, to balance your bank statement, to clean your house, to organize, to enjoy more quality family time, to just not feel so rushed and frazzled, which will reduce stress and possibly help you to be more patient and kind and less prone to anger, due to your hastiness. Maybe you spend too much time looking at emails that contain ads that you don't even need. Unsubscribe to these; don't let an invader steal your time, your goals, your peace. What people might have the potential of cluttering up your life? Maybe it is someone who takes advantage of your family time, of your cleaning time, of your Bible study time, of your organizational time, of your work time. Choosing to clear the clutter—no matter what it is—does not provide permission to be selfish, but rather it helps you to free yourself from the controls that are preventing you from walking on the path of righteousness that

God has for you. Take time to use God's wisdom to discern what is steering your daily routines and how this affects you, both in a positive and in a negative way.

Think about other things that you want to accomplish, like vacuuming the living room floor. We clearly need to clean the clutter off the floor before we vacuum. If we don't do this, we are not able to clean the floor. We can't vacuum. The clutter is in our way. It will become a distraction and a frustration. The clutter blocking our progress will make us want to quit because it takes more time to vacuum if we must pick this up than it does to vacuum with the clutter cleared. So clear the clutter. If you get new furniture in your house, you take the old furniture out first before you bring the new furniture in. Analyze what is standing in the way. What needs to go to achieve your goal?

Question #7: "What will I see, hear, and feel when this goal is achieved?" You can also ask this in the negative: "What will I see, hear, and feel if I don't achieve this goal?"

It is a very productive exercise to envision the goal and outcome you desire by using your senses. This is powerful. When you engage your senses and imagine what you will hear or see or feel, it actually makes the goal seem doable, achievable, and within your reach. This helps your brain get ready to believe that you can achieve it—that it is possible and that you are going to succeed. This is called self-efficacy in psychological terms, but in spiritual terms, you can see that this is faith and hope, not overconfidence—an honest outlook, as you believe that God will help you. Maybe what you will see is a better body with more muscle; maybe you will hear fewer creditors calling you because you paid your bills; maybe you will feel more peace because you finally are keeping your house clean and organized. Just imagine your outcome. Athletes envision doing their skill perfectly. By doing this, they are practicing for success, practicing perfectly. Just watching a skilled athlete or listening to a skilled musician makes the athlete or musician stronger to perform the skill themselves. Envision the outcome, think on it, and realize how wonderful this will look, sound, and feel.

In the opposite direction, you could envision the outcome that doesn't look or feel great. By doing this, you actually trigger your brain to have the motivation to stay away from that outcome. Just like we want to stay away from a hot stove or from a stinky and dirty pen of pigs, we will want to stay away from a negative outcome because it is not desirous. It is a very fruitful exercise to envision both the positive outcome and then the negative if you don't achieve your goal. This envisioning will help you, and that is where your brain comes in. Don't rely on self-will or self-control for all of this. You have got to think about it before you get into a situation that is difficult. Here is a caution, however. Spend more time dwelling on the positive outcome. We do want to focus on the mindset of success and not failure.

Question #8: "Who can support me in this?"

Although God calls us to trust in Him at all times and for all things, He does not demand that we do this alone or without support and help. In fact, He is glorified more through the humble efforts of many working together out of a spirt of love and humility than with the achievement of what might be perceived as a solo effort. Think about it. A mother and father need lots of support and help from others to encourage and provide assistance while raising their children. A church needs lots of different avenues of help and support; a pastor cannot do it alone; neither can a Sunday school director or a worship leader. An Olympic athlete who wins the gold medal does not achieve it alone. Expert coaching and dedication and support of many others helped the efforts on a consistent basis. Even a surgeon needs so much help in the operating room. There are so many other people who are helping to achieve the goal or the task at hand; the expert surgeon needs their help.

So it is with you. Who can support you in this? You are strengthened by loyal people who really understand your goal, your struggle, and your need for support. Who cares and loves you enough to support you when you get discouraged and are ready to quit and give up? Who is humble enough to walk with you in this, even if they feel a bit uncomfortable that they aren't joining you? Who won't turn away from you and watch you fail but will instead be there to empathize, confront, and challenge you to get back on track? We all need accountability and support. Think of three individuals who will be committed to you out of love and understanding to help you on this path. It is not easy; you need faithful friends who are not ashamed, afraid, or hesitant to stand in the gap for you when you are tempted. God will always make a way, and He uses our brothers and sisters in Christ to strengthen us, not to be our competitors or our intimidators. He also uses people who do not believe God's Word to strengthen you. They can definitely be an inspiration to you. They can be accountability for you. They can be someone who might be a better cheerleader for you than someone else who does not have the same struggle. Think about it. Who can be there for you?

Question #9: What is one action step you can take in your brain, body, and beliefs right now to move in the right direction immediately? This is a loaded question. This means that you must come up with three action steps: one that your brain is going to do; one that your body is going to do; and one that your beliefs, your faith, or your heart is going to do.

Only you can determine what you might need to do right now. Think about your goal; maybe it is to get better sleep so that you won't be so tired and so moody the next day or in general. Let's organize our goals and what we can do in our brains, bodies, and beliefs by recording our goals and actions in a chart with five columns. Take out a sheet of paper or make a journal of about fifteen pages. At the top of the first column, write the word *Goal*. At the top of the second column, write the word *Brain*. At the top of third column, write *Body*. At the top of the fourth column, write *Beliefs*. At the top of the fifth column, write *Scripture*. What could you do in your brain, body, and beliefs this week to help you get on the right path to achieving your goal? Let's pretend that we all have the goal to sleep more. In your goal column, write your goal of "to sleep more," but let's be specific by writing, "I want to sleep thirty to forty-five minutes more each night." Consider your brain.

Possibly just thinking about going to bed earlier is enough, along with saying to yourself, "I am going to go to bed fifteen minutes earlier for a week; then I will try for thirty minutes." See how it feels. Or envision yourself with extra energy and a better mood when you have slept more. Then make yourself do this, no excuse. That is the body part—actually doing it. The belief part could be this statement: "Sleeping more gives me more energy and helps me to be in a better mood; it is good for my body to get rest. I believe this will help my productivity." This is the belief part.

Here is what your chart could look like:

Goal	Brain	Body	Beliefs	Scripture
I want to sleep thirty to forty-five minutes more each night.	I will think about going to bed fifteen minutes earlier for a week. Then I will try for thirty minutes.	I will go to bed fifteen minutes earlier.	Sleeping more gives me more energy and helps me to be in a better mood. It is good for my body to get rest. I believe this will help my productivity. Negative: having a lack of sleep makes me feel lousy.	Proverbs 3:24: "When you lie down, you will not be afraid; when you lie down, your sleep will be sweet."

You could also envision the negative of this: "How will I feel the next day if I don't sleep enough?" We all know what that looks like. Later on, we'll talk more about sleep, but we all know that if we don't sleep enough, it's going to have an impact on the next day. So you can think about both the positive and the negative outcomes.

So many scriptures indicate God's concern for our sleep. Proverbs

3:24 is a good one: "When you lie down, you will not be afraid; when you lie down, your sleep will be sweet." Write this in the fifth column under your scripture heading.

Let's pretend that your goal is to get off caffeine. What could your brain focus on here? Maybe focusing on the fact that caffeine is a stimulant and it is actually controlling you would be a good point to ponder. Possibly admitting this is enough. Your body action could be to physically buy decaffeinated coffee and cut intake gradually for a while by reducing your caffeine to one half each week until it is negligible. Your belief? Maybe saying a Bible verse to yourself, such as Psalm 18:1, "I love you, O Lord, my strength," would be enough to get you through the lag you might feel. Don't worry. We have twelve weeks to work on this. I will guide you through many action steps, using scripture to strengthen and help your faith and your health.

We must think on the truth. This is an active process; it is a choice. Choosing to think on the truth and what is good for your whole person will help you to do action in all three areas—your brain, your body, and your beliefs. God's path is not disorderly or chaotic. It has a purpose for eternal good. It is not always easy and requires us to make disciplined sacrifices. Forget what you might want for a while. Maybe you need to quit buying certain things for a while to pay off credit card debt. Buy what you actually need by living within your boundaries. Don't be greedy. Be content with your needs being met and your credit card payment going down as you are able to use funds to pay down what you owe. Think of the stress this will relieve.

Remember, the Lord said in His Word to take every thought captive to the obedience of Christ. What we think and dwell on really matters. You can think yourself into depression. You can think yourself into temptation. You can think yourself into many things. Think on what is true, lovely, and just. Taking every thought captive to the obedience of Christ is not just a pleasant suggestion; it is a command, and it is a command that has science backing up the tremendous reasons why. As Jesus said, "If you love me you will obey My Word." Obey His Words, all of them; they are life and health for you and for me. He also said, "If you don't forgive from your heart, neither will God forgive you."

This affects your life and health. This is a heart condition that impacts you and then of course what you do. These are not part of a morning exercise routine that gets the heart rate up, but they are part of the morning and evening exercise routine that we should be doing in our hearts to ensure that we are staying up at the plumb line that God has for our standard. What we do is going to impact us. Carrying around a bag of toxic thoughts as well as a lack of forgiveness is exhausting. Our actions affect us. If you get up off the couch, your heart rate will increase automatically, and this will increase your energy. Of course, if you are sitting on the couch all day, you are going to want more caffeine. Think about all three areas of your complete being—your brain, your body, and your beliefs. It all matters.

Below is a chart I created with three goals: 1) losing twelve pounds; 2) getting more organization in my house; and 3) paying off my credit card debt. Read through it to see how different goals could be addressed by your brain, body, and beliefs as well as scripture.

Goal	Brain	Body	Beliefs	Scripture
Lose twelve pounds.	Envision myself exercising and actually losing the weight. I will look and feel better with more energy. My clothes won't be tight.	Clean the pantry out of the snack food that I eat too much of. Start walking every day or engage in another form of exercise. Make this a part of my day.	Eating right and exercising helps to manage weight and energy. I believe God will help me in this so that I can glorify Him in my body, having energy to do His will.	Psalm 18:29: "With your help I can advance against a troop; with my God I can scale a wall."

Organize my house.	Envision junk being removed from my drawers and viewing area.	Physically pick up things that I see; throw them away, give them away, or put them in the appropriate places. Choose twenty-five items per day until this is completed to my satisfaction.	Say to myself what is true. God wants my life in order. God helps me to keep my life in order. He helps me to walk in a path that has purpose.	Psalm 23:3: "He refreshes my soul. He guides me in the paths of righteousness for his name's sake."
Pay off credit cards.	Envision the zero balance on the card with no interest due. Envision the balance going down.	Refrain from buying at least five to ten things this week and add this amount to your credit card payment. Make this a habit each week.	Focus on the truth that the borrower is servant to the lender. Think about being free from the master of the credit card company that has control over you.	Psalm 37:16: "Better the little that the righteous have than the wealth of many wicked."

Just a word about the chart. Concerning any goal and looking at Psalm 18:29, remember, God wants to help us, but He wants us to turn to Him. He longs to grant us what we need at just the right time. Also, concerning house organization, look at all the clutter we all have. There are so many things we do not need. These things are in our way. Clothes have holes in them, or socks don't have matches; items are broken and useless. If you have clutter in the way, it is going to be a lot harder to do God's will. Get the cutter out of your life; make your life easier so that you can hear His voice and do His will and be available for Him. Lastly, think about the goal of ridding yourself of debt. The credit card companies have the right to charge you interest and tack on fees to your balance. They have the right to call you and give you a bad credit score. Think about the freedom you could have from that. Put off things that you have been wanting for a while. It's okay. Just put them on hold for now.

At this time, I want to draw your attention back to Psalm 1 and the law of the Lord. You already believe that God's Word is nonnegotiable. You might have a hard time obeying it all the time or feeling like obeying it, but you know in your heart that it is true and profitable for reproof, instruction, and training in righteousness and that we are to live by it. Think now about the goal that you have to improve your health, to improve your life. I want you to determine your own law of health for your goal. As you consider the positive outcomes of following through on the nonnegotiables of your own law of health, compose your own psalm of health. Mimic Psalm 1 as you do this. Of course, this is not to lessen the great value of Psalm 1 of the Bible. The idea here is to transfer the truth over to your daily life to make it relevant to your specific goal or your specific area of conviction that you think the Lord really wants you to work on.

Here are a couple of examples for you. One is a general law of health, and the second is a law of financial health. These are not meant to be judgmental at all. I can relate to all of the temptations and failures that these two attempts at a psalm communicate. Complete understanding on my part is present here. I understand almost every temptation or weakness. I completely understand, and I empathize. I love to share this understanding with people and to help them. I love it when people ask for prayer about their struggles. I think it is wonderful. The truth sets us free, and there is strength in helping other people bear their burdens and allowing others to bear your burdens with you.

Concerning these examples, I present these to you with the full expectation that you heed God's Word, that you have a fear of the Lord, that you believe the vocabulary and the intent of scripture is for truth and to set us free and to bring us life. This is done in love and with grace. So my psalm 1 here, which I have composed, might sound pretty harsh, but it comes from my heart, a heart that understands. I understand in both action and in conquering challenges in my own life. This also includes constantly dealing with some of these challenges on an ongoing basis. It is a process; we are never done.

How healthy is the competitor who does not walk according to the way of the unhealthy, nor stand in the way of gluttons, nor lounge in the comfort zone of the sluggard.

But their motivation is in the law of sound health, and in this law they daily focus with consistency, reminding themselves constantly of the benefits of its principles.

And they shall be like a strong athlete who is nourished wisely and who makes prudent habits a lifestyle, a nimble athlete who is energetic and motivated and useful for independent living and helping others.

Their efforts will not be ineffective, and all will produce goodness.

The unhealthy are not like this but are like couch potatoes without self-respect or ambition, useless and ineffective.

Therefore, the unhealthy shall not stand on the podium of success, nor gluttons in the field of athletes.

For the Great Physician is completely aware of the unhealthy and their needs, choices, and mistakes.

But the way of the healthy responds according to the God-ordained manner in which He created them, to heal and honor Him with what they think, what they do, and what they believe, which causes them to be healthy in their brain, body, and beliefs.

Here is another one created about financial health:

Blessed is the man who does not walk in the counsel of Wall Street, nor sit in the chair of the creditors, but his delight is in the law of good stewardship, honoring and remembering constantly what was given to and provided for him.

He shall be like a wealthy and generous man who shares with the poor and needy; he will give without sparing, and he will never be one to use usury.

His bank account will never run down, and whatever he buys will prove useful.

The greedy and stingy are not so but are like the scrooge who has no joyful future; therefore, the greedy and stingy will not stand with bankers, nor the rich and selfish in the community of the generous.

As we conclude, you have an assignment of four action steps:

1. Read Psalm 1 every day this week. Read it aloud as many times as possible.
2. Compose your own psalm called My Law of Health. Mimic Psalm 1 and start with the same words, "Blessed is the man who does not ..." Fill it in with details pertaining to your health goal, just as I shared with you earlier. Be creative. Let God strengthen you through this.
3. Immediately clear any clutter you see that is hindering you from your goal.
4. Ask three people to support you in this; ask them to check on you often.
   It can be daily. It can be a text; it can be phone call. Don't think you have to go through this alone, and don't think it has

to be somebody who appears to have it all together. It can be anybody; it can be someone with the same struggle who would love to see your success.

Well, give yourself a high five if you are ready to tackle this. Remember, small hinges swing big doors. Each step you take in the right direction will be progress. Don't beat yourself up. God is your strength. This concludes our introductory lesson for the twelve weeks of Health through the Psalms. Next week, we begin with the topic of environment. Bye for now.

WEEK 1

DECLUTTERING FOR BLAMELESS LIVING

Welcome to week 1 of my Health through the Psalms program. I am glad you have decided to join me and hope that you have firmly established a goal for your health as well as the big *why* you want this. I also hope you were able to implement the action steps we discussed last week by reading Psalm 1 every day and asking three people to support you in this endeavor. Hopefully, you implemented your brain, body, and belief action steps also. Before we begin our topic for week 1, which is environment, please be reminded that none of this is medical advice; rather, it is my effort to do good, to seek peace, and to pursue it by using scripture and providing information to you so that you might be encouraged to see how the brain, body, and beliefs affect your health and how these are uniquely connected in all individuals.

We will be using Psalm 101 for week 1, so you should get that handy. Prior to reading this together, I want to mention some important aspects about the topic of environment in the context of a garden. We all understand that for plants to thrive, they must have good soil; they must have sunshine; they must have water; they must have weather that isn't too harsh; they must have some type of protection. A garden that thrives indeed has a gardener who is dedicated to the specific needs of what is growing in the garden. Even before the seeds are planted, the gardener uses knowledge and principles to select a good location, to get the soil ready, and to consider what the plants need—when to plant, when to water, how much sunlight. There are so many details

1

to consider in establishing the environment for the garden. Both the internal and the external inputs are significant in the overall success of plant growth. The weather, the water, the sunlight, and the richness of the soil all matter. So it is with you.

Consider your environment and consider that you are the soil, and what you produce is the fruit. Consider both the internal and external inputs that are part of your environment. These impact you greatly; in fact, they might control you much more than you realize. Just like the gardener meticulously cares for the garden by watering, nourishing the soil, selecting the location, pulling weeds, and planting seeds at the right time, we must meticulously care for ourselves by assessing our environments, not just on a whim but with honesty and sobriety, being watchful and vigilant. This includes the environments of our brains, our bodies, and our beliefs. They all matter.

Here is a warning from Proverbs: "As a man thinks in his heart, so is he." Think about this. What you believe and think matters. They affect each other. If you do not believe that God can work through His Word to transform your brain, body, and beliefs, then it probably won't happen. If you do not believe that the psalms I am presenting to you have anything to do with your environment, your stress level, your habits, your health, and your peace of mind, then you will not benefit from this study like someone who is all in and believes that God's Word is powerful and active and is beneficial for instruction, reproof, and training in righteousness—and, in fact, for health and every aspect of life.

We do not have as much integration in our lives between different disciplines of expertise. Many people go to their pastor for spiritual counseling, then they go to their doctor for their physical health (and many times mental health), and then they go to their therapist for counseling. My goal is to tie all three of these together. I am trying to fill the gap between all of these experts. In general, the pastor does not talk about what you are eating or how you are sleeping. The doctor does not challenge you on your spiritual convictions and if you are adhering to what you say you believe. The therapist might tackle some of this but may only have the social component as the point of focus. Again, I am challenging you to allow this study to bridge the gap between all three areas so that you will have peace in your brain, body, and beliefs. I am challenging you to think that incorporating all three together using God's Word will benefit your entire health so that truly as you think in your heart, so will you be. In biological and psychological terms, we say, "Your psychology dictates your biology." Do not settle for what someone else told you that you are or what you have always believed you are—such as, "Oh, I am someone who deals with depression." Or "I am someone who will always be fat." Or "Heart disease runs in my family, so I for sure will have to have cardiac surgery and will probably have a heart attack." Or "I will always be poor; there is no way I could make more money." Take the challenge and hope differently. Remember that I am not giving medical advice. I am only using God's Word to be the source for improvement in your life. You do not need to sit in a pit of a poor mental state or in a state of poor health.

Let's take a good look at your environment right now. Your environment includes all things that affect you in your brain, body, and beliefs. It includes your sensory capabilities—what you see, hear, feel, touch, and smell. It includes your emotions and what affects your emotions—physical touch, tones of voices, others' facial expressions and attitudes toward you. It includes toxins that come your way, such as plastics, noise, falsehoods, conflicts, rumors, gossip, unbelief, complaints and arguing, negative social interactions, and your thought patterns. It includes how much someone touches you and how much you touch others. It includes what you think and believe, who your friends and coworkers are, how your family influences you, and what social media does to you. It includes your habits and lifestyle, the choices you make daily, even minute by minute. It includes what you say and what you spend time reading and listening to. It includes what conversations you participate in and how you contribute and respond to these. It is enormous. Learn to control your environment as much as you can or at least learn to manage it the best you can. You don't have to be the weak recipient of toxins, whether they are environmental, social, or emotional, but instead you can be a leader to muster the change to make all realms of your life better. Don't let the environment of others become your environment, unless of course their environment is good for you and you know it is part of the path of righteousness God has for you.

Let's look at the power of your senses, especially your sense of sight. We have millions of sensory neurons in our nervous system, and most of these sensory receptors are visual. Wow! How powerful our sight is. Ears that hear and eyes that see—the Lord has made them both. Think about how you have been greatly affected your whole life by what you have seen, both innocently and in a sense of unawareness but also by choice, by the willful and knowledgeable choosing of viewing movies, pictures, and other people or events. We have learned valuable skills and lessons from this, but we also have had toxic visual experiences and encounters as well. These affect the environment of our brains, how we think and feel, and then of course ultimately our own emotions, behaviors, health, and even our spiritual walk.

Remember, "as a man thinks in his heart, so is he." Who are you? How are you behaving? What are your habits? Who are your close confidants? Who are your heroes, your podcast commentators, your Instagram likes, your Facebook friends? Who are the newscasters, editorialists, or authors you follow? What stores and websites do you frequent? What luxury items and memberships do you value? How do you spend your free time? What relationships do you prioritize? These all matter.

Let's move on to our discussion of our environment using God's Word as our guide. Please look at Psalm 101 and read it aloud.

Psalm 101

1   I will sing of your love and justice; to you, Lord, I will sing praise.
2   I will be careful to lead a blameless life; when will you come to me? I will conduct the affairs of my house with a blameless heart.
3   I will not look with approval on anything that is vile. I hate what faithless people do; I will have no part in it.

4   The perverse of heart shall be far from me; I will have nothing to do with what is evil.

5   Whoever slanders their neighbor in secret, I will put to silence; whoever has haughty eyes and a proud heart, I will not tolerate.

6   My eyes will be on the faithful in the land, that they may dwell with me; the one whose walk is blameless will minister to me.

7   No one who practices deceit will dwell in my house; no one who speaks falsely will stand in my presence.

8   Every morning I will put to silence all the wicked of the land; I will cut off every evildoer from the city of the Lord.

Now let's take this apart verse by verse.

Look at verse 1: "I will sing of your love and justice; to you, Lord, I will sing praise."

Do you start your day with praise to the Lord, who gave you your day? Or do you start your day with feet dragging on the floor, disappointed at how tired you feel and dreading what you have to do? Think about it. Would we not all agree that we should thank the Lord for the day and instead of having the attitude of "having to do," might we instead have the attitude of "we get to do"? The Lord's love surrounds us. Create the environment of a grateful attitude from the beginning. Start your day with this verse. Set it straight from the beginning that your environment begins with praise to the One who gives you love and justice. We can't grumble, complain, or be hopeless if we are verbalizing praise to our Lord.

Look at verse 2: "I will be careful to lead a blameless life; when will you come to me? I will conduct the affairs of my house with a blameless heart."

Again, how are you conducting your affairs? Are you creating an environment of blamelessness, of integrity, of praise, of hope, of faith? Are you conducting your affairs with the same profession that you make on Sunday when you are around other Christians? You cannot separate what you believe from how you conduct yourself. How you behave shows what you believe. Are you quick to give grace? Are you quick to sing praise? Are you quick to walk in complete integrity with every word? Are you speaking the truth of God's Word in one breath and using profanity in the next? Are you telling someone about God's forgiveness one moment and criticizing a coworker the next moment? Do people see a Jesus bumper sticker on your car as you run a red light? Are you living in such a way that no one can say anything bad about you? Are you avoiding even the appearance of evil? This takes great effort. Consider the environment you create by how you are conducting yourself. What you do and how you behave and speak teaches others about who you are, and it teaches them how to treat you. Be quick to listen; be quick to obey; be quick to admit mistakes and wrongdoing; be quick to humble yourself; be quick to consider what are healthy options; be quick for godliness in all manners of conduct. This will create an environment around you, and this environment will be powerful; it will affect the environment of others. Your decisions to lead a blameless life, even though you miss the mark at times, will be a message.

On to verse 3, "I will not look with approval on anything that is vile. I hate what faithless people do; I will have no part in it."

As already mentioned, we have more visual sensory receptors than other sensory neuron receptors. These are powerful advantages to learning and obtaining information as well as for protection. Our pupils dilate when we are stressed; this is a fight-or-flight mechanism for survival. God made us this way, but this advantage can be a great disadvantage if we are not careful about what we view. What internet sites do you view? What magazines and advertisements grab your attention? What television shows and movies do you allow into your home? What group texts and emails do you get from different groups that promote hate and carnality and links that lead to false or evil pieces of information that do nothing but toxify your brain and heart and create a feeling of hatred toward others? What jokes and stories do you take part in with "faithless people," conversations that are nothing but Godless chatter or even worse are downright lewd, false, hateful, immoral, full of mockery, judgmental, prejudice, unforgiving, and detrimental to the well-being of others, especially the weak and downtrodden? Don't strengthen such an environment by your passive participation. Remove yourself from them and lead a blameless life. Don't allow the filth, wrongdoing, or slackness of faithless people, even if they claim to follow Christ, to soil your soul and testimony. Live in a manner worthy of Christ.

And by the way, practice gratitude by thanking God for the eyesight you have. The eye doctor must be meticulous and delicate while assessing this small member of your body. Just a tiny scratch on your eye can incapacitate you until you get relief. Until Jesus healed the blind man as recorded in John, chapter 9, no one had ever healed anyone who was born blind. Think of the poor child born blind who has no reason to lift their head because they do not have the visual stimuli to look up; there is nothing apparent to see, and so they do not develop their neck muscles as a typical child who has adequate sight would. Do not despise this small member. Care for yourself by caring for what you view with the gift of your eyesight.

Verse 4: "The perverse of heart shall be far from me; I will have nothing to do with what is evil."

Again, just because another individual claims to follow Christ does not mean they are living a blameless life. It does not mean they have chosen to allow the transforming work of God into their life. It does not mean that they are honoring God with their bodies and minds and with what they believe. You will have to take a stand for the truth. The perverse of heart includes unforgiveness; it includes anger, rage, malice, blasphemy, filthy language. It includes pride, arrogance, foolish talk, even duplicity. Have nothing to do with it. How can someone say they love God and hate their brother? Yes, you and I agree that this should not occur, but how often do we see this played out? We know the right words to say, but knowing and doing are two different things. We must judge our own hearts, and if our hearts do not condemn us, then we know we have peace with God. However, take heed that you do not allow the sin of others to distract you. He who walks with the wise will grow wise, but a companion of fools suffers harm. Keep the environment of your own brain, body, and beliefs clean before God by having nothing to do with evil, by having nothing to do with the hidden sins of the heart, the attitudes shown in secret. Guard your heart with all diligence.

Verse 5: "Whoever slanders their neighbor in secret, I will put to silence; whoever has haughty eyes and a proud heart, I will not tolerate."

Jesus said in Matthew chapter 7, "Judge not, lest you be judged." How do you reconcile this word from Jesus in view of this verse from the psalms? I think it has to do with the attitude of your heart. First of all, if you hear the slander of anyone, you should be concerned with both the individual who is slandering and the individual who is being slandered. This is the attitude of love for both. Keep in mind the definition of slander. Slander is the crime of making a false spoken statement damaging to a person's reputation. This is very serious. If you call someone out on slandering their neighbor in secret, you are not judging; you are only stating what is true. Stating what is true is not judgmental or sinful, unless it is done in an unloving way or with a wrong motive, in a way that it not after what is good and true.

The same is true about haughty eyes and a proud heart. These indicate scorn along with the high-mindedness of oneself toward others, which is clearly a violation of the law of love that Jesus has commanded. Just as we would not tolerate someone coming into our homes or even near us with a flaming torch to start a fire, we should not tolerate the tongue that could set a more damaging destruction ablaze with secret slander. However, this secrecy could prove to be a friend to the situation. If done in secret, you are able to privately confront and clarify the falsehood of slander, as well as set the record straight with the truth. The fear of man is a snare. Do not be familiar with a cowardly spirit. Be strong in the Lord and in the power of His might to stand for what is true, even when it is uncomfortable, difficult, unexpected, and with the possibility that you might lose a connection with someone who slanders. It might not make you popular, but it will make you a person of integrity and trustworthiness. It will be part of a blameless life, all done with humility.

Verse 6: "My eyes will be on the faithful of the land, that they may dwell with me; the one whose walk is blameless will minister to me."

I am so grateful for my pastors. They are men of God's Word. They are men of integrity. They are men who are not ashamed of the gospel of Christ and consistently preach sermons and give counseling, with God's Word and wisdom guiding them. They are faithful in my land. I am also grateful for their wives. I know that when I go to their wives for anything, I will be approaching faithful women; women who minister to me; women who are guided by God's Word; women who are leading blameless lives. I am not saying that any of them are perfect, but if I go to any of them with slander on my lips, they will speak truth; if I go to them with complaining, they will confront with grace; if I go with arrogance or a haughty spirit or a lack of hope, they will actively point me to the scriptures that will nurture me. Believe me; my eyes are on them, the faithful of the land; I will allow them to minister to me.

I also am familiar with people who could minister to me but who are not faithful people of the land. They might be friends or just frequent acquaintances, but they may not confront me with the truth of God's Word. They possibly will listen and understand; they might laugh with me at my weaknesses and failures, but they might not respond with a blameless outlook that considers our eternal good. This does not mean they are bad; it only means that I need to be honest about who ministers to me. Yes, sometimes we just need understanding, but more often, we need faithful people of the land to spur us on to blameless living. This takes an effort.

Also consider that some individuals are not beneficial for you to be around at certain times of your life. If you are trying to get healthy in the financial area, you probably should not hang out with people who are talking about their vacations or their new car or the house that they plan to buy. If you are training for an event, you probably should not hang out with others who have no idea what this entails and who certainly are not living in a way that is supportive of what you need at this time. If you are a mother trying to establish a home environment conducive to raising children, you probably do not need distractions that would hinder this. Think about it. A college student needs a study environment; a surgeon needs a sterile environment; a mechanic needs an industrial environment; a palace needs a kingly environment; a bride needs a wedding environment. All of these situations are in need of faithful people who are supportive of the goal of the environment.

Verse 7: "No one who practices deceit will dwell in my house; no one who speaks falsely will stand in my presence."

This is a challenging concept. How do we dwell in this world and avoid those who practice deceit? How do we dwell in this world without standing in the presence of falsehood? It does surround us. How do we minister to people and show hospitality if we never invite those who practice deceit into our homes? This takes a wise approach, an approach that includes love and truth. A huge difference exists between someone who practices deceit and someone who happens to miss the mark here; a huge difference exists between someone who consistently hides what is true as opposed to someone who, through a series of temptations, finally gives in to a deceit or a falsehood because they failed to take heed immediately.

But let's not worry about them right now; let's start with ourselves. Are you practicing deceit in any way? Are you lying to your employers? Are you lying on your tax returns? Are you lying to your child's teacher? Are you lying to yourself or to God? Speak the truth in your own heart. Does deceit have a part in you? After all, you dwell in your own house. Clean your house first before you start worrying about your neighbor. And what about this. Again, forget about your neighbor. He who practices deceit is readily found on the internet, on news sources, on blogs, on websites you frequent; these entities are the masters of deceit leading many astray. We are letting these into our homes every time we look at them, and not just the houses we live in; we are letting them into the homes of our hearts. We are letting them into the minds of our family members who hear or see them or who hear us repeat what they report or contain. Consider these very personal aspects of deceit and falsehood before you ponder others who might be practicing deceit or speaking falsely.

Verse 8: "Every morning I will put to silence all the wicked in the land; I will cut off every evildoer from the city of the Lord."

Again, let's make this personal. Forget about others in your vicinity right now; forget about the world as a whole. Think about the wickedness that could be found in yourself, in your own brain, body, and beliefs, and how you must silence it. What thoughts do you allow every morning? Thoughts of dread rather than praise? Thoughts of complaint rather than gratitude? Thoughts of self-will rather than thoughts about God's purpose? Thoughts of judgment rather than of grace? We must put these to silence. They are wickedness in the land of your heart and mind, and they affect the health of your brain, body, and beliefs. Take action and cut off these evildoers from the city of the Lord, from the city of your own heart; cut them off from the temple of the Holy Spirit that lives inside of you.

As we leave today, I want to remind you that tying God's Word into every aspect of our lives impacts our health. We must strive to apply it to our brains with what we think, to our bodies with what we do, and to our hearts with what we believe. God's Word is true. It matters for training in righteousness. Even the great basketball coach Pat Riley of the Los Angeles Lakers knew these were all connected. He developed a tracking system to monitor the improvements of his players over time and asked them all to strive for a 1 percent improvement each season. His program was called CBE for Career Best Effort. His belief was that the value of the player wasn't just about what their best statistic was. The value of the player connected these three aspects. He put it this way: it's about giving your "best effort spiritually and mentally and physically." It all matters.

OK! Take a deep breath. It's time to pull out your journal with your five columns. This same template will be used for all twelve weeks. If you want to download a copy from my website, please visit www.dynamotruth.com. You will find this and be able to print it off; otherwise, your own journal copy is fine. Writing things out in your own handwriting is very effective in making change. It requires action on your part; it engages different parts of the brain; it makes you own it. Please label your columns as follows: column one is *Environment*; column two is *Brain*; column three is *Body*; column four is *Beliefs*; column five is *Scripture and Action Steps*.

Here is a chart for financial health and decluttering for blameless living:

Environment	Brain	Body	Beliefs	Scripture and Action Steps
Declutter for Blameless Living Think about the people, organizations, activities, stores, and so forth that are in my environment. What needs to go? What people or locations do I need to avoid for better financial health?	Clear the clutter from your brain and focus on what helps you in this area. What hinders you?	Remove yourself from tempting situations that are difficult for you right now. This could be conversations, invitations, organizations, and so on. Look at the services you are paying for that you don't even use. Cancel these services. Stop purchasing unnecessary products that are clutter, things that are nonessential.	What do I believe about money? Does it belong to God or to me? Am I to do what I want to do with it, or am I to look to God about how I spend? Is debt OK? How should I invest for the future?	Read Psalm 101 daily. Apply it to my life. Judge myself. How am I treating others? How am I eating and sleeping? Where and when am I not blameless? Clean up my environment in all three areas: brain, body, beliefs. Go to the store and buy only three necessary items; leave immediately. Pray.

Remember, all of this pertains to the topic of your specific health goal, whether it is about your physical health, mental health, financial health, relationship health, spiritual health … even your work health. The chart above just tackled financial health and definitely would need to be tweaked by each individual—in fact, by all of us because we all are able to improve in all areas of our lives. We are in process; God is forever transforming and teaching us. We will never be done. Realize that if you are not blameless in one area, with even a little bit of slackness or disregard, then you are going to suffer the effects of it, and so will others. It all matters. Just remember that you are targeting your specific goal, and all of these are part of accomplishing this in the twelve-week period. Do not feel overwhelmed. Take it slowly with honesty and a serious attitude. However, you must be creative and thoughtful to come up with specifics. If you would like a personal coaching session on this, please email me, and I will be happy to help. In the meantime, let's proceed and see if you can tackle this.

In column one, we are addressing your environment; let's take a sample idea for financial health. Think about the people, organizations, activities, stores, websites, and printed material you have in your environment. What needs to go? Are you hanging around people who don't know how to manage their money or people who have plenty of money and spend freely? Both of these extremes could be toxic to you. On the one hand, there is no example, no insight, no chance for obtaining wisdom from those who are not good stewards of their money; in other words, they don't know how to use it in a responsible and productive way. On the other hand, you have people who might not need to be as concerned as you and have the liberty to purchase and do whatever they want. Listening to their conversations might not be the best influence at this time. You probably should consider separating yourself from this for a while and try to find others who are succeeding in dealing with the same dilemma or goal as you, someone who lives within their means and is organized and wise with how they utilize every penny, someone who shows great contentment in this way of living. Get around faithful people of financial prudence, people who understand and do what is beneficial for financial health. Incidentally, if you have another goal of, say, losing weight, you might have to separate yourself from your buffet buddies for a time. No matter what your goal is, you might have to find another group to minister to you for a while.

Don't be ashamed of this. It is being prudent; it is not being judgmental. You are seeing danger ahead and taking another path.

Moving on to your brain column. Clear the clutter from your brain and focus on what helps you in this area. If you spend time thinking about all the things you want, even if it is in the distant future, you might be hindering your self-control as well as your level of contentment. Instead of thinking about what you want or thinking about what others have that you would like, or thinking about what you don't have, try instead to think upon what you do have and be grateful for it. Remember, as soon as you wake up, "I will sing of your love and justice; to you, O Lord, I will sing praise." Instead of thinking about the better vehicle or kitchen or clothing you want, think about making your current vehicle, kitchen, or clothing better by how you care for it or by some small improvements you could make. Be creative; think on what is good. Do not dwell on what you want at this time. Dwell on what you have that is good and be grateful. Possibly think about what others need rather than what you want or what you might be giving up and refraining from buying right now. Everyone wants more or bigger. As my pastor has said, first he wanted a garage, then he wanted a two-car garage, and after he got both, he wanted a bigger garage. This is the human condition—always wanting more, never satisfied. Only God is our true satisfaction. Dwell on the contentment that He gives you each day with His love and truth and providing for your needs. What tremendous wealth this is in itself.

Moving on to the body column. What you do matters. What can you do right now to help your financial health? First of all, remove yourself from situations that are difficult for you in this area; maybe this could be conversations, activities that cost too much money, organizations that drain your money month after month, small purchases that add up to quite a bit over time. Consider what you do that is costing you money. Maybe you are disorganized and pay bills late and have late fees that add up to a grocery store run each month. Maybe you are paying for services that you don't even use anymore, like a gym membership or a subscribe-and-save membership that really isn't saving you anything. Write down all of your family and your personal activities and assess what actually is needed. Asses what these are really costing you. What products do you buy? What lotions, perfumes, food products, gas stations items, clothing articles, or leisure paraphernalia could you omit from your life? What items, such as clothing, junk, furniture, or nonessentials, could you liquidate? Find items with price tags still on them and return them to the store.

Again, this will be different for everyone. Clear the clutter from your environment to make it easy to do what is in line with your goal. When you clear all this clutter, you might notice your physical health improving. Sometimes certain lotions and foods could be causing us some physical harm that we don't even notice; even quick food choices that we make at gas stations that are not healthy cause us harm and also money. They could even trigger memories that might push us to spend money. By ridding our environment of these, not only do we have more space and less clutter, but we save money, we reduce exposure to toxins, and we have more time on our hands due to the fact that we don't use them, organize them, or spend time shopping for them.

Move on to the beliefs column. What do you really believe about money? Do you believe that God provides this? Do you believe that you are to honor Him with a certain portion of it? Do you believe that you should save a certain amount of it each month? Do you believe that a certain amount of debt is OK or that investments are mandatory? Do you believe in researching options or in leaving it up to some financial investment counselor? Go to scripture to see if what you believe is actually based on God's principles. Don't just follow someone else's example. Go to God and ask Him to give you direction here. Remember, you are to live a blameless life. This includes using wisdom and godly principles in all areas of your life. It is not wise nor is it godly to refrain from helping the poor. It is not wise nor is it godly to hoard what you have or to be a spendthrift; whether you have plenty of money or little money, your financial behavior is a reflection of your spiritual condition. In fact, all of our behavior is a reflection of our spiritual condition, as Psalm 101 clearly shows us. Wise and godly choices must be made in every area of our lives at all times, not just on Sunday, not just when the bills are due, not just when we see someone in need or when we are in need. Ask yourself this question: am I blameless in my financial life? I'm sure all of us have some improvement we could make in this area.

Please remember that we are talking about *environment* this week. It is important that you see that you are responsible for keeping your environment clean, safe, functional, in harmony with your goals, and blameless. We can't control everything, but if it is in our power to act, we must take action, and this includes action in cleaning up our environment.

We become like those we are around. Don't let the environment of others become your environment. Research shows that those around us affect us. One study reported that people had a 57 percent increased chance of becoming obese if they had a good friend who was obese. I am sure that this correlation could be made in most areas of our lives. We become like those we surround ourselves with; remember, he who walks with the wise grows wise. We can create a blameless environment just by the words of our mouths. Think about a common question you get daily, "How are you?" and you respond with the rote answer of "Fine." Your response could have an overwhelming effect on both you and your listener if you incorporated an answer based on your beliefs, as you tie your brain and body into this by using your creative thinking and your own mouth. When asked, "How are you today?" consider responding with one of the following statements based on the truth:

I am surrounded by peace and love twenty-four seven.
I am blessed.
I am accepted.
I am loved.
I am humble.
I am beautiful in the sight of God.
I am wise.
I am forgiving.
I am pumped up.
I am hydrated.
I am rested.
I am de-stressed and calm.

I am organized.

I am financially stable.

I am healthy in my brain, body, and beliefs.

You could change the day just by how you answer, and it might give you an opportunity to share more.

Lastly, column five—*Scripture and Action Steps.* Clearly, our scripture this week is Psalm 101, but take your particular goal and actually use a Bible concordance to find scriptures pertaining to it. For financial health, you might consider these words: money, rich, poor, needy, debt, borrower, usury, giving, firstfruits, treasures, lust, pride, greed, gain, hungry, thirst. Go to God and ask Him to direct you. You don't need every verse in the Bible. Just one verse is powerful. Use it for your training in righteousness.

These are the action steps that I have for you this week; feel free to add more:

1. Read Psalm 101 aloud each day this week, the more the better. Read upon waking, aloud.
2. Apply Psalm 101 to your life. Judge yourself; be sober; be honest. How are you treating others? How are you eating? How are you sleeping? Look for areas where you are not blameless, not just in the financial area but in all areas. How you are in one area is going to affect how you are in other areas.
3. Clean up your environment, the environment of all three—brain, body, beliefs.
4. This action step is specific to those who are working on getting financially stable. Go to the store and buy only three things that you need and that are nutritious. This would be a good exercise for everyone, no matter what their goal is.
5. Pray. A sample prayer is below.

Just a word about these action steps, especially number four. Doing this will help you to do something in accordance with your belief that you should not spend money unwisely. You should not impulse buy. You should not just grab something because you saw an advertisement or because it looked good. Going to the store and controlling what you buy in accordance with what you decided prior to going into the store is an exercise in self-control. This self-control will permeate other areas of your life. You might be challenged with talking too much. This type of self-control might cause you to think, *Oh, I really don't need to say that. Oh, I don't really need to express everything I think or all of my opinions.* Learn to refrain. This is powerful.

> Lord, I will sing of your love and justice; to you, Lord, I will sing praises. I will be careful to live a blameless life, and I give this area of health to you. Lord, show me how to clean up my environment. Show me how to live a blameless life in all aspects, especially in this area right now. Lord, please surround me with faithful people who are blameless, who do not slander, who are not perverse in their hearts, and who do no evil. Lord, help me to put to silence all the wicked in the land, especially in the land of my own brain, body, and beliefs. Lord, please minister to me and help me to allow the companions who truly minister to me to dwell in my presence. Lord, I will sing of Your love and justice, and I will not tolerate the proud of heart, especially my own. Thank You, Lord.

This concludes our study on environment using Psalm 101. More could be said, but this can be a starting point for you to create an environment that not only honors God with a blameless life but is healthy for your brain, body, and beliefs. It all matters. Bye-bye for now.

WEEK 2

MOVEMENT OUT OF OPPRESSION

Welcome to week 2 of the Healing through the Psalms twelve-week program. Last week, we focused on blameless living and cleaning up the environment of our brains, bodies, and beliefs by keeping toxins out and getting rid of toxins that already made their way into each area of our brains, our bodies, and our beliefs. If you haven't already applied the action steps, I encourage you do to so because it really sets the stage for how important our environment is, both externally and internally. This includes our personal environment, the environment of our family, the environment of our work, and the environment of others. Because they all have an effect on us, we must be aware to meticulously care for ourselves by realizing what surrounds us and accepting what we must do to guard ourselves. If we are slack in our attempt to clean up and to keep clean or blameless what is within us or what directly surrounds us, we have a weak link in the chain of our health, and it will affect all areas of our lives. Living a blameless life is part of this.

Please be reminded that none of this is medical advice, but rather it is my effort to do good, to seek peace, and to pursue it by using scripture and providing information to you so that you might be encouraged to see how the brain, body, and beliefs affect our health and how these are uniquely connected in all individuals. I am passionately diligent about sharing this information with you. Mental health has a huge impact on our physical health. Guarding this is very important. Whether you are currently dealing with challenges in this area or not, your attention to what affects your mental health is necessary. Do what you are able to do to support what your professionals advise.

This week, we will be using Psalm 25 as our scripture to focus on our health topic of movement and a health goal of dealing with oppression. Before we begin, however, I want to remind you of what the truth is about you. God made you. You trust in Him. You have gone to the cross to be forgiven and made righteous in the sight of God. You are clean before God because of what Jesus did for you. You are blameless before God; you are accepted; you are loved. He is faithful and will never leave you. God does not change. He is patient, kind, just, loving, wise, and sovereign. We cannot begin to name the attributes of God, but one attribute that is important here is that he is *faithful*. No matter what we do, He will not tire of us; He will not turn away from us; He will never leave us to fight our enemies alone. He is our strength and shield.

Because you trust in the Almighty, you know and believe that He is your defender against all enemies. Oppression is an enemy. No matter how you are oppressed, it is an enemy, but remember, God uses our enemies to strengthen us, to teach us, to develop us, to keep us humble, to show us His strength and glory, and to accomplish His purposes. We will always have enemies around us. Consider how you might be oppressed right now—oppressed in your body, oppressed in your brain or your beliefs, oppressed in your emotions, in your social interactions, in your work goals or advancement, in your academic endeavors, in your marriage or in your parenting, in your effort to share the Gospel with others, in your financial goals, in your single life, with no family surrounding you or supporting you, or in your church. My attempt this week is to use the health topic of movement to help you see the connection of moving out of a state of oppression, any oppression, into a spacious place that God has for you, the path of righteousness that God has for you. Even if you are in a dark valley, God has you on His path, and He is able to refresh your soul. Remember, goodness and mercy follow you all the days of your life, for He is with you. His Word is your hope

You might wonder, *How in the world do my disappointments or oppressed feelings or shyness or frustration in my work advancement or social connections have anything to do with my health, with how I am feeling, with how high my cholesterol is, or what my blood pressure is, or if I feel tired and sluggish, or if I am overweight?* You may wonder many things, but be assured that this has everything to do with your health because it is all connected. If you feel any type of oppression, whether it is social, physical, or spiritual; whether it is work related, family related, academically related; whether it is due to shyness, embarrassment, shame, regret, fear … you name it—any type of oppression will cause you stress, and stress is behind inflammation in your body, and inflammation is behind disease. This includes mental disease.

Think about someone who is about to give a speech and who has fear about public speaking. Their hands get clammy, they sweat, their blood pressure goes up, they lose their appetite and might become queasy in their stomach. Their body is reacting to this stress that comes from fear or anxiety, which is oppressing them at this time. This is true for any type of feeling that causes us fear or stress. It triggers us. We are never going to avoid stress, but we can learn to deal with it wisely. Recognizing what is going on and how it affects you and moving in the right direction to deal with this is important. Let's look at what is going on.

When you are stressed by anything, whether it is physical, mental, environmental, or emotional; whether it is by relationships, unforgiveness, fear, shame, shyness, or intimidation by others; no matter what the stress is, your brain responds. The part of your brain that responds is called your amygdala. This is the emotional center of the brain that responds to stress but does not know why. Its purpose is to protect you, but if your brain thinks that you need constant protection, it will keep you in a fight-or-flight mode, which will harm your health, both physically and mentally. Your cerebrum, which is the rational part of your brain, specifically your prefrontal cortex, theoretically knows why you are stressed, but your amygdala does not. It does not matter if an enemy with a gun is chasing you or you are just afraid to start a conversation with someone; your brain triggers your adrenals to secrete cortisol, which puts you in survival mode. Over time, constant stressors like this become problematic because they cause your body to be stressed so that something called silent inflammation might ensue in the form of high blood pressure and other issues that affect your physical health, not to mention your emotional and mental health. It's all connected. Any stress affects your sleep and blood sugar regulation. It affects your relationships and your ability to manage other areas of your life. We want to move out of this in all three areas—brain, body, and beliefs.

Let's turn our attention to Psalm 25 now and read it aloud.

Psalm 25

1   In you, Lord my God, I put my trust.

2   I trust in you; do not let me be put to shame, nor let my enemies triumph over me.

3   No one who hopes in you will ever be put to shame, but shame will come on those who are treacherous without cause.

4   Show me your ways, Lord, teach me your paths.

5   Guide me in your truth and teach me, for you are God my Savior, and my hope is in you all day long.

6   Remember, Lord, your great mercy and love, for they are from of old.

7   Do not remember the sins of my youth and my rebellious ways; according to your love remember me, for you, Lord, are good.

8   Good and upright is the Lord; therefore he instructs sinners in his ways.

9   He guides the humble in what is right and teaches them his way.

10 All the ways of the Lord are loving and faithful toward those who keep the demands of his covenant.

11 For the sake of your name, Lord, forgive my iniquity, though it is great.

12 Who, then, are those who fear the Lord? He will instruct them in the ways they should choose.

13 They will spend their days in prosperity, and their descendants will inherit the land.

14   The Lord confides in those who fear him; he makes his covenant known to them.

15   My eyes are ever on the Lord, for only he will release my feet from the snare.

16   Turn to me and be gracious to me, for I am lonely and afflicted.

17   Relieve the troubles of my heart and free me from my anguish.

18   Look on my affliction and my distress and take away all my sins.

19   See how numerous are my enemies and how fiercely they hate me!

20   Guard my life and rescue me; do not let me be put to shame, for I take refuge in you.

21   May integrity and uprightness protect me, because my hope, Lord, is in you.

22   Deliver Israel, O God, from all their troubles.

Although the history and theology behind Psalm 25 are important, it is not the focus of our discussion today. However, looking at this to see the depth of emotion, truth, and hope it conveys helps us to see the connection it has to the topic of oppression and movement away from oppression, as well as the movement God has both toward us and with us to deal with oppression.

We will look at a couple of verses at a time today.

Look at verses 1–3: "In you, Lord, my God, I put my trust. I trust in you; do not let me be put to shame, nor let my enemies triumph over me. No one who hopes in you will ever be put to shame, but shame will come on those who are treacherous without cause."

Here are a couple of takeaways from these verses: trust, hope, shame, enemies.

First of all, you trust in the Lord. Without question, He is your God. He is sovereign; He is almighty; He has a path for you. This path includes peace. This is your hope. This is huge and powerful. Remember your hope; remember the great and mighty God you trust in. Because you trust in Him, you no longer have any reason to feel shame; no reason for condemnation; no reason for rejection. You belong to Him. Jesus is forever interceding for you. This is fluid and active. This is the truth. Remember that *your* enemies are His enemies. Oppression is an enemy. Oppression might stem from shame, or it could stem from lies, which are also your enemies, vicious enemies in fact. You must be active in the movement of your mind to take every thought captive to the obedience of Christ; you must be active in the movement of your body to separate yourself from what is shameful, including slackness in blameless living, so that what you believe is your reality. Do not let carnality be your reality. You are to conduct the affairs of your house with a blameless heart.

God's Word is to move us in the direction of godly living, and this includes what we think and what we do. You must be active in the movement of your faith to apply this. It is not enough to just pray this. You must own it, embrace it, and dwell on it. This is powerful and good stuff. *You hope in the Lord.* Your trust is in Him. No one who hopes in Him will ever be put to shame. He is your defender. How dare anyone cause you to be oppressed by shaming you into a position of stifling your movement to embrace the spacious and free path of righteousness God has for you. This path includes reaching out to people, not feeling shame even before you are able to say a friendly word to someone or make a request or give a speech. How stifling this is! Oppression in the area of our mind or emotions is almost worse than oppression in our bodies because we can't see it; we only feel it, and feelings are powerful contributors to our mental and physical health. Even if what you think and feel is not true, if you think it is true, then you are functioning in the realm of that truth, and your brain and body will respond to this. You must use the movement of your faith to combat anything oppressive because you are responsible to obey the Lord while you trust and hope in Him. Consider His promise—He will not let you be put to shame.

Verses 4–5 say, "Show me your ways, Lord, teach me your paths. Guide me in your truth and teach me, for you are God my Savior, and my hope is in you all day long." Some action verbs to consider here are *show, teach, guide*, and *hope*.

We are to continually let God instruct us. Just because we hope in Him does not mean we have grasped all that God has for us or desires for us to know and experience. We must allow Him to show us His ways and teach us His paths. We are to willingly let Him guide us in His truth. He is our Savior. We hope in Him. Why would we want to move in the direction of our own will, our own desires, or our own strength? Do you see how what we discussed last week concerning Psalm 101 and our choice to live a blameless life continues to be relevant? Do you see how it is to be a continual and active effort of movement on our part? Even the truth that Jesus continually intercedes for us shows movement. He is not just sitting at the right hand of God. He is continually interceding for us. This is the one we hope in, the one who instructs us, the one who will not let us be put to shame. In Him is our life and strength. Be active in your movement to let God show, teach, and guide you while you hope in Him.

Verses 6–8 seem to bring up the topic of when we don't live a blameless life. Ponder them again: "Remember, Lord, your great mercy and love, for they are from of old. Do not remember the sins of my youth and my rebellious ways; according to your love remember me, for you, Lord, are good. Good and upright is the Lord; therefore he instructs sinners in his way."

I love some of the takeaways here. *Remember. Do not remember. Instruct. Sinners.*

It is a very important concept that nothing about God is stagnant, and He doesn't want us to be stagnant either. Just as Jesus did not suffer the shame of the cross and cease from action but continues to intercede for us, we are to continually look to God. Yes, we call out to God and ask that He remember His great mercy and love and to not remember the sins of our youth, even the rebellious ways, but we must also have active faith and admission here. Might we be rebellious at times, even if only a little? Rebellion is a serious condition. Samuel told Saul that rebellion was as the sin of witchcraft. It might not look like we practice witchcraft, but every time we are rebellious, we are tainting our souls by this awful attitude and choice. You might not appear rebellious on the outside, but God knows your heart. Are you putting on the right facade, but inside, your heart is far from God? Even if you aren't doing anything that looks rebellious, are your thoughts rebellious? Are your silent behaviors rebellious and causing you to live a life that is not blameless, a life that does not move in the path of righteousness

God has for you? Is this oppression that you feel due to the fact that you are not living blamelessly? If so, you might consider that your admission and movement from this type of living might free you from the oppression that hinders you. God wants you to have peace by living a life that considers Him. He established righteousness for those who are oppressed, but we must move in the direction that He has demanded. This is a command; this is an action; this is not an option. It is His demand given out of great love and faithfulness.

Don't be disheartened by this. The psalm even makes the point of dealing with current sin. In the same breath that the psalmist pleads with God to forget about the sins of his youth and his rebellious ways, the request is made to remember that God is good and upright. In addition, He instructs sinners. An allowance is made. Yes, we might be sinners, but God is still upright and good, doesn't remember our sins, and continues to instruct us. So move close to God and let Him show you His goodness and instruction as you also allow Him to alleviate the oppression you feel. It doesn't matter what your past movement has been. No shame awaits you as you move in the direction of God's mercy. Move on with Him, away from shameful living and the oppression that might come from this, into the freedom and peace that God has for you.

Verses 9–13 point to important concepts: humility, forgiveness, demands, iniquity, fear of the Lord, and prosperity. Read the verses again:

> He guides the humble in what is right and teaches them his way. All the ways of the Lord are loving and faithful toward those who keep the demands of his covenant. For the sake of your name, Lord, forgive my iniquity, though it is great. Who, then, are those who fear the Lord? He will instruct them in the ways they should choose. They will spend their days in prosperity, and their descendants will inherit the land.

Humility should always be a priority, all through the day, every day—humility toward God, toward others, and about ourselves.

Proverbs instructs us like this: "Do not be wise in your own eyes; fear the Lord and shun evil." It states later that the fear of the Lord is to hate evil—pride, arrogance, and evil behavior. Consider how this again ties into blameless living and in creating an environment of health, of goodness, of peace in your brain, body, and beliefs. If you are not humble, if you are not allowing God to teach you, if you are not faithful in keeping the demands of His covenant, then you might feel ashamed; you might feel oppressed; you might have stress, all due to the fact that you have the wrong movement, a movement that is away from His covenant. But take heart. Notice how the psalmist prays for God to forgive not for our sake but for the sake of His great name because He is loving and forgiving. This promise is for you and for me. This promise is for the whole world. Remember this as you seek to understand and relate to others. This same promise is for them too. Do not be hesitant to respond to others with the humility that comes from believing this. You are not the only one who deals with oppression.

Even though the iniquity is great, He is loving and forgiving. But what is iniquity? Here is the definition: gross injustice or wickedness, immoral behavior. Are any of us free from the gross injustice or wickedness we may have in our hearts and minds every time we judge someone? Aren't we wicked every time we have a rebellious movement in the realm of immoral behavior or in simple disobedience to the demands of His covenant? Of course, this would cause shame. This would cause oppression—and rightly so. Move away from this and let the oppression go. We should feel no shame; there is no condemnation for those who are in Christ Jesus, but if you are in Him, so should you walk with Him by living a blameless life. When we do not behave or live in a way that reflects our beliefs, we have duplicity. This causes stress, which causes shame because our own hearts are condemning us. If your own heart does not condemn you, then you have peace with God and no reason for shame. He will not let those who trust in Him be put to shame, and this indeed is peace for your soul.

Moving with obedience to God allows Him to instruct us further, to have reason to confide in us. Think about those we confide in. We confide in those who show that they care about us, who love us, who are interested in us, who understand us, and who are trustworthy. Remember, we probably confide in those who are faithful people of the land as we discussed last week. The fear of the Lord is the beginning of wisdom. When we fear the Lord, He is able to show us His covenant. When this happens, we then grow in wisdom, and this wisdom shows us not only how to see danger ahead but also to see the escape we have from the snare, from the temptation, from the oppression. It all matters.

Verses 16–18 tie this together: "Turn to me and be gracious to me, for I am lonely and afflicted. Relieve the troubles of my heart and free me from my anguish. Look on my affliction and my distress and take away all my sins."

Yes, it all matters. If we are not the faithful of the land, living a blameless life, and fearing the Lord, how can God show us His ways? If we do not trust in Him and humbly go to Him for mercy and relief, how can He be gracious to us and relieve us from our loneliness, our affliction, the troubles of our hearts, or the anguish of our souls? These are super stressors on our brain health, our physical health, and our spiritual health. These affect our relationships, our behavior, our well-being, our movement toward success and goals, and our movement toward the end goal of living a life worthy of Christ. These cause us distress in our emotions and can lead to anxiety, depression, false contentment, and even continued movement away from God, just because we do not know the demands of His covenant and therefore do not keep them. If we say that we trust and hope in the Lord, if we call to Him to remember His great love and mercy, if we ask Him to forget about the sins of our youth and give us relief from our distress, then we are responsible for learning from Him, keeping the demands of His covenant, and truly embracing His grace by our response and admission that we need Him and that we are at fault for moving in a direction that is not part of the demands of His covenant. It all matters.

We will wrap up Psalm 25 by looking at verses 19–21: "See how numerous are my enemies and how fiercely they hate me? Guard my life and rescue me; do not let me be put to shame; for I take refuge in you. May integrity and uprightness protect me, because my hope, Lord, is in you. Deliver Israel, O God, from all their troubles."

These are the takeaways I want you to see here:

- Enemies are numerous.
- They hate fiercely.
- The plea for rescue and no shame again.
- Integrity and uprightness for protection.
- Others, all of Israel, not just self.

Remember, oppression is an enemy. It harms your health. It stifles you. It causes stress in your entire person. Your enemies hate you, and your enemies hate your Lord. We do not need to fear them, but we must recognize them. Whether your enemy is a person who intimidates you, mocks you, rejects you, scorns you, tempts you, or lies to you; whether your enemy is your own sin that causes you to have a lack of integrity and uprightness, your own sin that is rebellious and is causing your movement away from God and His peace, away from God and living according to the demands of His covenant, away from God and the escape from the snare, away from healthy choices you could make for your physical health (like choices that cause your high blood pressure, your weight gain, your hormone imbalance, your poor sleep, your selfishness, your carnality, your arrogance)—no matter what or who your enemies are, they are God's enemies. Our thoughts can be an enemy to God and to us. Our lack of obedience is an enemy to God and to us. Our rebellious ways are an enemy to God and to us. Even if you know you should not spend money on something, or should not eat something, or should quit having your focus on yourself and reach out to someone, if you do not have the movement to obedience with integrity, you are functioning as your own enemy. It is no one else's fault.

All of this is not just about you. Maybe your financial choices, food choices, avoidance of people, lack of forgiveness, arrogance, or opposition to instruction are limiting the work of God not just in you but in all of Israel, in the whole body of Christ, in your brothers and sisters, whom you are to love and encourage. Truly, this is not just about you. Your choices affect your family and those close to you, those who care about you. It is about the environment you create by your choices and what you do and think. Move out of your comfort zone; move into the realm of freedom, the realm of the fear of the Lord, the realm of integrity and hope for rescue. The Lord will not allow you to be put to shame. Do not fear moving in the direction that is required of you, no matter what realm of your life it is—in exercise, in shopping, in relationships, in giving, in serving, in kindness, in turning the other cheek, in keeping silent about the offenses that may have been dealt to you. Do not hesitate to let God give you the strength for the movement that will release you from the oppression of any snare. It all matters.

Now it is time to pull out your journal with your five columns. Remember column one is your topic, which is *Movement*; column two is *Brain*; column three is *Body*; column four is *Beliefs*; and column five is *Action Steps and Scripture*, which you already know is Psalm 25.

As we work through this, we are using the topic of oppression, whether it is emotional oppression, physical oppression, mental oppression, or oppression from events, from people, from poor finances, from past choices, from regret, from failure, from disappointments, or from food. Any oppression is an enemy, but God can use it for good, for instruction and training in righteousness, to keep you and me humble and attentive to His teaching and guidance.

I want to focus on the topic of emotional oppression because I think there are many people who deal with this, and it relates to other types of oppression. I have dealt with the fear of others, fear of failure, fear of rejection. I have dealt with the intimidation of others, scorn of others, mockery of others, and lack of support and interest from others that caused me to feel worthless. I have dealt with people who ignore and don't respond to kindnesses or attempts at reconciliation. I am not talking about the world here. I am talking about my brothers and sisters in Christ. This is why it is so oppressive. They know the truth but aren't doing it. I am guilty of this too, however; I have known the truth and haven't done it. I can't be judgmental; I can only be hopeful that God will release me from the snare of this oppression so that I will move in the direction that is not blameless.

In your brain column, let's think about the actions we can take to rid ourselves of this oppression as we hope in the Lord to release us from the snare. This is causing our brain to *move* in the right direction. To move is an action. You must choose to think on these things. I would suggest these certain thoughts for your mind to dwell on: *I am accepted. It is not my fault* (or if it is, admit it and deal with it). *I am not responsible for how others respond to me. God wants me to reach out to others even if I fear their response. It is not just about me; it is about the whole body of Christ; it is about redeeming all of Israel in Christ Jesus. I am a part of that.*

Also, try this rehearsal in your mind. Envision speaking to someone when you are afraid and feeing oppressed. Envision speaking to the one who intimidates you or someone who has mocked you. You may need to be prudent and avoid some situations, but do not shrink back. If it is another believer, there should be unity, and you may be part of establishing this. If you continue to have this movement of shrinking back, you could be part of the problem of this oppression. This could also oppress the other person. Envision the situation and choose to follow through on it. Envision several situations and ask God to give you the strength to hope in Him that you will not be put to shame as you move forward.

Move to your body column. I must be honest with you. If you need to develop confidence and inner abilities of strength, there is nothing like exercise to do it. This is advantageous for the health of all areas of your life. If you are not exercising, you would benefit by adding this to your daily schedule, whether it is intense or mild cardio, resistance training, or just walking. Even if it is only ten minutes a day, *do something* and be consistent. Five times a week would be wonderful. It is so beneficial to have movement in your physical life to fully experience confidence and inner stamina. Research shows that people have better physical and mental health when they exercise. It improves brain function and promotes better blood flow to all areas of your body. Take this seriously. You cannot expect to move out of the snare of oppression if you are not willing to move your body. Your confidence will improve. Your mental health will improve. Your physical markers will improve. It will strengthen your posture, your self-confidence, your energy. It will improve your sleep and resilience. It will decrease your stress, and this is definitely something we all desire; we want to get stress out of our lives because it harms our health. If we pray daily for God's peace and His protection, we are responsible for receiving this instruction of truth so that He is able to do more and more in us. Take action. Move.

Another movement you could implement is deep breathing. This helps to calm us. It tricks the amygdala, the emotional center of the brain, to believe that there is no stress. Doing this will calm you. This benefits you as you approach a situation that causes you stress from oppression, whether it is people, activities, environment ... you name it. It benefits you when you do this as part of your day even when not experiencing stress. You could do this in the morning as part of your morning routine. You can do this as you are lying on your bed at night. I suggest the 5-5-7 method where you inhale through your nose into your belly for five counts, hold for five counts, and exhale through your mouth for seven counts. It helps relax you so that you feel less stressed so you can fall asleep. It also has many other health benefits. We will talk more about this at another time. You could also use the 4-7-8 method. Just exhale longer than inhaling.

Finally, move in the direction of what you envisioned. God brings us into a spacious place. David had fear; he had oppression; he had opposition. He was the king of Israel. If the king of Israel needed God to act on his behalf to release him from the snare of oppression, to get relief from loneliness and other anguish, don't think you don't need it. Move into freedom and hope in the Lord and the fact that He protects you from shame. Move out of your shyness, out of your fear of rejection, out of the control that intimidation has on you. If you are oppressed by hiding that you want to be healthy, move in the direction of continually making healthy food choices. If you are hindered by the shame of holding finances from God, move in the direction of cancelling your involvement at events and other engagements if they are not in accordance with what God has for you. If you are oppressed by what food is doing to you, move away from it. Leave the kitchen; avoid the aisles in the store that have snares waiting for you. If you are stifled by the fear of what others at the gym will think of you, give it to God, your defender. The truth is that many people at the gyms applaud and respect people who begin exercising. They remember what it was like at that time and know how much better their lives are because of this choice. They are not oppressed by lack of movement anymore.

I cannot stress enough that it is important to move no matter what it is, whether it is exercise, speaking to people, encouraging, doing good to others, actively implementing God's Word in your life, or actively seeking peace with others or yourself. Psalms has this interesting peace of psychology: "When I obeyed your commands, then I understood your statutes." Read that again! This indicates that the understanding came after the obedience, after the doing. Every time we do something, we are changing our brains. What we do strengthens the synapses and connections in our brains. It strengthens the neuronal pathways. This is called neuroplasticity, and it is a very important aspect of the human condition. What we do matters, just like what we think matters. We cannot separate these aspects from our spiritual condition. Every time you do an action, you are strengthening the action in your entire being. Do not underestimate the power of taking action and doing what you know is good. This is important in habit formation, as it strengthens the connections in your brain. Each time you do something, it will be easier the next time. We will talk more about this at another time. But remember, when you envision doing something, it empowers you to actually follow through on it.

In your beliefs column, please consider what you believe about movement. Do you really think that physical exercise will help you in this area? Do you really believe that deep breathing will help? Do you really believe that envisioning your movement in a situation will help? In fact, do you really believe that Psalm 25 is for you, for every area of your health, for helping you to move out of shame and oppression into the release from the snare, into relief and freedom from loneliness, from anguish, from disappointment? If you don't believe Psalm 25 is for you and you say that you hope in the Lord, you have duplicity. Confess it. Accept what is true! God is for you. Recognize what is going on! You feel intimidated and oppressed. Care for yourself. Believe it and move with it. It all matters.

Let's close it up with action steps. This week, your action steps will be related to oppression in the emotional and social sense. Although I give you specific action steps, I want you to develop a couple of action steps specific to the particular area of health you are tackling, whether it is relational, financial, physical, parental, educational … you name it. Determine where you might feel oppression in any area.

Chart for Moving Out of Oppression

Topic	Brain	Body	Beliefs	Scripture and Action Steps
Movement out of oppression	Think about actions to move out of oppression. Think on these things: *I am accepted.* *It is not my fault.* *I am not responsible for how others treat me.* *God wants me to reach out to others even if I fear their response.* *It's not just about me.* *It is about the whole body of Christ.*	I will exercise my mind and my body. I will do deep breathing for five minutes twice a day. I will move away from food or people that oppress me. I will obey God rather than feel oppressed by my own conscience.	Do I really believe physical exercise and deep breathing will help me? Physical exercise and deep breathing help to calm me.	Read Psalm 25 aloud daily. Envision a challenging situation where you are afraid to speak to someone and develop a strategy to act on this by speaking to them first. Exercise! Give thanks daily for the Lord's love and faithfulness. Continue to live a blameless life with no regret.

Here are action steps for those dealing with emotional or social oppression:

1. Read Psalm 25 aloud daily—the more, the better. Try to memorize verses in it.
2. Select a challenging situation that oppresses you. Envision the scenario and develop a strategy for tackling it. Possibly it could be that you are the first to speak to three people rather than waiting for them to speak to you. Possibly it could be that you address someone who intimidates you, or who you feel does not have time for you. Say something positive, such as, "It is very nice to see you today," or "I am glad you came," or "I hope you had a good week." Branch out of your comfort zone. Maybe call someone up who is in need and ask them if there is anything you can do for them. Be creative. Just do something to *move* out of your oppressive zone.
3. Exercise. Exercise. Exercise. Exercise is Miracle Grow for the brain. It detoxifies your body, reduces stress, makes you feel better about yourself, helps with depression, increases metabolism, improves cognition, and is invigorating. It has so many benefits. Use it to your advantage daily.
4. Give thanks daily for the Lord's love and faithfulness, for the fact that He will not let you be put to shame even though you are surrounded by numerous and great enemies, including any thoughts that are enemies.
5. Continue to live a blameless life and keep your environment clean. Conduct your affairs in such a way that you feel no shame from regret. Persevere in this.
6. Pray!

Here is a sample prayer if you need help with this. Just pour your heart out to God.

Lord, I lift up my soul to You. You are God, and I trust in You. Lord, do not let me be put to shame. No one who puts their hope in You will ever be put to shame. Show me Your ways, Lord; teach me Your paths. Lord, I know You are loving and forgiving. You are good and upright, and You instruct sinners, and this includes me. Lord, help me to remember this and receive Your instruction. Help me to fear You and to remember that You will not allow me to be put to shame. Lord, even though I am afflicted and in distress, even though I am lonely and afflicted, even though my enemies are numerous and fierce, You will guard my life and rescue me. Lord, I take refuge in You, and I ask You to protect me with integrity and uprightness. Thank You, Lord, for delivering all your people from oppression. Amen!

I hope you are able to see the connection between what we discussed last week about environment and this topic of movement. We make an effort to clean up the environment of our brains, bodies, and beliefs, but it takes movement to do this and to keep it clean. We create an environment by the choices we make, even by speaking to someone first. Just like Jesus died on the cross for us but continues to intercede for us, we must make an effort to clean up our environment and then continue to move in the direction that God has for us, to keep it clean and free from what oppresses us.

This wraps up our discussion on movement, using Psalm 25 to help us out of oppression, out of snares, out of whatever is stifling us into a true hope in the Lord, into a true condition of no shame, into true peace in all areas of our brains, bodies, and beliefs. It all matters.

WEEK 3

MINDSET AND GRATITUDE

Welcome to week three of my Health through the Psalms twelve-week program. This week, we will be discussing mindset using Psalm 103 as our scripture. None of this is medical advice, but rather it is my effort to do good, to seek peace, and to pursue it by using scripture and providing information to you so that you might be encouraged to see how the brain, body, and beliefs affect our health and how these are uniquely connected in all individuals. Again, I am passionately diligent about sharing this information with you because it all matters. I am trying to bridge the gap between what you and your doctor know, what you and your pastor know, and what you and any counselor know will benefit your health. I want to encourage you to succeed in implementing this information as you learn more reasons why.

So far in our study, using the psalms for health, we have tackled the topic of environment and the topic of movement. We emphasized in our first two weeks that we must strive to keep our environment clean and free from as many toxins as possible. This includes the environment of our brains, our bodies, and our beliefs. We took a look at environmental toxins, toxins from thoughts, relationships, words, noise, people, activities, habits, and lifestyles—anything that would dirty up our brains, bodies, or beliefs. We also focused on how living a blameless life is part of this process. When we discussed movement, we dealt with the effort on our part to move in all three areas—brain, body, and beliefs—by thinking thoughts and starting to exercise as well as taking action to actively move out of what is oppressing us. I gave you the challenge to answer the question of whether or not you really believe that God's Word is relevant in your health and challenged you to move your belief in the direction of finding this significant.

As I said, today we will discuss the topic of mindset and use Psalm 103 as our belief foundation. First, let's define mindset. I think this definition nails it quite nicely: mindset is the established set of attitudes held by someone. This could sound a little vague, or even more, it might sound too encompassing, so I would like to include a couple of words to establish a bit more about it. Attitudes are a huge part of how we think and make decisions, how we behave and react, and how we plan and persevere, as well as how we give our attention to certain ideas and pursuits. Our focus is very important in how we maintain our habits, which affect our lifestyle and all aspects of our person. In other words, our mindset determines our actions. This is definitely affected by our attitudes, which might or might not be grounded in solid thinking and knowledge. When we determine to have a mindset, or a set of attitudes, toward a certain idea or goal, we are making our brain focus on this. By focusing on this, we are actually strengthening the synapses in our brains, which will influence our actions. This type of determination in our thought processes helps us to move more easily in doing the action associated with it, which will then help in establishing the habit. All of this together, the choice to think, to determine, to focus, and then to act, actually changes the brain. This was not known when I was a child, but now it is scientific information that gives hope to many. Don't give up on anything concerning the brain. Learning disabilities, poor memory, anxiety issues, and a host of other brain-related challenges can be alleviated with our intentional choice to help ourselves in this area.

Even your attitudes change your brain. This is called neuroplasticity, which basically means the brain changing. So your mindset, your set of attitudes, affects your focus. It affects your priorities. It affects your habits and, therefore, your life. Do you see why having the attitude of Christ matters, as well as the attitude of believing God's Word and the attitude of establishing a clean environment and moving in the right direction of God's commands? It actually changes your brain, which will affect your body and your beliefs. Your set of attitudes is powerful. What you think and do and believe … what attitudes you allow to permeate your thoughts change your brain. Your willingness to determine your mindset, your focus, and your set of attitudes with the goal of moving in the right direction changes the environment of your brain. The connection to God's Word is so important. This is why we meditate on it day and night. Meditating on it makes us focus and have the same mindset or the same set of attitudes as God Himself. This actually changes our brains, and this will affect our health, but most importantly, this changes and improves our spiritual health. All three are connected. God wants this for us.

Be reminded that, as we discussed from Psalm 25, this is not just about you or me. This is about God, about the whole body of Christ. It is about the world and how we connect to it for good, for the eternal good that God has planned. God wants us to move out of our environment into a spacious place, into the world. Jesus commanded this. We must have the mindset for this. If we are only interested in our little environment, and if we are oppressed by a mindset that limits us, we are determining our actions to reach others for him. The Lord instructs us to reach out and love others, to minister to them, to consider others better than ourselves. This is doing the will of the Lord. This is our ultimate goal of health—to do His will. Of course, we can have the personal goal of health and happiness, but this isn't just for ourselves; it is for our families, our friends, our church, and the whole world.

Three Perspectives

While we discuss Psalm 103, I want to focus on it from three different perspectives: the mindset toward time, the mindset toward action, and the mindset toward relationships. Concerning time, I want you to consider the past, present, and future. Concerning action, consider God, the concept of rest, and you. Concerning relationships, consider you, your circles, and all of heaven. Let's read Psalm 103 aloud now.

Psalm 103

1   Bless the Lord, O my soul, and all that is within me, bless His holy name.

2   Bless the Lord, O my soul, and forget not all His benefits

3   Who forgives all your iniquities, who heals all your diseases.

4   Who redeems your life from destruction, who crowns you with loving kindness and tender mercies.

5   Who satisfies your mouth with good things, so that your youth is renewed like the eagle's.

6   The Lord executes righteousness and justice for all who are oppressed.

7   He made known His ways unto Moses, His acts to the children of Israel.

8   The Lord is merciful and gracious, slow to anger, and abounding in mercy.

9   He will not always strive with us, nor will He keep His anger forever.

10 He has not dealt with us according to our sins, nor punished us according to our iniquities.

11 For as the heavens are high above the earth, so great is His mercy toward those who fear Him;

12 As far as the east is from the west, so far has He removed our transgressions from us.

13 As a father pities his children, so the Lord pities those who fear Him,

14 For He knows our frame; He remembers that we are dust.

15 As for man, his days are like grass; as a flower of the field, so he flourishes.

16 For the wind passes over it, and it is gone, and its place remembers it no more.

17 But the mercy of the Lord is from everlasting to everlasting on those who fear Him, and His righteousness to children's children.

18   To such as keep His covenant and to those who remember his commandments to do them.

19   The Lord has established His throne in heaven, and His kingdom rules over all.

20   Bless the Lord, you His angels, who excel in strength, who do His word, heeding the voice of His word.

21   Bless the Lord, all you His hosts, you ministers of His, who do his pleasure.

22   Bless the Lord, all His works, in all places of His dominion. Bless the Lord, O my soul!

Perspective of Time

As you look at Psalm 103, I want you to notice how the past, the present, and the future are indicated and are of value to us. Connecting these three segments of time in relation to God and ourselves can be useful. Time is always changing. A moment in time can bring a dramatic shift in circumstances, physically, mentally, and spiritually. A moment in time can turn sadness into joy; it can turn hunger into fullness; thirst into quenching; hope into reality; craving into satisfaction; yearning into rest; even labor into delivery.

Although we are often reminded to avoid dwelling on the past as it pertains to our mistakes, regrets, failures, and other things, such as disappointments, it is not wise to forget what is important as it pertains to what we should remember, dwell on, and learn from. The psalmist here calls to mind many reminders of what God has done in the past. Here are some of them:

- He made known His ways to Moses and His acts to the children of Israel.
- He hasn't dealt with us as our sins deserve and hasn't punished us according to our iniquities.
- He has removed our transgressions far from us.
- His mercy has been from everlasting.

These are past actions that are very important to remember. Israel and none of us should forget about the past in this respect. This past establishes our present situation and environment. Remembering these things is encouraging. It helps our mindset. It helps the attitude of our minds. It helps our focus. All of what God has done is an admonition to and for us, so that we can learn and depend on Him more and more; so that we take heed to what it teaches; so that we can be encouraged to persevere. This takes a mindset on our part to have the attitude of gratitude for all of it, as well as a focus on it. Dwelling on the past in this respect is profitable and will help us to improve our mindsets. If we are stuck in a moment that is difficult and we feel disheartened while we are waiting for improvement or relief, we surely could be tempted to lose hope; however, remembering events such as these from the past is a reminder of what God has done. It is for us in the present. Also, remembering how long those in the past had to wait to see what God would do, to see the deliverance and freedom that He promised, is important. Some of this was not seen by many of His faithful ones but was seen by their posterity. Remembering this while we wait for our Lord is comforting.

Now to the present, which is always changing from one moment to the next. Think about what is going on in the present here in this psalm. It is personal; it is about the individual and how God is working in his or her life now, not in the past but now. This is relevant, and it shows great healing in the health of the psalmist, in his brain, his body, and his beliefs. He commands himself to bless God and not forget the past. God still forgives him and in the present heals his diseases. He redeems him from destruction, crowns him with good things, and satisfies him for his benefit as He renews his youth. God is still merciful and gracious. He is still slow to anger and full of mercy. This is present tense. We can't point to the past and say, "That was then; this is now." God is current. This should change the attitude of your mind and shift your mindset to help you focus on what is good and true. This should cause an attitude of gratitude to well up in you, and this is the best attitude to have. It is as far from grumbling, complaining, and lacking faith as we could possibly be. This changes your brain as you move into the realm of realizing how God worked to change the environment of the past for all of Israel, and He still does so in the environment of your soul as He establishes righteousness for all who are oppressed. This includes you and me, and it means now—not then but now.

Ponder the future here. The psalm does not keep us in the past or in the present but encourages progressing forward with speech that will inspire movement to take place and to continue in motion. Once a word is spoken, something else happens—either a thought or idea in your brain is triggered, and then an immediate action or a response occurs. It is not enough that the psalmist remembers the past and realizes the present but that he moves forward with a response. The cue or command was given to remember and realize. So now it is time to respond, which will be in the future. This is fluid. It is not just enough to remember the past and realize that God did something. We must respond to effect good change in our future. The psalmist responds with a mindset of words that command. We will talk about this in a bit.

Perspective of Action

Now let's look at the psalm from the perspective of action: God's action, no action or rest, and our action. Remember our health is fluid and is influenced by what we do. Our bodies want to be in a homeostatic state, which means they want to be balanced. Our brain loves stimulation and change, but our body likes routine. Similarly, our spiritual state is fluid; God does not want us to be stagnant. He wants us to do His will, to always abound in the work of the Lord, to be moving on. We are to grow. We are to give what has been given to us. We are to keep things moving. Lack of movement and action is usually ineffective unless a choice has been made to remain still out of prudence.

Consider God's actions. He forgives, heals, redeems, crowns, satisfies, executes, made, is, has not dealt, removed, pities, knows, remembers, and has established. This is a lot of action on God's part, and these actions are specific and determine a lot. God is not stagnant, nor does He change. We can count on this. Our mindset should have a focus that includes these powerful abilities of God. His action for us, with us, and toward us, as well as his action throughout the world, is relevant.

What about no action—in other words, rest? Actually, to rest would take a choice. We don't just rest. We decide to stop what we are doing and rest. God did this on the seventh day after He completed creation. He rested, and we are also to rest on the seventh day. In relation to the psalm, I view that while God keeps working as He heals, forgives, establishes, redeems, pities, satisfies, and so on, we are in a state of rest or receiving. It is almost as if we are passive while He performs work on our behalf. We do not have the power to heal disease or satisfy longings or remove transgressions, but He does. It is OK to rest in this sense as we allow Him to do the work, and as we choose to be in a relinquished state of rest for this purpose. Our mindset focused on this aspect would definitely shift our attitudes.

The psalmist also has action, however. I don't imagine his doing anything but realizing what is true and good and responding by praising the Lord, resting, and receiving the benefit of God's action. However, he moves forward with speech to command others to action, to praise the Lord. As we discussed concerning environment and oppression early on, think about how powerful this is in establishing an environment of praise and faith, an environment to move one out of oppression, an environment that would definitely affect your mindset and the mindset of others to move into gratitude. God inhabits the praises of His people. There is no judgment or word against giving praise to God. We can never go wrong here. Even if there is no fig on the vine or fruit on the tree, we can still praise Him. Even if He doesn't deliver us, we can still praise Him. Even if our mother or father abandons us, God is to be praised because He is good, and everything He does is good. Whether here or with the Lord, we can still praise Him. This will change your brain, body, and beliefs through a total mindset shift toward gratitude.

I want you to see the connection of the action of praise to many environments. Remember, this is not just about you. It is about all of Israel, the whole body of Christ, and the world. We are members of one another, and we are to be hands to help the world. When we take action on this command to praise as the psalmist did, we change the environment of our brain. This influences our emotions, our faith, our choices, our actions, and our whole mindset. It also influences and affects those around us. It establishes an environment of focus on God and His purpose rather than on self and stagnation. This will definitely be influential in touching the lives of others as well as establishing a safer and more blameless environment. After all, how can we have sin when we have praise? Furthermore, look at the fact that all of heaven is influenced by this command to bless the Lord. Wow! Can you imagine this? The words of your mouth telling all of heaven, the ones who do His will and His pleasure, the ones who minister to us who believe, the ones who excel in strength to "praise the Lord." These are the ones who do His Word. Think of the environment we are creating, telling them to do this. How can this be? Try it with belief. I challenged myself just this morning to do this. I am waiting to realize how this is going to benefit my day and the day for those around me. How will it change things? I do not know, but I do know that if it was an action for the writer of the psalm, then it should be action for me too. I will respond by heeding it and receiving the benefits. I do know that giving praise is a positive action for my whole being. God is worthy of it too.

I hope you are able to see strong connections between all we have discussed so far concerning the brain, body, and beliefs and our environment, movement, and mindset. Our environment affects our brains and bodies. It affects our movement and action. Our movement and action affect our mindset. We can change our brains by moving; it changes the environment of our brain and therefore our other environments. It even has an effect on the systems of our bodies. This is important because it has further effects on our genetic expression. This is why I am discussing things in this order, to bring up the topic of our genes. Epigenetics is a current health principle, highly researched and studied by scientists today. What we do and what influences us contribute to our genetic expression. I won't go into this now, but it is something to consider with a curious mind. We know that many of our behaviors bring health or sickness, bring peace or mental oppression, bring spiritual growth or stagnation … it all matters. A lot of people will blame a problem on their genetics and never take ownership of how their environments, their actions, and their mindsets helped to contribute to the problem. Yes, God created us with our own personalized DNA, but what we do, how we have been nourished, and so much else has shaped us and will continue to. All of this affects the expression of our genes.

Please also consider this aspect of what God has done, is doing, and will do, as well as past, present, and future—to the fact that what you realize about what He has done, how you receive concerning what He has done, and how you respond to what He has done, is doing, and will do shifts your mindset and your life. It will impact you and those around you. Again, realize, receive, and respond to what God has done, is doing, and will do. As you look at Psalm 103 and as you take action steps, realize, receive, and respond to what the psalmist has taught us through Psalm 103, as well as what was, is, and will be for you, your circle, and the whole world.

Chart for Mindset of Gratitude

Topic	Brain	Body	Beliefs	Scripture and Action Steps
Mindset of gratitude	Think about God's goodness, past, present, and future.	Write statements of gratitude to the Lord and other people.	Do I really believe that God is good and that I have reason to be grateful? Am I truly grateful on a daily basis?	Read Psalm 103 aloud each day! Thank God for the help He is giving you to reach your goal. Pray!

Let's conclude today with action steps concerning our mindset. No matter what goal of health you are tackling right now, your mindset matters. I will leave it to you to select some action steps specific to your personal situation, whether it is health, financial, relational, or anything else, but no matter who you are or what your goal is, I want your specific focus this week to be on the mindset of gratitude. This is one of the most important aspects of our entire being. I think gratitude is the antidote for everything. We can't go wrong with it. It shows we are grateful; it shows we realize that something was given to or done for us; it shows a right response of humility by expressing thanks. Being in a state of humility, in my opinion, is the absolute safest state to be in. God is close to you and everyone when we are humble. As it says in Proverbs, "Do not be wise in your own eyes; fear the Lord and shun evil." Here are my suggestions:

1. Read Psalm 103 aloud each day—the more, the better. Memorize some of the verses. Read it with faith and expectation. Realize, receive, and respond to what it says.
2. Write it out in your journal. Write specific verses. Relish in it.
3. Write down at least one thing per day that you thank God for.
4. Daily, write three statements of gratitude to the Lord for what He has done, is doing, and will do.
5. Actively express gratitude each day to at least three people who have done something for you in the past, three people who are currently doing something for you, and three people who are going to be there for you in the future.
6. Concerning your particular goal, thank God for the help He has given, is giving, and will give to establish you and your habits to function with success.
7. Pray!

Here is a sample prayer incorporating Psalm 103:

> Lord, I praise You; I praise You with all of my being, with my mind, my mouth, and my heart. Lord, You have forgiven me; You have healed me; You have redeemed me from destruction and have crowned me with loving-kindness and tender mercies. You know what I am, and You have great compassion on me. Lord, You have done this from old; You are doing this now; You will continue to do this. You have established Your dominion, and

Your kingdom rules over all. The ministering spirits who excel in strength bless Your name and do Your bidding. Lord, I realize for all time that You are God, and I receive all You have for me with this response of gratitude. Thank You, Lord. I will praise Your name with all of heaven as I realize again and again and receive again and again and respond again and again to what You have done, are doing, and will do. Praise the Lord!

The Lord is slow to anger. He is kind, people. He understands our struggles, and yet He doesn't look away and avoid us. He never has disdain for us. I love that. He never has disdain for us. He hears us when we call. This is the same Lord who has established His throne in heaven and whose kingdom rules over all. Embrace this truth no matter what your struggle is. Instead of clinging to your struggle, cling to the God who commands angels who excel in strength and do His will. It is what has been true, is true, and will be true. Realize, receive, and respond!

Next week will be exciting. We will continue to keep our environment clean as we move forward out of oppression with a healthy mindset and talk about one of everyone's favorite topics—food. Bye-bye!

WEEK 4

FOOD THAT TRULY SATISFIES

Welcome to week four of my twelve-week Health through the Psalms program. Congratulations on sticking with this and seeking improvement in your health or just optimizing your health with extra tidbits of effort. This week, we are going to discuss the very controversial, yummy, and important topic of food, using Psalm 104 as our scriptural foundation for discussion and guidance. This will be another aspect of improving your health. Hopefully, you are realizing more and more how you are able to bridge gaps in your health.

Review

Before we look at Psalm 104, let's take some time to review what we have discussed so far. In week one, we talked about environment and how we could clear the clutter from our lives by living a blameless life. Psalm 101 was our scripture, and although we usually think of environment as what is outside of us and how it affects us, we considered ourselves and how we affect the environments of our minds, others, and the rest of the world. We analyzed our personal environment, considering our mind and thoughts, our physical environment, and our spiritual environment, which we can't see but affects us greatly. We also looked at our outer environment, considering the effects of toxins from other people as well as environmental toxins in food and products we buy. We talked about how our words affect our environment, both personal as well as those of others and all of heaven, as we considered how we can praise the Lord and tell His angels, who excel in strength, to praise Him also.

During our discussion in week two, we talked about movement and used Psalm 25 as our scriptural basis. We emphasized that we must have a priority of movement in our lives, mentally, spiritually, and physically. God wants us to be growing and moving forward. Yes, there is a time to be still, but even in this, we are actually moving forward with obedience because God has told us to rest. We also reminded ourselves that our minds should be moving with active thoughts that are good and true and that all of this leads to the movement out of oppression into a spacious place to do God's will. Finally, I gave you the challenging action steps to move, including committing to a consistent effort to exercise by starting where you are able—walking, lifting weights, anything that would ensure physical movement, because this is very important for your health, brain, body, and beliefs.

In week three, we discussed the topic of mindset using Psalm 103 and emphasized that our mindset is very powerful in how it helps or hinders us in moving forward with action. When we think about what we are going to do, we actually have more ease in doing it. This mindset also helps with reaching goals and obtaining new habits. Your action steps challenged you to focus on the mindset of gratitude as I conveyed that I think this is the most important mindset to have—an attitude of gratitude. Remember your mindset is your set of attitudes. This is important to evaluate. I also challenged you on this, as I posed the valid question, "Do you really believe that God's Word has any relevance in your health?" Proverbs states that as a man thinks in his heart, so is he. This is huge because if you do not have a mindset or set of attitudes to believe that God's Word can help you in this area, you will not benefit as much as you would if you really believed it and were 100 percent committed to it. What we believe really matters. It is important to realize what you are believing and how it affects your mindset.

Anecdotes

I am going to share three anecdotes with you about all three of these topics. All three of these are from just this week, and I feel ashamed, regretful, humbled, and instructed. I realize my responsibilities, failures, and acts of foolishness and disobedience, both in my brain and body. I receive what God has shown me, and I am responding by moving forward with a changed mindset and a willingness to improve the environment of myself and others.

My first anecdote is about the loft area, where I work with my sweetheart Mollie, and that of my desk, where I do my office work for my husband's business as well as my writing and videos and Zoom meetings. My desk had been so cluttered and had much filing that needed to be done, as well as documents to process that I wasn't sure what to do with or where to put. Many extra items were on my desk that were not functional for the purpose of that environment. I said to my daughter, "Maggie, when you come home tonight, this awful mess will be gone, and it will be stiflingly organized and functional. It will look like our beautiful upper room, which has absolutely no clutter. I am going to get this done." It took effort on my part, and I almost gave up, but I purged, organized, filed, and dealt with much that I had put off with my procrastination—something that really affects us and indicates that we are avoiding a troubling issue. I'll be honest with you. The fact that I voiced the goal to my daughter actually helped me to do this. I completed the task; Mollie's educational area and my desk and office area look great. I cleaned this environment up, and let me tell you, it feels fantastic. I get an endorphin rush every time I look at it. This feels so good. I hope you understand that even a small accomplishment can do so much. This also reflects who I am. I don't want to be a disorganized person. By cleaning this clutter out of my life, I moved forward as an organized person. It is a continuous process.

My second anecdote is a more serious one about the heart. Psalm 101:2 says, "I will be careful to live a blameless life. Oh when will you come to me? I will conduct the affairs of my house with a blameless heart." In all honesty, I have not been at all blameless in my heart and my mind with my thoughts, attitudes, and what I have been thinking about people and situations. Because of this, I have been creating a toxic environment in my person as well as in others, as my environment has negative effects on them. So, my family is and would be the main recipient of this poor thinking and behavior. It is no small matter to dismiss anything that is vile. I was the vile one—not others, not the environment, not the world. Remember, I said we need to take a look at ourselves and whether or not we are the cause of a toxic environment; we need to look at ourselves first and evaluate how we are living and if we are living a blameless life before we get carried away with the rest of the world that is not blameless and might be full of perversity and vile behavior because we are just as guilty. It starts with each individual, and I admit to you that even as I am passionately diligent to help people obtain peace in their brains, bodies, and beliefs, I am even more passionately diligent to be at peace with God by living a blameless life.

My third anecdote is about praise. I haven't felt much about praise lately. I have felt that God has been quiet. I have been dwelling on what I want instead of being thankful for what I have. I have steadily been traveling downward in my thoughts and beliefs. In fact, a very wise woman, a biblical health coach herself, challenged me and told me that she heard "feeling sorry for myself" in what I was saying. It stung. Why did it sting? It stung because it was true. My clutter, my poor mindset, my lack of moving forward with true and good thinking really has stained me. So I have admitted it and repented of it, and now as I realize and receive this, I am responding with movement forward with praise, to establish an environment that is blameless, and this honors God and helps my health.

All of these topics—environment, movement, mindset, and now our topic of food—are important for a very good reason. They affect the expressions of our lives. They affect our bodies, how we heal, and how we deal with challenges and stressors. They affect our emotions and how we think, learn, feel, make decisions, and treat people. Because they affect us so much, I am taught by those who know more than I that they affect us down to the cellular level; they affect us down to the genetic level. This is important for the whole life span, not just at conception. Our genetic expression doesn't stop when we are born. It continues as we develop. If this is not nurtured in a healthy way via our environment, our movement, our mindset, and our food, we are hindering what God has made. The goal of knowing and implementing the wisdom of this information is that it will reduce stress in our brains and bodies and in our beliefs. By reducing stress, we reduce the chance of sickness and disease. If we have health issues because we do not take care of ourselves, God is not at fault. The responsibility is ours. We are to honor Him with our bodies. Let's try to do this as we make choices for a blameless life to improve our environment, our movement, our mindset, and now our nourishment as we talk about food.

Finally, on to Psalm 104. We are going to stop and discuss while we read this one.

Look at verse 1: "Praise the Lord, my soul; Lord, my God, you are very great; you are clothed with splendor and majesty." The psalmist opens up with praise. Remember, praise is a mindset. The attitude of gratitude is a huge antidote for challenges. We used Psalm 103 to look at an attitude of gratitude last week. This type of attitude changes your brain; it changes your mindset; it changes your environment and that of those around you; it impacts your decisions and what you will choose to do. This mindset of praise also gets the focus on God and not on the self. This is beneficial for all of us. Having our focus on self limits us. Yes, we should know ourselves, evaluate ourselves, judge ourselves, and understand what is going on with ourselves and what we need, whether it is sleep, rest, food, time to ourselves, or relationships. However, focusing too much on ourselves might negatively impact us as well as others, as it shifts our mindset from the good of others and moving forward to our finite selves, which limits us; it actually inhibits reaching our goals. Having an attitude of gratitude and a mindset of gratitude is an automatic jump out of any kind of stagnation or mindset that limits growth or improvement. Keep it a priority in your day.

Look at verses 2–6:

> The Lord wraps himself in light as with a garment;
> He stretches out the heavens like a tent and lays the
> beams of his upper chambers on their waters. He makes
> the clouds his chariot and rides on the wings of the
> wind. He makes winds His messengers, flames of fire
> his servants. He set the earth on its foundations; it
> can never be moved. You covered it with the watery
> depths as with a garment; the waters stood above the
> mountains.

God has established an environment of splendor and power not just with and around Himself but in all of heaven and earth as well. This is not just a stationary environment either; it is an environment of movement. See how He makes the winds His messengers, His servants flames of fires, the earth unable to be removed from its foundations, yet we know it is in motion around the sun. The waters are in the deep, and water is fluid, always flowing, yet the waters above the mountains are in place to provide rain for the earth. The environments He created are purposeful and are for health, for growth, and for moving forward to do good, to do His will.

Look at verses 7–10:

> But at your rebuke the waters fled, at the sound of
> your thunder they took to flight; they flowed over the
> mountains; they went down into the valleys, to the
> place you assigned for them. You set a boundary they
> cannot cross; never again will they cover the earth.
> He makes springs pour water into the ravines; it flows
> between the mountains.

I love this! God establishes an environment, yet He does not stop there. He keeps moving forward with speech by commanding the creation in this environment. Remember, wise speech nourishes the soul. God's Word is food for us, and it is our health. Truly, this is good for us to do. Sometimes we just have to say what needs to happen to prompt or promote it to happen, to prompt and promote our own action, our own moving forward, our own obedience to God and to what we really believe. Think about this direction. Can you imagine running a family, a classroom, a business, or a country without using words, without giving some type of command to the environment that belongs to us? We can't command the environment of others, but we sure have the right and responsibility to command ours. Do this. Take a stand even if it means you are commanding yourself. Get the environment of yourself blameless and in order before worrying about everything else.

I do this often, especially when I feel a bit depressed or if I feel like I am dealing with pride. I love the last verse of another psalm, of Psalm 42: "Why are you downcast, O my soul? Why are you so disturbed within me? Put your hope in God, for I will yet praise him, my Savior and my God." What a reminder to us to get the focus on our Lord and His greatness rather than ourselves. Another verse that comes to my mind often is in Proverbs: "Do not be wise in your own eyes; fear the Lord and shun evil." This reminds me to take heed, to be careful to live a blameless life. We must be in constant awareness to keep our environments clear of all toxins, and the toxins of our own thoughts and emotions are nothing to scorn.

Now verses 11–15.

> They give water to all the beasts of the field; the wild donkeys quench their thirst. The birds of the sky nest by the waters; they sing among the branches. He waters the mountains from his upper chambers; the land is satisfied by the fruit of his work. He makes grass grow for the cattle, and plants for people to cultivate— bringing forth food from the earth; wine that gladdens human hearts, oil to make their faces shine, and bread that sustains their hearts.

These verses indicate to me purposeful, functional, and loving aspects of God. He not only created the heavens and the earth with a beautiful design and established an environment of purpose and function, but He also established this for the living creatures, the animals and mankind, for us. He created an environment not just for our physical health but also to "gladden our hearts" and to "make our faces shine" and to "sustain our hearts." Of course, God wants us to delight in Him, but look what He put in place so that we could have delight. Look what He put in place to ensure that we have what we need. Our whole environment is from Him. He made it purposeful and functional. We are the ones who have cluttered it up with toxins and junk. We may have not done this on purpose, but our lack of paying attention to our environment through our lack of blameless living, through lack of movement, and through a mindset of slackness and lack of gratitude have brought unhealthy consequences. We aren't condemned, however; we are redeemed. We are forgiven, blessed, chosen, and accepted. Remember, although God does not change, He is fluid, and His creation is fluid. His creation, the environment He created, has cycles, and these cycles have established patterns of clearing clutter from the earth. These established cycles cause our bodies to grow and heal, our hearts to mend, our brains to learn, and our beliefs to grow in faith. This is why we take heed, so that we can move forward with beneficial actions that promote improvement and avoid harm.

On to verses 16–18.

> The trees of the Lord are well watered, the cedars of Lebanon that he planted. There the birds make their nests; the stork has its home in the junipers. The high mountains belong to the wild goats; the crags are a refuge for the hyrax.

Again, God shows the care He has for His creation by how what He created is beneficial for the creatures He created. I love how the trees belong to the Lord and are well watered, by Him of course, by His command. I love how He provides places for the birds, the storks, the wild goats, and the hyrax to have homes. Think of all God manages, not just us; He manages all of creation. He keeps all of the different environments free from toxins. He is blameless in what He does; everything He does is good, including watering the trees, which the animals use and which man uses, the beautiful trees of Lebanon. Just imagine! If He can keep clutter out of all of this, surely we could manage ourselves and our homes with more consistent and similar attention.

Look at verses 19–23:

> He made the moon to mark the seasons, and the sun knows when to go down. You bring darkness; it becomes night, and all the beasts of the forest prowl. The lions roar for their prey and seek their food from God.

Again, these verses show that God continues His work for all of creation. The seasons are timed, as is the day. Because of this, we are guided in how we plant and harvest seeds; we are guided on when to sleep and when to work as well as when to eat. We are reminded that this comes from God. Just as the mighty lion seeks its food from God, so should we. With a mindset of gratitude, we should approach the topic of food. Our food comes from God. We are nourished because He cares for us. He sends rain on the just and the unjust, and this rain nourishes the soil and the plants that we need for food. We might plant, water, and harvest, but He causes the seeds to grow. He commands it, and therefore, we have food. All of creation has food because He established the environment for the continuation of food production; this is fluid, a constant process.

Just a quick mention about the sun going down. God established a set pattern for our sleep-wake cycle. We should not disregard this. We follow His lead and care for ourselves by sleeping when He intended for us to sleep. Of course, seasons of time exist when we might not be able to ideally follow this, such as when a new baby arrives, when urgent matters dictate no sleep, or when we must work a night shift, but in general, we are harming ourselves by disregarding the indication that we are to sleep and rest. God commanded a day of Sabbath to focus on Him and to rest. He knows we need this. He made us this way. It is up to you to decide how much sleep you need and when exactly to go to bed and when to get up, but consistency and a good sleep environment matter for good health. Again, we should not scorn the little things that add up to huge impacts on our lives and the lives of others. If you deprive yourself of the sleep you need, you are behind the body's increased efforts for consistency and homeostasis because lack of sleep stresses your body and stress is behind illness. Remember this. Stress is behind illness, no matter where the stress comes from. It all matters. You are nourishing yourself by wisely making sleep an important part of your daily priorities. This is food for emotional health, brain health, physical health, and spiritual health, as it shows obedience to what you believe is good for you, which is God's command to rest.

Look at verses 24–26:

How many are your works, Lord! In wisdom you made them all; the earth is full of your creatures. There is the sea, vast and spacious, teeming with creatures beyond number—living things both large and small. There the ships go to and fro, and Leviathan, which you formed to frolic there.

Again, we are returning to a mindset of praise to the Lord. He is acknowledged as one with wisdom; he is acknowledged for the environment He created, a spacious environment full of life, an environment that allows man to do work as ships made from His trees go to and fro for the purpose that provides for needs. Also, an indication is made about play. The Leviathan in the sea has a place to "frolic." I see indication of no stress, of pleasure, of peace, of ease in the connection with God. If God mentions that the Leviathan has a place to frolic, surely He is concerned with the concept of play in our lives. It isn't just about work and accomplishment. We are to enjoy, to play, to be about more than just struggle. God cares about us enough to give us this type of reprieve. This, too, is part of health, and God has established it. Here is the definition of frolic: "play and move about cheerfully, excitedly, or energetically." What a picture of health this is. If our children don't do this, they are sick. I remember how awful it was when my kids would just lie on the couch with a fever or other common immune challenge and how relieved I was when they started jumping on the couch. We might not embody this energy as a ninety-year-old, but every age needs some frolic.

Let's look at verses 27–30:

> All creatures look to you to give them their food at the proper time. When you give it to them, they gather it up; when you open your hand, they are satisfied with good things. When you hide your face, they are terrified; when you take away their breath, they die and return to the dust.

Finally, we are going to talk about food. First, let's acknowledge that it comes from God. He gives it to us. It comes from His hand. It is to satisfy us. God satisfies us with good things, and food is one of them. How terrified we would be if we did not have food. I have heard it said that complete chaos and social upheaval would occur if six meals were missed. We don't work the land as independent gardeners and farmers like our ancestors did. We rely on others to plant, nourish, and harvest the crops, but it all comes from God. Do not forget this. Egypt had a famine. God knew it was coming. Ireland had a famine. God knew it was going to happen. We are reliant on God for food, for our crops to grow, for the rain showers to come, for absolutely everything. We must be humble and grateful for this, for every morsel that goes into our mouths. Remember this. Our food comes from God, not the grocery store.

When I was a little girl, my father, who was a farmer, would sometimes tell us to pray for rain. When the rain would come, we would sit out on the east porch with my mom and dad and relish the rain. We would listen to the thunder. It is a special memory, a time of rest and gratitude. The attention was a physical posture of unspoken gratitude. Yes, I am sure my mother and dad said, "Thank God for this good rain," but it was also a time of rest, of a healthy connection to God and to each other, of the mindset that what we need comes from God. This memory is a treasure to me now that my dad is ninety-two and my mother is eighty-nine. My dad, the farmer, was dedicated to this godly occupation, basking in what God gave while his children observed. The visual is still powerful … my father's giving of thanks to *my Father*, who gave. For this, I will be eternally grateful. We did not give passionate thanks like the psalmist gave so often, but our hearts gave thanks.

A quick word about table prayers. I am going to be honest here and admit that often I say quick prayers of grace before a meal rather than taking a complete pause to really embrace the truth that, in giving thanks, I am acknowledging the Almighty in a personal and holy way, in a way of respect by giving thanks to whom it is due. Giving thanks helps our bodies. Research shows that taking this moment to give thanks actually improves digestion and nutrient absorption, which will further help our body and our brain health. When we are nourished this way, we are more energized and less stressed. Experiencing health this way gives us more stamina to walk in the fruit of the spirit, to obey God, to do what we know we should do, to do His will. It builds resilience. It is for us, to help us. This is not to hinder us; it is to nourish us. How can God use us if our bodies and brains are not functioning at their optimum ability? We can improve this. It doesn't mean that we are to become "super"; it only means that we are being who God made us to be; we are made in His image, and His image does not include being too tired or undernourished to be able to do His will.

Now that we have taken a moment to acknowledge that our food comes from God and that we should thank Him for it each time we enjoy it, let's finish the psalm with the good words of praise.

Look at the final verses, 31–35:

> May the glory of the Lord endure forever; may the Lord rejoice in his works; he who looks at the earth, and it trembles, who touches the mountains, and they smoke.
> I will sing to the Lord all my life; I will sing praise to my

God as long as I live. May my meditation be pleasing to him, as I rejoice in the Lord. But may sinners vanish from the earth and the wicked be no more. Praise the Lord, my soul. Praise the Lord.

We cannot go wrong when we praise the Lord. It is this mindset of praise that should be the ultimate priority for our health. This creates the right environment for health. It keeps us moving forward. It is right and good to give the Lord thanks and praise. It is good to have sweet meditation of Him, meditation that is pleasing to Him. We have so much reason to rejoice. Not only is this a command, but it is part of every relationship, acknowledging what is good about others, and God is good. It all matters.

The Topic of Food

Now what we all have been waiting for—the topic of food. We have already discussed that food comes from God, but moving forward, we are going to define what food is, why it is important, who you are when you approach food, how you approach food, where you approach food, and other spicy connections. We are also going to address some of its impact on brain health and spiritual health as we consider our beliefs.

What Is Food?

First of all, let's take a step back and realize what food actually is and then compare it to what is presented to us as food, as well as what we allow ourselves to ingest. Food is to be nourishment; it is to feed our brains and bodies with the nutrients that they need to function the way God intended them to function. This includes growth and development, healing, energy, and most of all homeostasis so that everything stays in working order.

Here is a definition: "Food is any nutritious substance that people or animals eat or drink or that plants absorb in order to maintain life and growth."

For the sake of clarity, we will just define "nutritious" as something that is actually good for us and provides nutrients that we need. However, these nutrients are what our own personal bodies need. In other words, what one person needs is different from what another person needs. In addition, there are thousands of different aspects, details upon details, of what is good for us and what our bodies need. I will present information about this later, but I think we all have enough knowledge and wisdom to realize what is good for us and what we need, as well as to admit what isn't good for us and what we don't need, but I am going to give you my view in my own words as I see it. This is not a nutrition course; this is just some basic information.

Considering our modern American diet and how we prepare and process food, I am going to challenge you to just accept that real food, which is nutritious for us and which provides what we each need, is not in a bag or a box. I challenge you to realize that real food is what you see in gardens and fields. Accept that real food has traveled very little from the field or the garden to your fork and gut. Accept that real food does not have added ingredients in it. Accept that real food is easily identified, and you don't wonder what it is actually made from; in other words, it doesn't have an ingredient list, nor does the FDA need to approve it. Do you get the picture? The truth is real food is whole food; it is in its natural state and not processed with extra ingredients to make it more flavorful or addictive.

Real food is what God made and is similar to how He made it. Real food has vibrant colors that God established. Real food has great diversity with many different nutrients that the body needs. Think of blueberries, strawberries, raspberries, carrots, spinach, and peppers. No one made it another color. Real food has vitamins and minerals according to how God made it. No one added them in to make the food "better" or more nutritious. Real food has different nutrients combined wisely and in such a way that they have more powerful nutrition due to the effect of synergy when combined. The nutrients are better absorbed together. An example of this would be an apple, which contains natural sugar combined with fiber. The fiber slows down the delivery of this natural sugar, called fructose, into the blood. This slow delivery of the sugar is quite unlike drinking a soda with several teaspoons of sugar and no fiber. The slower delivery of the sugar from the fruit into the bloodstream helps to maintain the homeostasis the body needs and strives to maintain. A quick spike in blood sugar can get us into trouble. I could go on and on. I think you get the picture. Food is to nourish and satisfy us, not to make us crave. Remember, God satisfies us with good things. Proverbs says the sluggard craves and gets nothing, but the desires of the diligent are fully satisfied. Psalms states that God satisfies the longing of every living creature. It is hard to indulge in real food beyond what you need to be sustained and be nourished. However, food that has been tampered with usually creates cravings that drive us beyond what we actually need. An example of this is when extra sugar is added to fruit to make it tastier. Not only is this more stressful for the body, but it also increases our cravings for it. This increased desire for the extra tasty treat causes many of us to overeat, and therefore, weight gain is bound to occur.

It is also very important to consider the quality of the food you eat, and this can refer to whether it is organic or nonorganic, if it is a GMO food or non-GMO food, as well as if it is disguised in a bag or box as a real food. Although I will not go into these details now, it is important to understand that the quality of what you think might be good is actually not the quality you think it is. Take time to evaluate the quality of the food you eat. Be curious and notice. You will learn a lot and begin to see easy ways to improve this aspect of your food selection.

Why Is Food Important?

We already discussed that food is important because it nourishes us and provides what we need to maintain growth and development, to provide what we need to heal, and to provide not just what the body needs but what the brain needs as well. If we do not nourish ourselves appropriately for this, we will get sick, we will fail to be at our optimum thinking and physical level, we will not have the right amount of energy, and furthermore, we will not be able to do God's will the way He intended, and this is the ultimate goal of health—to do God's will.

God wants us to nourish ourselves, but He has given us food for this, and this food doesn't include junk because God does not make junk. As we continue to discuss the topic of food, I want you to consider four key factors in evaluating how nutritious the food you eat actually is and in deciding what you might want to eat. These factors are the quality of the food, the quantity you are eating, the timing of your eating, and the variety of food you are eating.

Hippocrates, the father of medicine, said long ago, "Let food be thy medicine." Often, we are hurting ourselves by what we are eating or not eating. Often, we are hurting ourselves because we think a certain food is good for us, but it really isn't. It might be good for other people, but it might wreak havoc for you or me, and you and I might be unaware of this. We know about obvious allergic reactions to things like peanuts, dairy, eggs, and gluten, but sometimes we have a bad reaction to something we ate and do not realize it. So, in essence, good nourishment is what works for your body, not what works for someone else's body. We all have different needs, and these needs change during the course of our lifetime. God created such a variety that we are sure to find what our bodies need. He has prepared for this in advance.

Who Are You When You Eat?

You might find this to be a strange question, but many health professionals challenge their clients with this question. Please realize who you are when you eat. Are you a weight trainer? Are you a dancer? Are you a businessman who doesn't exercise much? Are you a self-employed entrepreneur who is overworked and stressed? Are you a mother who is constantly concerned about her family? Are you a Christian speaker who inspires people to grow in the Lord and learn of Him? Are you a person of diligence and self-control? Are you a disheartened pastor or youth group leader? Are you being who you are or who you want to be when you eat? Do you like who you are when you eat? Are you being true to what is good and profitable while you eat? Again, who are you when you eat? Does the quantity of what you are eating match who you are and what you need at your particular phase of life? This matters. We need different quantities at different periods of time: young versus old; pregnant versus not pregnant; leisure versus work time; ill versus healthy; premenopausal versus postmenopausal.

I guess what I am trying to say is this: analyze who you are as you eat. If you are a stressed and undisciplined individual when you eat, you probably will not select food that is good for you, nor will you eat it with pleasure, which will hinder your nutrient absorption. If you are not true to yourself and you do not eat according to what you believe about how you should eat, you are creating conflict in yourself. This could result in a lack of enjoyment and gratitude for the experience of eating because you might feel guilty for not doing better in this area. If you are a person attempting to lose weight and want to be this when you eat, yet you eat too much of the weight-promoting, nonnutritious foods, you probably feel regret even before you are done eating your meal. You possibly eat without awareness of this negative feeling. Analyze what is going on. Be curious. Realize it and receive what God wants to show you, and respond with an action to help yourself choose to be who you want to be and to eat what is good in such a way that it is good for your brain and body. This is the first step. Realize it.

When Do You Eat?

When you eat matters. Do you eat too soon in the day? Just a note here. Breakfast is not the best time for many people to eat. You need to determine this for yourself, but giving your digestive system a rest through the night with a fast is good for both your brain and body. Don't feel that you must eat as soon as you get up just because you have been led to believe that breakfast is the most important meal of the day. Decide what is best for you. The fact is that breakfast is not the best meal for some people, and postponing the first meal until later in the day is actually good for their health.

Do you eat supper right before you go to bed? Again, not a good idea. This means you are probably rushed; it means your digestive system must work while you sleep; it means you probably did not eat with anyone. These are important matters. Eating in a relaxed state at least two to three hours before you go to bed and eating with someone are contributors to increased nutrient absorption. Timing matters. Refraining from eating three hours before bed is one of the steps in the overall plan according to the Alzheimer's protocol for better brain health, developed by Dr. Dale Bredesan. Doing this with other strategies has shown cognitive improvement in individuals who are developing dementia and other cognitive impairments. Again, realize what is going on and care for yourself by making a change for the better. Small changes can bring big results. Eating too close to bedtime, especially if it is your big meal of the day, impairs the quality of your sleep, which further affects your health. Our goal is to reduce stress so that we will have peace in our brains and bodies. We believe this is true, so implementing an action to respond to what we believe further helps homeostasis. God established a sleep-wake cycle with the rising and setting of the sun. There is a reason for this. He wants us to sleep at night, not eat.

Do you eat when you are not hungry? Or do you eat only when you are hungry? Many times, we eat out of boredom, or we eat because we are stressed, or we eat because we are around other people who are eating. I have found myself eating in all of these situations when I am not actually hungry. It is hard to refrain, but if I really analyze whether or not I am hungry or what I am actually doing, I am better able to respond in a beneficial way and refrain from eating. Eating is stressful on the body, so eating when we are not hungry makes things more difficult for the digestive system. This can also lead to other problems like constipation and poor nutrient absorption. Your body can only handle so much. Overconsumption of food could also lead to cognitive stress because you are uncomfortable and regretful. I have experienced all of this. I also have experienced eating due to the fact that I am procrastinating because I do not want to do something. Then I feel regretful because I ate too much, and I did not get the other job done. This causes stress, not good.

God does want us to eat at certain times. He has called us to enjoy feasting with togetherness and celebration, but He has also called us to fast. We fast regularly at night when we sleep. We are able to increase this time if we do not eat right before bed and if we possibly put off our first meal in the morning. This has physical benefits that I won't go into now, but God implemented a regular fast at night. He knew we needed it and why.

How Do You Eat?

How you eat is important, so do not laugh. Realize how you are eating. Do you chew your food enough? Do you eat fast or slowly? Do you eat standing up or sitting down? Do you talk while you are eating, or do you eat alone? Do you eat one bite at a time while you prepare food for others or while you clean up the mess? If you do not focus on how you eat and if you eat in a state when you are stressed or not attending to the fact that you are eating, you actually impair your digestion and don't enjoy it as God intended. God wants us to enjoy our food. We do this when we slow down and realize that we are eating; we do this when we chew our food many times before swallowing; we do this when we enjoy the company of someone who cares about us. All of this is what God wants for us. He satisfies us with good things, and this includes peaceful meals that nourish us and are shared with others. You can rest while you eat. You can enjoy God while you eat. You can be replenished while you eat just because you stop what you are doing, you give thanks, and you eat with purpose. This is how we should eat. It can be a spiritual experience, possibly like the Last Supper, because you slow down and share the experience with God or with another person.

Where Do You Eat?

Yes, where you eat matters. Do you eat at a table sitting on a chair? Do you eat at the computer? Do you eat in the car? Do you eat in front of the TV? Do you eat at work? At a restaurant, at a friend's house, at the café in your gym? Where you eat impacts how you eat and what you eat, as well as if you are eating with someone. If we are not in the right location for the purpose, our choices for good actions are limited. Yes, this might occur sometimes, but if it is daily or too often, we are depriving ourselves of a lot of enjoyment and nourishment as well as overloading our efforts of self-discipline as we make choices more difficult; this also causes stress. Chances are if you are not at a table when you eat, you might be eating out of a bag or a box, which means you probably are not eating something quite so healthy. You also might be stressed and eat too fast without chewing your food. You could be alone with no one to share the experience, and therefore have no social benefits. All of this together leads to impaired digestion and possibly lack of satisfaction, both of which are not God's plan for "satisfying us with good things."

Connection to Brain, Body, and Beliefs

The who, what, why, when, where, and how questions lead us to evaluate if what we are doing is working for us. Maybe your constipation is rooted in eating too fast and not chewing your food. Maybe your loneliness is due to never eating with anyone. Maybe your stress is due to the fact that you won't sit down to eat because you want to get the kitchen cleaned up. Maybe the clutter in your car is due to the trash you leave behind because this is where you eat on a daily basis. Maybe your weight gain is because you eat out too much and don't realize how much or what you are eating and how it is affecting you, not just physically but mentally and financially. Maybe when you eat or what you eat has impaired your sleep so much so that you have given up on feeling rested and getting along with people because you are too tired to care. Maybe any of this causes you stress, money, joy, or other emotional upheaval and causes you to feel oppressed and not worth much to anyone, including God. Do you see how all of this impacts your mental state and your spiritual state? How can God use us if we are not healthy? How can we do God's will if we can't even manage ourselves or if we feel unworthy and condemned? He will help us, but just like we must seek after wisdom and pursue peace, we must search diligently for what is actually going to nourish us and then proceed wisely. It all matters.

Conclusion and Action Steps

Let's wrap up today by remembering again that our food comes from God and that we should have a mindset to praise Him for it. We should be in the right environment when we eat, an environment that helps us to calm down so that we can enjoy our food with someone, an environment selected by a person who is committed to living a blameless life and who is trying to conduct the affairs of their house with a blameless heart. Remember, this isn't just about you and me; it is about others also. It is about each circle of people we influence, our children, our church, our coworkers, and the rest of the world. God wants to gladden our hearts. He wants to make our faces shine. He wants to sustain our hearts. Every time we make a wise choice, we are teaching others. When this includes others who are weaker than we are, we have a huge responsibility to display a blameless life. Do we really want our children to think that their bag of chips was a good snack? Do we really want to teach our children that eating in front of the TV is what God wants for us? Do we really want to teach our families that always working late and never eating with the family is what God planned for us? Do we really want to live such a rushed life that we eat in the car and are constantly making a mess that causes more work for us and keeps us from connecting with other people? Do we really want to throw more money at food because we aren't planning meals at home and therefore spending too much at restaurants and gas stations? Again, God established creation with good things for us, but we must realize it, receive it, and respond to it.

Please take out your journal with the five columns. Remember, the columns are labeled *Topic, Brain, Body, Beliefs,* and *Scripture and Action Steps.*

Topic	Brain	Body	Beliefs	Scripture and Action Steps
Food that truly satisfies.	Am I hungry?	Get to a table to eat with someone at least three hours before bed.	Do I believe food comes from God? Should I thank Him for this?	Read Psalm 104 aloud each day.
	When am I full?			Memorize verses 14–15 and 27–28.
	How will I chew my food?			Refrain from eating anything out of a bag or box.
	What am I eating? Will it nourish me?		Do I believe that when, where, how, and with whom I eat is important?	Chew each bite thirty times.
	Think about the quality, quality, timing, and diversity of my food.		Can food really be my medicine?	Give thanks for your food. Don't take it for granted. Engage the cephalic stage of digestion— thinking about it.
				Stop eating when you are 80 percent full. Not too much!
				Follow other action steps.

Under *Topic*, please write our topic of food.

Now to your brain column. In this column, let's focus on your state of hunger when you eat. Are you hungry? When are you full? Think about how you are going to chew your food. Think about what you are eating and how it will nourish you. Think about where your food came from. Think about how you are enjoying it. Think about what is going on—that you are being nourished by what God gave you.

In your body column, this is what I want you to write and do: Get your body in the right location to eat—at a table at the right time to eat—long before bedtime and with people. Physically get your body where it needs to be.

In your beliefs column, please write what you believe about food. Do you believe that your food came from God and that you should thank Him for it? Do you believe that what, where, when, why, and how you eat matters for digestion? Do you believe that your digestion and what you eat matter to your health? Do you agree with Hippocrates, the father of medicine, "Let food be thy medicine"? Write what you believe about food

Following are your action steps for this week on food. I have a lot of action steps for you this week. Do your best. Don't beat yourself up! Every little step matters, no matter how small.

1. Read Psalm 104 each day aloud. Memorize verses 14–15 and 27–28.
2. Refrain from eating anything out of a bag or box.
3. Take time to consider these four aspects of what you eat: quality, quantity, timing, diversity.
4. Eat with someone at least once a day at a table. Make it last twenty minutes. Put your fork down between bites.
5. Notice how hungry you are before you eat and after you eat to determine when you should eat and when you should stop. Stop before you are completely full—80 percent.
6. Chew each bite of food thirty times to ensure slow eating. Remember, the small pieces ensure better digestion and further action in the stomach so that you absorb nutrients better. Be grateful for those teeth you have and use them. Just as you are grateful for your eyes and ears, be grateful for that set of teeth.
7. Pray gratefully before eating anything. Your attitude of gratitude is huge; don't take it for granted. Engage this cephalic stage of digestion.
8. Eat the last meal at least three hours before you go to bed. It helps get the overnight fast going.
9. Practice reading food labels after you have read the supplemental information to this lesson, which discusses very basic nutrition

concepts, ingredient labels, and action steps for a super jump to stimulate change.

10. Pray! A sample prayer is below.

Just a word about the second action step to refrain from buying anything out of a bag or box. Do you remember when we had the action step to go into a store and only buy the three items on your list? You can also do this at this point by making the plan to go into the store and avoid the food aisles that have the junk food in bags and boxes. Tell yourself you will not buy any of it. This will help establish the habit of refraining from the temptation. Even if you just go into the store to buy a few items, you will benefit if you consciously avoid the bad aisles, the tempting aisles, the unhealthy aisles. Believe me, I know where they are. Some of those items call my name. I still must actively refrain from this temptation.

Also, about the quality, quantity, timing, and diversity. Go back and review this information. Remember, the quality of the food you eat is important. Know what it is and where it came from. Rinse your produce well. Remember the quantity, not too much. Remember the timing—stop eating three hours before bed and not too early in the morning. The overnight fast is good for you. And diversity—remember the colors of the rainbow. Incorporating variety helps us to ingest the nutrients that God has created our bodies to need.

Let's pray.

Lord, You are good, and You created a good creation, which is for Your pleasure and for us too. You prepared the environment so that we could be nourished and satisfied. Lord, our food comes from You. You bring forth grass for the cattle; You bring forth food from the earth; You gladden our hearts and make our faces shine, and You sustain our hearts. Lord, You created the seasons and marked the days to guide us so that we know how to live, when to eat, when to sleep, when to plant food, when to harvest it, but, Lord, You make it grow. You have given us a reason to rest and enjoy, even to frolic. Lord, please help us to make choices to eat the food You want for us in a way that You want for us and when and where You want for us. Help us to realize what is good for our bodies and our brains, which ultimately shows what we believe. Lord, You satisfy us with good things, and we praise You for this. Lord, we look to You for our food at the proper time and for all nourishment. Lord, our meditation of You is sweet, and we will continue to rejoice in You. Praise the Lord, O my soul!

Well, this wraps up our first four week sessions on environment, movement, mindset, and food and how they are important influences on our genetic expression and, therefore, our health. Next week, we will begin to discuss the next big topic of digestion as we break it down into four weeks to discuss how it impacts our health.

Supplemental Information: Basic Nutrients of Food and Food Labels

Welcome to the supplemental information for week four of my Health through the Psalms twelve-week program. This information is to focus on reading and understanding ingredient labels. None of this is medical advice, and none of this is a complete nutritional text, but rather it is my effort to do good, to seek peace, and to pursue it by using scripture and providing information to you so that you might be encouraged to see how the brain, body, and beliefs affect our health and how these are uniquely connected in all individuals. Again, I am passionately diligent about sharing this information with you because it all matters. I am trying to bridge the gap between what you and your doctor know will benefit your health and supporting you on following through with doing it as you learn more reasons why.

Today, we are going to discuss the six basic nutrients of food as well as the added constituents to packaged food. We will also tackle reading ingredient labels. Action steps will be given at the end. Because we must rely on the Lord to teach us what we each need and how we each need to live, we are going to use Psalm 25:4–5 as our scripture:

> Show me your ways, Lord, teach me your paths; lead me
> in your truth and teach me, for you are God my Savior,
> and my hope is in you all day long.

God teaches us as we go along. We must look to Him for guidance.

Six Basic Nutrients of Food

The six basic nutrients of food are vitamins, minerals, water, fat, carbohydrates, and protein. These occur in varying amounts in food, and the body needs all of them. Balance is important for homeostasis, so when a certain nutrient is ingested in more quantities than what the body needs and when the body is depleted of other nutrients, stress occurs. We want to avoid stress. We cannot trick our bodies. They need what they need.

First of all, your body needs vitamins A, D, K, E, B, and C. All of them are important for different and numerous reasons. We won't discuss these reasons, but let's acknowledge that when you get a variety of food, such as fruits and vegetables, peanuts and legumes, and some meat, you are getting vitamins. This is why diversity matters. Some fruits don't have certain vitamins, while others do.

Minerals include such things as iron, calcium, magnesium, zinc, phosphorus, and potassium, plus others. These help regulate body processes, such as making enzymes and hormones. They are also important for heart, brain, and muscle health. Our bodies will make enzymes and hormones naturally, but we must provide what the body needs by what we eat.

Water is definitely necessary. Our body is comprised of about 60 percent water, and we need to replenish this daily, all through the day. We need more if we sweat, of course, but our natural body processes require water to function at an optimum level. Our cells need this. It is vital for our health and energy as well as to help purify us, to get toxins out, to help keep the environment of our bodies clear of clutter.

Fats are important for hormone health and brain function, especially for babies and young children as their brains and body systems develop. Fats actually help the body to absorb certain vitamins. Too much fat is not good, but neither is too little fat. Again, everyone's body is different. Monitoring what you need is important—not too much, not too little. Quantity matters. Fats help keep you satiated and take longer to digest than carbohydrates. They do not spike your blood sugar like carbohydrates do, so they are a healthy option to help regulate this.

Carbohydrates are basically sugar, and there are different kinds, but we won't go into them. You get carbohydrates from fruits and vegetables, grains and bread, peanuts, and anything with sugar in it. All food is ultimately broken down into sugar or converted to what we call glucose and then utilized by the body, or it is stored. Carbohydrates give us quick energy, but they also increase our blood sugar quickly. This might lead to drops in blood sugar later, which might set you up for a plummet. Monitoring your intake is a wise strategy to maintain energy levels. Combining carbohydrates with fiber helps to slow down the delivery into the bloodstream.

Finally, my favorite—protein. Protein is so important for the body. We need it for muscle development, for strength, for repair on the cellular level, for wound healing, and so much more. We need adequate protein, and many people do not get enough because they are eating too many carbohydrates. It doesn't take much meat to get your daily protein requirements met. Determining how much protein you need would be beneficial for your health. As we age, we lose muscle, and if we do not get enough protein, this muscle loss is accelerated, and this impairs our health. Carbohydrates and fats give us energy but they do not build muscle. We need the amino acids from protein for building muscle. So if you lift weights, you would be wise to take a look at your protein needs and ensure that you are getting enough. Also, as you age, it is very important to get adequate protein to help maintain muscle. Just a quick comment here: it is my opinion that each day you should be getting at least a half gram to one gram of protein for each pound you weigh. So if your weight is two hundred pounds, you should get at least a hundred grams of protein and possibly more per day, depending on who you are and what your individualized needs are. Your gender, age, lifestyle and exercise routine will impact what your body needs, and it is important the you prioritize your protein intake and digestion for your long-term health, especially as you age.

This was a super quick review of the six basic nutrients of food. It was not at all to teach you a deep level of understanding, and you probably knew most of it. It was only an introduction to this as we proceed to our topic of reading food labels.

Food Labels

When we look at food labels, we will find certain things: calories, fat, protein, carbohydrates, fiber, added sugars, as well as the minerals potassium, magnesium, sodium, and calcium, along with other minerals and vitamins. In addition, we will look at the ingredients that are added to the product but not listed in this section. Go to your pantry and select any item. It can be bread, beans, pasta, soup, Jell-O, a candy bar, chips, canned meat, cake mix, or tortillas. From the fridge, you could get out milk, cheese, butter, vegetables, yogurt, or juice.

Let's look at the label from the top down.

Please find the number of calories.

Calories are significant. However, it is more important to note what the calories come from. This is why we want to look at everything else. If a food is high in fat, the number of calories is prone to be fairly high in the item. If it is high in carbohydrates, the item could look like a lot but might not have as much nutritional benefit as another choice. If it is high in protein, it provides a nutrient your body needs. It is not enough to just look at the number of calories; you need to realize where the calories are coming from, whether it is fat, protein, or carbohydrates. This is important because these affect us differently and are needed by the body in differing amounts. It is also important to understand what the serving size is and how many servings are in the container. Please find this on the label. It is not just important to know the number of calories in the item. It is also important to know what the calories are composed of. This is why we look at fats, carbohydrates, and protein.

We must have good calories so that we are well nourished. We also need to know how many servings are in the contents of the package. You might think you are eating only one serving when in actuality you could be eating three servings. Know what and how much you are eating.

Please find the number of grams of fat.

Although we need fat in our diet, fat from a packaged food is usually not the kind of fat we need. Be sure to know if it comes from a healthy source. Seed oils are not a healthy source of fat because they provide too many omega-6 fatty acids and are inflammatory. We do not need as many omega-6 fatty acids as we need omega-3 fatty acids. Foods such as fatty fish, eggs, and flaxseed are healthy options for omega-3 fatty acids. Omega-6 fatty acids can be found in seed oils and other foods, but we don't need too many of them. Again, we are only touching on the topic. Know what you are eating.

Please find the number of grams of protein.

We need protein. Usually packaged food is not high in protein unless you eat a protein bar, but you must be careful to really notice what is in that protein bar. Many of them are advertised as having lots of protein, but in actuality, they might have only a moderate amount, along with a bunch of added sugar and carbohydrates. They put these additions in the item so that they are tastier for us and so we will want them. Again, know what the calories you are eating contain so that you can monitor what you are actually giving your body.

Please find the number of grams of carbohydrates.

Carbohydrates are usually sweet, and we like them. This sweetness touches our brains and can be addictive if it is coming from refined sugar. If the carbohydrates are not coming from naturally occurring sugar in the food, this means added sugar was put into the product. This is when it becomes problematic for you. Know what you are eating. It is hard to overeat fruits and vegetables, but when added sugar is included with them or included in a product to make the item more palatable, it is harder to resist, and therefore, the quality decreases while the quantity of what we might eat increases. We usually eat these types of food when we are tired and stressed or when we decide to relax in front of the TV or at a social event. Just know what you are eating and realize what it is doing to you and how it makes you feel. Realize who you are being when you make this choice because it will impact who you are. Realize your goals, not just for now but for your whole life span and for your children and your grandchildren

Within this number of carbohydrates, please find the number of grams of fiber.

We all need dietary fiber. Depending on who you are, male or female, and other factors, it is recommended that you get anywhere from twenty-five to forty-five grams. There is much discussion about this. Your digestive health is impacted by your fiber intake. Fiber feeds your microbiome, which we will discuss later when we talk about digestion. The health of your gut is linked strongly with the health of your brain and the rest of your body systems. What you eat matters. Your daily food intake should include fiber. This is where diversity comes in: if you do not have a lot of color in your diet, you may be lacking fiber due to the fact that you are not getting healthy fruits and vegetables. Meat does not have fiber; fiber comes from plants.

Within this carbohydrate number, find the number of added sugars.

Added sugars are important to note. These are what will increase your blood sugar too quickly. If all of the carbohydrates are from added sugar and not from the fiber or the natural sugar in the food, it has been tampered with so that it will be more tasty and palatable. This will tempt you to eat it and possibly too much of it. When you eat something like this, you are putting yourself in a position to want more, and you may have to utilize self-control to stop. This is difficult for many people and is especially difficult when we are already stressed or challenged by food in general. You will want to rethink eating it.

Now let's talk about the added ingredients. Answer the following questions:

How many are there?

Does it have sugar?

Where does sugar appear in the list? Is it first, fifth, last?

How many different names appear as sugar? There are over fifty names that could be listed instead of sugar. It is important to know this. Google the different names. It is purposely hidden so that it is not recognized.

Does it have seed oils? Soybean, corn, canola, and sunflower oils are inflammatory, not healthy. Coconut and olive oil are healthy for most people. Know how they affect you.

Does it have natural flavors?

Does it have colors or dyes?

Can you pronounce all the words used?

I want to challenge you on this: if the item in your hands has more than five ingredients, it should be questioned. It is no longer in the form that God made it and might have elements in it that could be questionable for your health. You should have known this already because it might be in a bag, box, or jar; however, many items in the freezer aisle are exactly in their whole food form in the sense that nothing has been added to them. Reading the ingredient list confirms this, but many times, cheese, sugar, salt, coloring, or other elements have been added. We just need to check and see.

Does it have sugar? If so, why does it have sugar? Sugar is addictive. The food manufacturers know this and deliberately add sugar to their products so you will want them in large quantities. More about this later. Now consider where sugar is in the list. If it is first, then the sugar is what makes up most of the ingredients, which means a lot has been added. This is not naturally occurring sugar either. It is refined sugar, which has the fiber removed from it. If you look up the different names of sugar, you will find over fifty possibilities. Food manufactures might add three or more different types of sugar to the product, which means more sugar is in it than you might think. If you are not aware of this, you will not realize how much sugar you are actually ingesting. This is why it is important to recognize the added sugars as we previously discussed.

Sugar spikes your blood glucose. Every time you do this, you are putting your body under stress. Stress leads to inflammation, and inflammation leads to disease. Type 2 diabetes is rampant in our nation, and sugar is the culprit. Also, Alzheimer's disease is referred to by some as type 3 diabetes, all due to sugar ingestion and poor blood sugar regulation. People do not know this. If you look at the history of our obesity epidemic, you will be able to trace it back to when we changed our diet theories to low-fat, high-carbohydrate foods and people started eating more packaged foods with added sugar. Again, we are only touching on this, but research it for yourself. Research the different lives that have been changed when individuals decided to say goodbye to sugar. Your health depends on it.

Seed oils are inflammatory. You do not need them. These are in many products to preserve the product but are damaging to your health. Noticing how often you see this is important. Quantity matters. Ingesting these on a consistent basis means you are getting too many omega-6 fatty acids, which are not good for you because they are inflammatory, causing stress and harming your health.

Natural flavors and dyes simply are not nutrition. So why are they in the product? They are there for the same reason as sugar—for flavor or appearance. Think of the bright color of chips or the fun color of cereals. What might these do to you? Many react negatively to these types of things and have severe digestive issues because of them. Possibly this might be you, and you haven't realized it yet. Even a slight intolerance is not good for your health.

Lastly, let's look at the long words you see on the label. Can you pronounce them? Advice is given that if you cannot pronounce what is on the label, you probably should not be eating it. This is a valid point to consider. Again, just know what you are putting into your body.

Why Does Food Contain Added Ingredients?

So why do food manufacturers put all of these added ingredients into our food? They do this for different reasons. Much is added to create a bliss point to optimize the taste of the food so that we will like it and want it. Many cereals would not be eaten if sugar was not added to them. Other elements are added to create a more desirable texture or to combine textures to make us like it—crunchy on the outside, soft on the inside. Increasing the shelf life of items is another reason for added ingredients. This reduces their cost even though it may harm us. The dyes help to create a more delightful and unique appearance of the item so our eyes will want it. Remember the power of sight? The food psychologists know all about this, as well as how the human desire mechanism works for wanting more. Also, when different tastes are combined, they become even more desirable, such as when fat, sugar, and salt exist together. Yes, this is delicious, but is the quality and is the timing when we eat such things beneficial? It leads to increased quantities and weight gain as well as stress.

This concludes the discussion on basic food information, but it is not at all the amount that could be presented or shared. It doesn't even touch on what is known. However, it is enough to get you to start thinking about and analyzing what you are ingesting. This is what I want you to do. Just think about it. At least try to know what is going on. Just like we need to look at our environment and ourselves and strive to live a blameless life, we must look at this aspect also. It all matters. If we want a doctor to help us, we must try to manage ourselves in such a way that we are attempting to keep our bodies healthy with the choices we make.

Journal

Please pull out your five-column journal.

In the first column, please write our topic of food labels.

In your second column, the brain column, please write what you should think about this information. What is in the food? Is it good for me? How much sugar? How much fiber? How much protein? Include other related questions.

In the third column, your body column, tackle this: How does this food make me feel? Does it give me energy? Does it promote the desire for more? Does it change my mood or my stool habits?

In your fourth column, your belief column, please ask yourself, does what I eat honor God? Does what I eat help me to do His will? Does what I eat help me to fulfill the purpose He has for me?

In your fifth column, write your scripture of Psalm 25:4–5.

Show me your ways, Lord, teach me your paths. Lead me in your truth and teach me, for you are God my Savior, and my hope is in you all day long.

Action Steps

Here are your action steps concerning food labels:

1. Memorize Psalm 25:4–5.
2. Ask God to show you what He wants you to know concerning this and what He wants you to do.
3. Remember, no condemnation. Seek to understand how your choices are affecting your body. Remember, all things are permissible, but not all things are beneficial.
4. Challenge: don't buy or eat anything with sugar or seed oils.
5. Pray.

Here is a sample prayer:

> Lord, You are good, and we praise You. Lord, please show us what we are to do. Lead us and teach us what You want us to eat. Our hope is in You. Show us how what we eat is affecting us. Help us to realize it, receive what You want us to know, and respond to what You teach us. Lord, help all of us to do what is good so that we have peace in our brains, bodies, and our beliefs. Lord, please show me, show everyone, what this is so that we have peace. Thank You, Lord.

Now, do not feel condemned about what you are eating or become legalistic about it. Just realize what you are eating. See what you can do to minimize what is not ideal. Make small changes. Do what you can; just try to do something, and the habit will grow and become stronger to do more and more. Create the environment you need to keep bad stuff out of your house, and then you won't need to deal with it. It won't be there to tempt you. Realize, receive, and respond.

Bye-bye. Hang in there. Next week is the cephalic phase of digestion.

WEEK 5

DIGESTION AND THE CEPHALIC PHASE

WAITING IN EXPECTATION AT THE
TABLES OF ANY CONCERN

Welcome to week five of my Health through the Psalms twelve-week program. I am glad you are sticking with this. Keep at it. Progress take time. Each intentional and healthy choice you make will have an effect for the betterment of your entire being.

The next four weeks will focus on four phases of digestion: the cephalic phase, the structural and mechanical phase, the chemical phase, and the microbial phase. We could actually refer to these as aspects of digestion rather than phases. This week, we will begin our discussion about digestion by focusing on the first phase of digestion, which is the cephalic stage. We will tie this into the connection it has to our physical and mental health as well as the connection it has to any type of activity we encounter, whether it is work, play, task completion, attending church, shopping, financial struggles, or even attending a sports or social event.

Introduction—Cephalic Phase of Digestion or of Anything

Our first week of discussion about digestion is focusing on the cephalic phase of digestion. However, I want to tie this aspect of digesting our food to any type of activity that we might be digesting. Please think about this: we might digest a conversation; we might digest a problem; we might digest information. In fact, years ago, many people read the *Reader's Digest* regularly. So consider that digestion doesn't just refer to food, but rather, it refers to how we might analyze or break down anything, whether it be a puzzle, a sermon, a situation, a conversation, or a budget. We do this all the time, and this is what digestion is—breaking down food so that we can better absorb the nutrients for the benefit of our health or breaking down a situation so that we are better able to analyze and deal with it.

The aspect of digestion is so very important because it affects the health of our brains, and the health of our brains affects our bodies. It affects our decision-making, our relationships, our financial choices, our habits, our mood, and our sleep. It affects every aspect of our lives, including our spiritual lives. We should not disregard this. It affects our understanding of scripture, God's Word, and the implementation and motivation of applying God's Word to our lives. Furthermore, it affects our tendencies and desires of even craving God's Word, which is our very food for life. We should not scorn this aspect of our lives. It is not enough to just pray about improving our health, our mental clarity, our energy level, or any other aspect of our lives if we are not going to follow through with choices that support this prayer.

Let's look at a few examples from scripture: Rahab wanted to be saved; she followed through by hiding the spies. The woman who bled for years and wanted healing broke through the crowd to touch the hem of Jesus's garment. Mary Magdalene wanted her Lord; she was at the foot of the cross and ran to the tomb. Our actions must support what we believe and want. Just praying about something without implementing the power you have to create the environment you need, the mindset you need, and the food you need, as well as realizing the impact you have on your genetics, is prayer without action, without faith. Fervent, effectual prayers are tenacious. They have meaning and include a mindset to implement what is necessary. Rahab, the woman who was bleeding, and Mary Magdalene had a mindset and focus on the Lord and followed through with action. They broke things down to be able to make strategic choices, which led them to what they desired … the Lord our God.

So why is this important? This is important because of the power of the cephalic phase of anything and especially the cephalic phase of digestion, which will impact our overall health. Cephalic refers to the head. Have you heard the old phrase, "Get your head in the game"? This is usually yelled out by a coach or father who notices that a player or child is not thinking about what they are doing, and therefore, they are not functioning at their optimum capability. It could be spoken to a whole team. This is relevant because digestion starts in our brains. Yes, in our brains. This is the first chance to get off on the right foot with the power of food as your medicine.

However, I want to branch out here and challenge you to realize, receive, and respond to this: digestion leads to absorption of nutrients, which leads to benefits, which leads to power, energy, and potential, which lead to progress, which leads to peace, which leads to health, whether it is physical health, mental health, financial health, relationship health, or work health. Yes, it matters this much. Your digestion affects every area of your life. If you don't feel good, how can your physical or mental health be good? How can your financial health be good? How can your relationships be good? How can your work performance be good? And most importantly, how can you do a good job living according to God's Word? I challenge you to realize this connection, receive it, and respond accordingly.

We are going to use Psalm 5 to break down this topic of the cephalic phase of digestion to help make connections to all of your health so that you will have peace in your brain, body, and beliefs. Verse 3 is our pivot verse, but the whole psalm will be used to make this more relevant. Let's read it now.

Psalm 5

1   Listen to my words, Lord, consider my lament.
2   Hear my cry for help, my King and my God, for to you I pray.
3   In the morning, Lord, you hear my voice; in the morning I lay my requests before you and wait expectantly.

4   For you are not a God who is pleased with wickedness; with you, evil people are not welcome.

5   The arrogant cannot stand in your presence. You hate all who do wrong;

6   You destroy those who tell lies. The bloodthirsty and deceitful you, Lord, detest.

7   But I, by your great love, can come into your house; in reverence I bow down toward your holy temple.

8   Lead me, Lord, in your righteousness because of my enemies— make your way straight before me.

9   Not a word from their mouth can be trusted; their hearts are filled with malice. Their throat is an open grave; with their tongues they tell lies.

10 Declare them guilty, O God! Let intrigues be their downfall. Banish them for their many sins, for they have rebelled against you.

11 But let all who take refuge in you be glad; let them ever sing for joy. Spread your protection over them, that those who love your name may rejoice in you.

12 Surely, Lord, you bless the righteous; you surround them with your favor as with a shield.

We are going to break this psalm down into different segments:

- verses 1–3, the mindset and focus of your brain
- verses 4–6, the wickedness of self
- verses 7–8, the house of God; the presence of God
- verses 9–10, the wickedness of others (notice we focused on ourselves first in this area)
- verses 11–12, the refuge, safety, protection, and hope we have in God

First, we are going to discuss what is meant by the cephalic phase.

I posit this to you: the cephalic phase of anything is the most important phase of its entirety.

Read the above statement again.

Why do I pose this statement to you? What is so important about a cephalic phase? How does it impact our health or any aspect of our lives? Digestion doesn't just happen, as other events don't just happen. A wedding doesn't just happen; a concert doesn't just happen; a closing on a house doesn't just happen; indeed, a feast doesn't just happen. Planning occurs, and this planning takes thinking; it takes an initial thought or impetus, and then the action follows.

Our minds and our thinking are very powerful. What goes into our brains and then the mental activity that follows have huge impacts on our person. Let me share this with you. Recently, I put a notification tone on my phone for each one of my children. Now, when I get a text from them, I know which one of my treasures texted me. I immediately have pleasant thoughts particular to that child. Not only does this put my mind on the topic of that child, but it also creates the pleasant mood associated with this child and even the present concerns that I might have concerning this child. I must say, however, that usually the impact is one of delight and love. Do you see what I am saying? I did nothing but be a passive recipient of what affected my brain, which affected my thinking, which affected my actions. Possibly I sent money to them, prayed for them, counseled them, or even drove to their location. It started in my brain first. Please do not diminish the point I am making here and take seriously what the apostle Paul instructed us, "Take every thought captive to the obedience of Christ." The thoughts triggered when I receive a text from my children are pleasant to me, but what about the thoughts that aren't so pleasant? Thinking on what is true, pure, lovely, and just is good for us; it affects our health. It's powerful. God knew this long before Paul wrote the words to address it. We must take our thoughts captive to the goodness and truth of the Lord. Even if thoughts are not pleasant, God is still good and instructed us to think on what is pure, lovely, just, and of good report.

Thankfully, God made us in such a way that we do not have to think much about digestion, as once we eat, digestion occurs without our conscious thought or instruction on the smooth muscle activity of digestion. This is quite unlike our skeletal muscle, which we consciously control when we decide to move. However, we do have the power to influence the process and benefits of digestion when we focus on the cephalic phase of this process.

Most people think digestion starts in the stomach. Others think it starts in the mouth. The truth is that digestion starts in the brain, even before we put anything into our mouths. The mere thought of food gets the process going. However, I would stretch it back even further to remind you that even as you are grocery shopping, you are affecting your digestion because it will later influence what you select to eat. Also, if you have not created an environment that is free from toxins, including bad food choices, clutter, or tempting items, you have influenced your digestion even before you get to your meal or snack, long before you approach the table. Furthermore, if you are not moving, you have influenced your digestion because exercise actually helps you to digest food. So many things to consider must be acknowledged here.

Just the mere thought of food activates secretions in your body that help digestion, such as that we salivate and our digestive enzymes begin flowing. Salivary enzymes and pancreatic enzymes are secreted. Hydrochloric acid and gastric juices increase. Bile production begins. The body gets primed for the activity, all because of what is going on in the brain. We might not notice this, but it is happening, and we can promote it by our thinking. All of these events prompt better digestion because they get the body ready to break down the food so that we are able to absorb it more easily. We want this. We want the food to be easy to absorb.

So why is this important? Doesn't our stomach just break it down for us? Yes, the stomach breaks down food for us by churning and by the hydrochloric acid's effect on the food particles while they are in our stomach; however, if we think about what we are going to eat and pause a moment to take a big breath and give thanks for the food God has given to us, other beneficial bodily processes occur. As I stated already, many secretions of enzymes and juices begin flowing, but the pause you take in getting your mindset on food and what you are going to do—eat—actually stimulates vagal nerve activity, which helps the process of digestion even more by relaxing the smooth muscle of your gastrointestinal tract. This is important due to the fact that we need all parts of the GI tract for the breakdown and absorption of the nutrients we require. Getting as many aspects of digestion ready even before ingesting food makes for easier digestion and less stress on the body, which is what will benefit nutrient absorption and overall health.

Benefits include the following:

- easier digestion
- better absorption of nutrients
- more energy
- better health
- better brain activity
- better mood
- better sleep
- better implementation of God's will, which is our ultimate goal of health

Why? If you aren't nourished, you are not in your optimum health in your brain, body, or beliefs.

Let's break it down using Psalm 5.

The Mindset and Focus of the Brain

When we think about food, we get in the proper mindset for digestion. We realize what is going to occur, and we are ready to receive it and respond accordingly by chewing, swallowing, and probably being relieved that we get to eat to satisfy our hunger (hopefully we were actually hungry). We have many aspects about eating to consider:

Am I actually hungry?

Am I relaxed to eat?

Who am I when I eat?

What am I eating?

Where did this food come from?

When am I eating? Too close to bedtime?

Am I eating with someone?

Am I thanking God for this?

Is the quality, quantity, timing, and diversity of what I am eating going to benefit me?

See all that you are able to consider. Look at verses 1–3 of Psalm 5:

> Listen to my words, Lord, consider my lament. Hear my
> cry for help, my King and my God, for to you I pray. In
> the morning, Lord, you hear my voice; in the morning
> I lay my requests before you and wait in expectation.

I absolutely love that this psalm is calling out to God to listen to his words, a lament, a cry to the King, to God Almighty. He does this in the morning before anything. Yes, before anything. Might we turn to God before we put anything into our mouths, or if we are struggling in this area, before we put anything into our grocery carts, before we take anything out of our fridge or pantry, before we put anything on our plate? Think about the power of this. We turn to God in our attempt to be healthy—to eat right, to get more energy, to heal, to be nourished, or to lose weight so that we can do His will, to live in a way that promotes walking in the fruit of the Holy Spirit, but most importantly to thank Him. This is our mindset of gratitude, which is powerful and nourishes every aspect of our whole person, our environment, and others and their environment.

Furthermore, turning to God as the first step gets the psalmist and us in the mindset that God does hear us and that we are able to turn to Him, and this puts us in a solid position to wait in expectation. We can do this whenever we turn to God—wait in expectation. He hears us; He answers us when we call; He satisfies us with good things; He understands our struggles, our desires, our current needs, and requirements. He has a path of righteousness for us to follow every day, and He helps us on this path.

So what table are we talking about here? The table of food? The drawing table? The table before our enemies? The bargaining table? The financial table? The communion table? Again, I challenge you to apply this to any area of your life—health, finances, relationships, work, habits, church, exercise, leisure, all areas of your life. Get your mind set on what is happening or going to happen so that you are ready for it, so that you are going to God about it, so that you wait in expectation for His help and His leading to do His will concerning it, whether it is eating, working, helping others, or even sleeping.

Why is this mindset important? Let's just tackle the area of eating right now. Mindset is important for many reasons. As we already mentioned, it gets our bodies ready to digest our food more adequately for better nutrient absorption by priming our bodily processes, thus beginning digestion before we even ingest the food. This leads to improved health and healing. Imagine the scenario that your body is not ready. Think of how you feel while you are in the dentist chair and you need to swallow. Have you ever noticed how hard this is to do when the dentist is waiting for you before he puts his utensils into your mouth again? I have. Or think of a baby who is being spoon fed. If the baby is not ready and expecting the spoon or the food, a mess is made. The baby is not prepared for the food, which means no chance for salivation to occur, no chance for gastric secretions to begin, no chance for smooth muscle relaxation. This unexpected invasion into their environment may cause stress, something we want to avoid, even for a baby.

Now again, let's stay on the topic of food right now. If we set our minds on the matter at hand and go to God for help and wait in expectation, we begin to see how He can lead us to make nourishing choices, to think about what we are doing, to plan ahead with prudence, to see possible temptations that might get us off track from reaching our goal or goals. Do you see how taking this moment to look to God with expectation helps you to implement action that will profit you? I hope you can see this. It is a little hard to willfully make a poor or unwise choice when you look to God before your moment of need and choose to wait in expectation for His help. This action allows us to step back and realize what we are doing, to be able to receive what He will offer, and then respond with the choices that are part of His will for us. All of this is good.

Let's branch out to other tables of concern that God has ordained for us: financial tables, work tables, the table before your enemies, the table of relationships, the table of communion. Do you see all of the different tables that we are bound to encounter during our days? What about the table of concern? We can go to God and pour out our lament to Him, cry out to Him in prayer, and then wait in expectation so that we are able to utilize prudence in how we proceed, so that we are able to be more aware of the dangers or temptations that are ahead, so that we are ready to implement the action He has for us to do His will in every situation. This is a mindset as well as a chance to envision what might happen and practice our response. By doing this, we avoid knee-jerk reactions that might get us into trouble or might get us off track. A foolish choice could lead to bad habits or sin or unintentional hardship.

Proverbs states that the prudent man sees danger ahead and takes a different path. I think the verse of Psalm 5:3 gives us clear indication that this occurs when we lay our requests before God prior to approaching any table. It gets our mindset ready so that we know and anticipate what to expect and put ourselves in a position to expect from God in the true sense He intended.

Let's take a quick look at verses 4 and 5. They speak about wickedness and that God is not pleased with it or with evil people. He hates all who do wrong; the proud cannot stand in His presence. What a reminder to us to walk humbly before Him at all times and in all ways. Just like we focused on ourselves before we focused on others when we discussed the environment, let's take a moment to focus on ourselves and the wickedness, the evil, or the pride that could be present in our own hearts.

Consider that wickedness or evil is anything that keeps us from doing God's will or from doing what is good for us. This might not always appear as wicked or evil. It could actually look like a good thing but in actuality be very wicked and evil. This could be in the form of distractions that we allow into our homes or environment; it could be in the form of temptations that we encounter because we did not keep our environment clear of clutter or toxins or the triggers to our lack of self-control or overconsumption; it could present itself in the form of falsehood by what we allow to enter our minds and then choose to believe; or it could be embedded in our pride as we make unrealistic goals founded in selfish ambitions. All of these could be distractions to get our mindset off of God, which will put us in a position to have poor digestion for the particular table we are encountering, especially the table of reverence or "throne of grace," the table of His presence.

Do you see the connection to digestion here? We are to be sober and vigilant and ready for what we might encounter, looking to God and waiting in expectation. This starts with self, not with others. This is part of health no matter what we are going to digest, whether it is food, conversation, a sermon, a business meeting, or even a time of fun. Prepare your mind and be sober. It all matters. We can wait in expectation for His help for all things.

Verses 7 and 8 remind us again about God's great love for us and that we can approach Him with reverence, and He will lead us in righteousness even with enemies present, even when we are at the table set before our enemies. Remember, our enemies can be distractions, temptations, lies, selfish ambition, toxins, clutter, past choices, regrets, and even people. Don't blame anyone, however. Just realize what is going on, receive what God has for you, and respond by waiting with expectation.

Now that we took a look at ourselves and are in reverence before God, we can take a look at the wickedness that might be in others, both people and situations. Verses 9 and 10 give clear indication that not a word from them can be trusted, that malice is present, that they tell lies, and that this is rebellion toward God. What might this look like? Again, this could be in the form of distractions, temptations, falsehood, or unrealistic goals and expectations. It could be in the form of flattery or manipulation. Therefore, we must not walk in duplicity but in wholehearted devotion and fear of the Lord. Fear Him only, not man. Live a blameless life; be careful to conduct the affairs of your own house with a blameless heart and not look with approval on anything that is vile.

Would those distractions be obvious? No, they might not be obvious much of the time. Think about the distractions you get from social media, from internet sites, from other people, or from your own poor planning. Think about the temptations that are purposely presented to you from advertisements, from those who want your money, from activities that might promote pride or selfish ambition. Think about the falsehoods you encounter daily from news stories, or presentation of information, or from people who speak falsehoods or twist information to manipulate you into doing what they want you to do, not what God wants. Consider yourself as you are influenced by the outside to have unrealistic expectations or goals, like a certain body image, a certain yearly wage, a certain spouse, a food or supplement that is a quick fix to your problem, or a quick moneymaking scheme or improve-your-health scheme. Enemies surround us; this is why we must present our lament to the Lord before we approach any table and wait in expectation. We need His help.

If we are in a state of waiting in expectation for God, we will be satisfied. We won't be craving; we might be yearning and groaning but not craving. He cares for us and satisfies us with good things. Look at the last two verses. He is a refuge for us—our gladness, our protection, our shield, our reason to sing with joy. Isn't God good! We begin our day crying out to Him by pouring out our complaint and waiting in expectation. At sunset, we end our day singing for joy in a position of protection and shelter. Our mindset matters.

So just like our digestion starts in our brain by thinking about the food we are going to eat even before we approach the table, in this case, the food table, verse 3 heralds the call to go to Him in the morning with our requests and then wait expectantly. In this way, the digestion of our lives will be broken down into manageable pieces just like the digestion of food. By the end of the day, we will be more nourished and less stressed as we are satisfied by His protection, refuge, and defense, all leading to a better brain, body, and beliefs—because we realized Him, received from Him, and responded to Him.

Returning to Rahab, the woman who bled for years, and Mary Magdalene, please realize that clearly they were waiting in expectation. This had nothing to do with physical food; it was for protection, life, health, and peace. The cephalic phase of their situation affected their behaviors and their focus. While they waited in expectation, God did the work. Take their lead. In the morning, lay your requests before the Almighty and wait in expectation. He is able. Nothing is too hard for the Lord. You will then sing for joy; you will be surrounded with protection; you will rejoice in the Lord. Just like the digestion in your body begins even before you eat, with the mere thought or sight of food, God responds after we pray, and even before we pray. The sovereign Lord has prepared the table you are going to encounter, which could even be a table before your enemies. Wait in expectation and let God break it down into manageable pieces for you for a better brain, body, and beliefs. It is a path of righteousness for His name's sake.

Let's conclude with our actions steps, scripture, and prayer. Please take out your five-column journal. Remember, you can download this from my website, www.dynamotruth.com. Column one is our topic, which is cephalic stage. Column two is *Brain*. Column three is *Body*. Column four is *Beliefs*, and column five is *Scripture and Action Steps*.

Topic	Brain	Body	Beliefs	Scripture and Action Steps
Digestion and the cephalic stage. Waiting in expectation at the table of any concern.	Ask the *"w"* questions: What am I eating? With whom? Where? When? How? Am I hungry? Does this food help me reach my goal? How will it benefit me?	Sit and wait before approaching my meal or any table of experience. Deep breathe for vagal nerve stimulation. Get in the right location to eat.	Am I laying my requests before God? Am I thanking Him for my food? What do I believe about Psalm 5?	Read Psalm 5 aloud every day. Memorize verse 3. Give thanks before each meal. Breathe deeply for two minutes before each meal. Anticipate distractions, temptations, and so on before eating.

Under column one, be sure to write *cephalic stage.*

Under column two, the brain, let's write our "w" questions: What am I eating? With whom? Where? When? How am I eating? Am I hungry? Does this help me to reach my goal? How will this benefit me?

Under column three, the body, please write this: "Sit and wait before approaching your meal as well as approaching any table of experience. Breathe deeply for vagal nerve stimulation. Get in the right location for eating at the right time. Let your body rest to prepare for digestion."

Under column four, write "Do I really believe that laying my requests before God and thanking Him for this food and thinking about what I am going to eat will help me to digest my food better? What am I believing about Psalm 5 as I approach the table of food or any table?" You will benefit more if you are all in and really choose to believe this.

Here are your action steps for column five:

1. Read Psalm 5 daily. Memorize verse 3.
2. Take a moment before each meal to give thanks and realize what you are eating. Realize what is going to happen; envision it and think about the digestive juices beginning to flow.
3. Breathe deeply before eating. Two minutes would be ideal.
4. Anticipate distractions, temptations, falsehoods, foolish decisions, and cravings even before eating.
5. Pray!

Here is a sample prayer:

> Lord, we lay our requests before You. We cry to You and thank You for hearing our lament. Lord, we wait in expectation for You. Nothing is too hard for You, Lord. You know our enemies because they are Your enemies. Lord, You know our temptations; You know each one of us; You know how we might sabotage ourselves with our own arrogance, our selfish actions, our distractions, our poor planning, our lack of gratitude, our thoughts that are from lies, which cause us to make poor decisions

and lead to unhealthy habits. Lord, You conquer our enemies for us, but we must wait for You, and we do. We thank You for our blessings, for our opportunities, for every table we encounter, even the table set before us in the presence of our enemies because You, Lord, prepared this for us, but You are with us. Lord, You are our refuge, our protection, our reason to sing for joy. Lord, we sing to You, we wait for You, we approach our table of food and all concerns with reverence to and for You, and with gratitude to You because we are in Your presence and You bless the righteous. You surround them with Your favor as with a shield. Thank You, Lord. We are better nourished because You give us peace in our brains, bodies, and beliefs. Amen!

This wraps up week five. I hope you learned something and will take a moment to realize that God is there to help you no matter what table you approach. Get in the right mindset and wait expectantly for your God. Call out to Him. Have a great week and wait in expectation for God.

You are doing a great job getting this far. Hang in there. Persevere. Endure for better health so that you are able to do God's will. Next week, we will talk about the structural/mechanical phase of digestion.

WEEK 6

STRUCTURAL/MECHANICAL DIGESTION

CHEWING ON THE REAL FOOD, GOD'S WORD

Welcome to week six! This week, we will be discussing another phase of digestion, the structural and mechanical phase. We could also use the term *aspects* of digestion rather than *phases*. Just be aware that they are very important to the whole process of being at optimum health.

Before we begin, let's review what we discussed last week concerning the cephalic phase to see how it relates to this aspect of digestion and actually promotes the effectiveness of it. Remember, digestion begins in the brain. Just the mere thought of food or of eating starts the process. It begins the secretion of saliva, gastric juices, and pancreatic enzymes, and it stimulates the vagal nerve, which helps us to rest and digest. In fact, just the smell of food triggers all of this. Thus, we have the incorporation of "smellvertizing" by our food corporations that want us to spend money on the food they prepare. They know that digestion starts in the brain. They know that the brain is powerful and that the mere sight or smell of food will stimulate the desire to eat. This is why they spend lots of time with the advertisements and food ducts that they put into their structures.

God has wisely incorporated structures into His creation too. He created us with the structures necessary to be able to digest, to be nourished, and to enjoy the food that He provides for us, for every living creature. The structure we will talk about this week is our mouth and what is in it. Think about the structure of the mouth and what is within and nearby the mouth. These include the tongue, the teeth, the salivary glands, and the muscles for chewing and swallowing. There is more we could bring into this, like the nerves and the different types of teeth, but this is enough to emphasize the importance of the mechanical and structural phase of digestion that occurs in the mouth, with the purpose of breaking down food into manageable pieces.

Before we dig into the breakdown of food, let's look at how we break other things down into manageable pieces in our lives with three analogies—money, books, and a loaf of bread.

Imagine that someone gave you a million dollars consisting of only one-hundred-dollar bills, probably secured with rubber bands in groups of ten bills. First of all, I am sure your mind would immediately start thinking about how you were going to spend the money (recall the cephalic phase of any process or table we encounter?), but before you spend the money, you would have to do something with it. You would not just take the whole wad or suitcase full of money and dump it somewhere. You would take the rubber band off the money and use it in the right increments to be utilized properly for your purchases—not too much, not too little, just the exact amount. You break it down so that you can use it. You break it down so that you are able to manage the whole of it for its specific purpose and, of course, utilize every last cent of it.

Imagine you have a book you are going to read. This book is organized for you, but you have to open it. It is in manageable pieces for reading, which include chapters, sentences, words, and letters. It would be very difficult to digest the book if it was not organized in such a way to break it down. Our mind breaks it down for us. We can't just put the book up to our head and get the information out of it. We see each letter, realize the words, attach meaning from the parts to make a whole, and then comprehend the meanings, which helps us to grow in knowledge, wisdom, understanding, and hopefully the ability to share this with others.

Imagine a loaf of bread. We don't just put the whole thing into our mouth or on our plate. We slice it into pieces so that we can manage it. After we do this, we might make sandwiches out of it, but even after slicing the bread, we must chew it. We can't just swallow the whole slice. It must be manageable. We take a whole, break it into parts, and then the parts are utilized for our benefits or purposes.

It is the same with the mechanical phase of digestion. The purpose is to break food down into manageable pieces so that we can better utilize the nutrients—the smaller, the better. Continuing this discussion, we will use Psalm 90 as our scripture. Let's read it aloud.

Psalm 90

1   Lord, you have been our dwelling place throughout all generations.

2   Before the mountains were born or you brought forth the whole world, from everlasting to everlasting you are God.

3   You turn people back to dust, saying, "Return to dust, you mortals."

4   A thousand years in your sight are like a day that has just gone by, or like a watch in the night.

5   Yet you sweep people away in the sleep of death—they are like the new grass of the morning.

6   In the morning it springs up new, but by evening it is dry and withered.

7   We are consumed by your anger and terrified by your indignation.

8   You have set our iniquities before you, our secret sins in the light of your presence.

9   All our days pass away under your wrath; we finish our years with a moan.

10   Our days may come to seventy years, or eighty, if our strength endures; yet the best of them are but trouble and sorrow, for they quickly pass, and we fly away.

11   If only we knew the power of your anger? Your wrath is as great as the fear that is your due.

12   Teach us to number our days, that we may gain a heart of wisdom.

13   Relent, Lord! How long will it be? Have compassion on your servants.

14 Satisfy us in the morning with your unfailing love, that we may sing for joy and be glad all our days.

15 Make us glad for as many days as you have afflicted us, for as many years as we have seen trouble.

16 May your deeds be shown to your servants, your splendor to their children.

17 May the favor of the Lord our God rest on us; establish the work of our hands for us—yes, establish the work of our hands.

I love Psalm 90. I love verse 14 where the request is made to satisfy us in the morning with His unfailing love so that we may sing for joy and be glad all our days. Isn't this just what God does? We lay our requests before Him in the morning (can anyone say *cephalic phase?*), and we wait in expectation, as Psalm 5 gives us permission, and He satisfies us just like it says in Psalm 104:28, "When you open your hand, they are satisfied with good things" and where it says over and over in the psalms, like in Psalm 101:1, "I will sing of your love and justice" or Psalm 103, "Bless the Lord, oh my soul, and all that is within me, bless the His holy name." Remember, the mindset of gratitude that correlates with the cephalic phase is one of the most powerful mindsets you can have, and this requires a choice. It doesn't just happen. God is inclined to satisfy us, not indulge us but satisfy us, nourish us, and bless us with good things. This is His inclination toward us, not to keep things from us but to teach us and to extend His hand to us constantly.

The verse in Psalm 90 that I want you to hold as your pivot verse for this week is verse 12: "Teach us to number our days, that we may gain a heart of wisdom."

Isn't it interesting that the psalmist is concerned with numbering his days, not his years here? He broke the year down into manageable pieces, just as Jesus said to do, "Do not worry about tomorrow, for today has enough trouble of its own." This is what I want you to focus on this week—how important it is to break food or anything down into manageable pieces so that you are able to handle it and be more nourished by it. Breaking anything down so that we are able to manage it more thoroughly and to our best benefit is so important, whether it is food, money, cleaning our house, organizing, or even dealing with relationships, one at a time.

I will break Psalm 90 down into manageable pieces for our discussion—not exhaustive, of course, just enough to provide a portion size that's beneficial to correlate God's Word and how it nourishes us to the mechanical phase of digestion and how this is important in nourishing our bodies and brains and beliefs.

Verse 1 says, "Lord, you have been our dwelling place throughout all generations."

Right from the start, I envision a structure, God as a dwelling place. I envision purpose and function for us. This is what God has given to us, a dwelling place for our spirits to reside, a structure. This is our body, made by God in His image, fashioned by Him for a purpose and with the functions it needs to accomplish this purpose. Remember, the most important purpose or goal of health is to do His will. This is the purpose of our body—to do His will in the flesh, not just for our benefit but for the benefit of others. Remember, our healthy lives are not just about us. Our healthy lives are about our families, our church, our inner and extended circles, the whole world, and the entire host of heaven. We move forward with this reminder of truth.

Verse 2 says, "Before the mountains were born or you brought forth the whole world, from everlasting to everlasting you are God."

Again, God created a structure, mountains. I do not know all of the functions or values of mountains, but they do contain gems, diamonds, coal, and treasures. They do show God's grandeur. They do provide homes for some of God's creatures. They even stop storms that aren't at a high enough elevation to pass over the mountain. They direct the flow of water. They provide challenges. They are something for God to move if He so chooses. This verse establishes again that God is from everlasting and that He brought forth the whole world, all with so many purposes and functions, all for His Glory and for our benefit.

Looking at verses 3–11, please notice these ideas: man's finite being and returning to dust, as opposed to God's everlastingness; time indicated by morning and evening; days that pass away, and even a thousand years; our death, our iniquities, which are set before him, our secret sins, and God's power and wrath.

Read them again.

3   You turn people back to dust, saying, "Return to dust, you mortals."

4   A thousand years in your sight are like a day that has just gone by, or like a watch in the night.

5   Yet you sweep people away in the sleep of death—they are like the new grass of the morning.

6   In the morning it springs up new, but by evening it is dry and withered.

7   We are consumed by your anger and terrified by your indignation.

8   You have set our iniquities before you, our secret sins in the light of your presence.

9   All our days pass away under your wrath; we finish our years with a moan.

10   Our days may come to seventy years, or eighty, if our strength endures; yet the best of them are but trouble and sorrow, for they quickly pass, and we fly away.

11   If only we knew the power of your anger? Your wrath is as great as the fear that is your due.

Do you see how so many huge ideas, such as time, conditions, and qualities, are broken down into manageable and more specific language and messages? Concerning God, we see precise phrases of "consumed by your anger; power of your anger; under your wrath; fear that is your due." Concerning man, we see that we are like dust, like grass that is swept away; we have a finish to our years; we are finite; we have iniquities that are known by God, our secret sins too. Concerning time, the psalm even breaks a thousand years down to morning and evening, which is something we can understand and manage. We can't even imagine a thousand years, let alone manage them. However, we can manage a day, and the wise man breaks the day up into even more manageable time frames of day and night. We use this organization for work and sleep. We clock into time clocks for work. We take breaks that are minutes long. Think of a long life lived well. The eulogy of such a life doesn't speak of the entirety; the life is broken down into manageable pieces, into the anecdotes that best reflect the value of the individual, the mortal who has passed away like grass. These are small bits that we in our finiteness are able to understand, to digest, to absorb for better understanding.

Now for verse 12, our pivot verse, "Teach us to number our days, that we may gain a heart of Wisdom."

I want this verse to reflect the pivotal moment of food entering our bodies after we have thought about it in the cephalic phase of digestion. Please make this correlation with me. Just as we eat food, or ingest it, chew on it, relish it, and realize we are eating it before we swallow it, we are also to eat the food of God's Word—chew on it, relish it, realize it, and swallow the truth of it so that we are transformed. We should not just gulp it down; we are to meditate on it day and night; these are manageable pieces and time frames. Do you see the correlation? If we swallow it whole, without any understanding, explanation, meditation, or consistency, and in fact, without even preparing our minds for reading it, we are somewhat like a starved individual who ingests a huge amount of food that makes them sick because they are not ready for it. God's Word is the same; we can't ingest the whole of it at once. We must daily nourish ourselves wisely with it, taking in the portions of it that might be particularly relevant to the needs we have at the specific time of life or circumstances we are in. It might be one verse, one chapter, one book, or maybe it is the entirety of scripture embraced so that we consider the whole counsel of God's Word. Realize now that we are to number our days to gain a heart of wisdom—not our years, just our days. We can manage this. Just like food, we manage it meal by meal, bite by bite, nutrient by nutrient, so that we gain a body of health. We also must manage God's Word daily, day and night. This is a manageable guide and goal for us. We chew our food, and we chew on God's Word, seeking Him not with our teeth but with our hearts.

Finally, verses 13–17.

13 Relent, Lord! How long will it be? Have compassion on your servants.

14 Satisfy us in the morning with your unfailing love, that we may sing for joy and be glad all our days.

15 Make us glad for as many days as you have afflicted us, for as many years as we have seen trouble.

16 May your deeds be shown to your servants, your splendor to their children.

17 May the favor of the Lord our God rest on us; establish the work of our hands for us—yes, establish the work of our hands.

The God who is everlasting is broken down into these descriptors: He has compassion; He satisfies; He causes us to sing for joy; He makes us glad; He grants favor to us; He establishes the work of our hands. He does this for us, the mere mortals who are like grass that is swept away; the mere mortals who are guilty of iniquity; the mere mortals who are only able to handle one day at a time, not a thousand years. So many diverse and good attributes of God are mentioned here. All of them are important, from wrath to power to compassion. All are a benefit to us. This makes me realize that I don't want to pick just one attribute of God and only rely on that for spiritual health, somewhat like we should not just pick one food and rely only on that for our physical nourishment and health.

Created with Order

We have discussed God's creation to lay a foundation for the fact that God created all with a functional purpose, to be enjoyed and used to honor Him and help each member. We looked at the entirety of the world and broke it down into mountains, seas, trees, creatures, food, and homes for His creatures. Now let's break this down even further and look at how He created us, and more specifically, how He created our digestive system so that we are able to break food down for the functional purpose of nourishment for health in our brains and bodies while we at the same time walk in line with our beliefs by giving thanks.

As we discussed last week, our digestion starts in our brains with the mere thought of food or the smell or sight of food. This stimulates our vagus nerve, which triggers the digestive processes of salivation, gastric juice production, enzyme secretion, bile production, and more. It primes our bodies for digestion. It promotes a state of rest so that we are able to digest.

Now let's turn our focus to what we can see and feel, beginning in our mouths. Think of the structures that we have for breaking food down. God gave us teeth and different kinds of teeth, some for mashing, some for chewing, some for tearing. He gave us a tongue that helps move food around our mouths so that we can chew it more adequately and move it in place for swallowing. He gave us salivary glands, which produce saliva and begin the process of breaking down carbohydrates and fats. He innervated all of this with nerves and muscles that control and give power to the process. Please do not take any of this for granted. My daughter had to be taught how to bite, to chew, to move food around her mouth, and to swallow. All of this is still not easy for her either. Please do not take your ability to chew and your understanding of chewing for granted.

Let's just focus on the aspect of chewing. Do not disregard this very important step in the health of our entire being. Just as God's Word should be approached with respect, regard, time, meditation, a willingness to absorb, learn, and be transformed by it, and a willingness to chew on it, our food should be approached with this same mindset. The purpose of chewing food is to break it down into smaller particles for easier digestion. Chewing also stimulates more salivary production, which enables the food to become a liquid bolus for easier swallowing. This increased liquid quality of the food enables the stomach to be even more effective in digesting the food as it gets churned by the stomach.

Protein digestion does not begin until the protein enters the stomach. However, when protein is chewed and broken into small particles in the mouth, the surface area of each piece increases. This increased surface area enables more contact with the pepsin and hydrochloric acid in the stomach. This then breaks the protein down into peptides and later into individual amino acids. Our bodies need the protein to be broken down to the amino acids so that they can be absorbed and then used to build up the proteins we need in the rest of our bodies. We need this for muscle development, for wound healing, for hormone production and other body processes, and for brain function. It is not important for you to understand all the what and why about protein. Just understand that chewing is what you can do to help your growth and health, just like opening your Bible and reading is what you can do to help your spiritual growth and health. God will meet you for both. The Lord said, "Taste and see," and Augustine heard, "Take and read." It all matters.

One final note about the importance of chewing and getting the food to a liquid state for easier digestion and absorption. This allows the body to use less energy to digest the food. It takes energy to digest food. In fact, to digest about one hundred calories of protein, the body uses about twenty to twenty-five calories of energy. If we do not chew adequately, not only do we deprive ourselves of the benefits of the nourishment, but we also make things more difficult for the body. The extra effort for the body to digest the protein or any food due to poor chewing is expended by the body; this creates stress and additional effort. The energy used for this will not be available for you; it decreases your energy for other processes; it decreases your energy to do God's will.

Correlation to God's Word

I direct you back to Psalm 90 and our pivot verse 12: "So teach us to number our days, that we may gain a heart of wisdom."

We number our days to make the most of each one, to use each day to seek after wisdom, to make the most of each day by meditating on God's Word, by chewing on His Word so that our souls are nourished, so that our spirits are fed, so that our minds are renewed, so that we are transformed, all for the purpose of doing His will.

I challenge you with this: teach us to number our chews and our food particles so that we may gain a brain, body, and belief of health, so that we do all that is good, so that we do God's will, so that we grow in understanding, to love Him more, to be nourished by Him. Remember, to do God's will is our ultimate goal of health.

It all matters. Every word of God is pure, flawless, and profitable for instruction, for reproof, for training in righteousness. Every nourishing bite we eat and chew is profitable for our health, for giving thanks, for realizing, receiving, and responding to God. He has given this food to us so that we are able to respond to Him and to the purpose He has for us. If we are better nourished, we are better able to think, to feel stronger, to have energy, to do God's will; we are able to have a physical condition to be able to grow in God's wisdom. Isn't this what we want? We are to seek after wisdom. Seeking better health helps the process of seeking after wisdom. Jesus said that we can't serve two masters. If we prioritize pie over prayer, we have put the Prince in a position below His Priesthood, and we have set ourselves up to be a spiritual pauper, portly and permissive, not prudent and purposeful. The mindset and awareness of this mechanical aspect of chewing on food along with the mindset and awareness of chewing on God's Word day and night are both beneficial for doing God's will and gaining a heart of wisdom. This is in accordance with the Potter's plan for the path of righteousness He has prepared in advance for us.

Another correlation I would like to point out is the concept of whole versus part. If we look at the human body, we see a whole person, yet this person is made up of parts just like the body of Christ. We have different experts who deal with these parts: brain experts, heart experts, bone experts, lung experts, kidney experts, hormone experts. We have pastors, teachers, counselors, coaches, trainers, nutritionists, and financial managers. If we look at man-made construction, we again see whole buildings, yet these buildings are made up of different parts that were directed by their respective experts: electricians, plumbers, painters, heating and cooling managers, et cetera. The foundation of the building, done by the cement experts, is necessary for the stability of everything else. It is not even seen by the rest of us, yet it is there, firmly holding its important position. If we think of a path or life journey, we are not equipped to navigate the whole at once or even to envision it.

We can only take one step at a time, somewhat like a toddler learning to walk. Do I dare bring up another analogy? How about the conception of a child? It begins with one cell, then two cells, then four cells, and eventually trillions of cells to make up the wonder of the complete person God created.

This is the same with God's Word. Every word of God is flawless. Every word is to be relished, to be chewed upon, to be treasured, and indeed, as it says in Isaiah about the one with whom God is pleased, "the one who trembles at my Word." Yes, we are to tremble at His Word. This means to have a healthy fear, with respect and time to be adequately nourished by it, so that we can learn of Him and do His will. Although growing in God's wisdom by nourishing ourselves daily to gain a heart of wisdom is far more important than the aspect of chewing our food for health, you must realize by now that God has fashioned us this way with His perfect wisdom. It is a daily spiritual lesson on the importance of gaining a heart of wisdom, on the importance of becoming like a tree planted by the river of water that brings forth fruit, on the importance of doing His will. As Jesus said, "My food is doing the will of God." How much better to taste and see that the Lord is good while at the same time nourishing ourselves by chewing on His Word and His food that He gives to satisfy us.

Conclusion

What a reminder that God in His wisdom has knit each of us together, that we are truly fearfully and wonderfully made, down to every last structure and detail of our bodies. Today, we focused on the structure of our mouth, the teeth, and the aspect of chewing, yet we see how very important this little member is. We use it to encourage others with wisdom, and we use it to encourage ourselves with the wisdom God has provided to us through His Word. We chew on His Word, and we chew on our food so that our entire person is nourished each day for the whole life span, so that we gain a heart of wisdom and a body of health.

We will conclude today with our journal once again. Please get your five columns out. Remember column one is our topic, which is chewing. Column two is *Brain*, column three is *Body*, column four is *Beliefs*, and column five is *Scripture and Action Steps*.

Please write the word *chewing* under column one.

In column two, please write what is true about this situation. Chewing my food into small particles helps for easier digestion, which will nourish my brain and body. This is a true statement whether you are a Christian or not. Think about your food being broken up into small pieces and becoming a liquid while in your mouth.

In column three, please write, "I will chew each bite of food thirty times before swallowing."

In column four, please ask, "What do I really believe about nourishing myself with God's Word and food? Am I acting according to what I believe? Am I chewing on God's Word day and night with the goal of gaining a heart of wisdom? Am I chewing my food enough to really get adequate nourishment?"

In column five, please write Psalm 90:12: "So teach us to number our days that we may gain a heart of wisdom."

Here are your action steps:

1. Read Psalm 90 aloud each day. Memorize verse 12. Read it thirty times this week.
2. Engage the cephalic phases of digestion by praying before each meal and thinking about what you are going to eat. This is still important.
3. Chew each bite of food thirty times before swallowing; notice how it gets liquefied.
4. Thank God for the wisdom and the physical nourishment He gives you.
5. Pray.

Topic	Brain	Body	Beliefs	Scripture and Action Steps
Chewing	Chewing my food into small particles helps with easier digestion, which will nourish my brain and body. Think about your food being broken up into small pieces and becoming a liquid while in your mouth.	I will chew each bite of food thirty times before swallowing.	What do I really believe about nourishing myself with God's Word and food? Am I acting according to what I believe? Am I chewing on God's Word day and night with the goal of gaining a heart of wisdom? Am I chewing my food enough to really get adequate nourishment?	Read Psalm 90 daily. Memorize verse 12. Engage the cephalic phase of digestion by praying before each meal and thinking about what you are going to eat. Chew each bite of food thirty times before swallowing; notice how it gets liquefied. Thank God for the wisdom and the physical nourishment He gives you. Realize how you are numbering your days to gain a heart of wisdom. Count the number of minutes you read your Bible and pray each day. Compare this to the number of minutes you do other things.

Here is a sample prayer:

Lord, we thank You for Your Word. It is pure; it is flawless; it is for our lives. Lord, help us to number our days so that we apply our hearts to gain wisdom. Lord, help us to realize that each day is an opportunity to grow in wisdom, to learn of You, and to do Your will. Lord, help us to realize that we do not need to know the complete path You have for us; we must just trust in You each step of the way, just as we trust in You for our daily bread. Lord, we want to chew on Your Word; we want to learn of You; we want to be nourished by food so that we can do Your will. Lord, help us to chew on our food just as we chew on Your Word for wisdom. Help us to realize, receive, and respond to the wisdom You give us and to the food You give us. Lord, we thank You that just as the power of Your anger is to be feared, so is the satisfaction that You give us to be regarded with great thanks. Lord, we thank You that You establish the work of our hands and that Your favor rests on us. Lord, teach us to number our days, that we may gain hearts of wisdom. Amen.

I also challenge you on some other things. No judgment here. Remember, our goal is to do God's will, to learn of Him, and if we are not doing this, we are not healthy. I challenge you to monitor your minutes, not the one thousand years; don't worry about what is going to happen in a thousand years. Don't even worry about tomorrow, just today, just the minutes of today. I challenge you this week to monitor your minutes. We are going to go with the theme of thirty. I challenge you to spend time in Bible reading and prayer, at least thirty minutes. If that is too much for you, then read thirty verses or give thanks to the Lord thirty times for something. If you are having trouble with your finances, I challenge you to put thirty cents or thirty dollars in a jar this week. Make this a habit. If you are having trouble with relationships, and you don't know what to do, I challenge you to go to someone thirty times to work on the relationship, or to thirty different people. If you are having trouble sleeping or are not getting enough sleep, I challenge you to go to bed thirty minutes earlier. If you are late to work, I challenge you to leave for work thirty minutes earlier. If you are not drinking water, I challenge you to drink thirty ounces. Let's just start there. Do something to move in the right direction with a mindset of praise.

Remember, our food, our movement, our mindset, our environment, and our chewing are important to health. If our environment is not clean, let's take thirty items and throw them away, or thirty items and put them away, or thirty items and give them away. If you have junk food or toxins in your house, throw thirty of them away so you don't have to think about them or deal with them anymore. Get rid of thirty temptations that you deal with daily. You can do it. Go to the Lord and thank Him. Let the Psalms run out of your mouth. Spew forth Psalm 103 with "Bless the Lord, O my soul!" Don't hesitate. Do this. Persevere. Endure. Detail upon detail. Small step upon small step. I cannot tell you what God is able to do through your action to respond to what He shows you, with the willingness you exert to respond to Him.

If you are struggling with wickedness in the land of your mind and heart, pray, "I will sing of Your love and justice. I will be careful to live a blameless life. Oh when will you come to me? I will be careful to conduct the affairs of my house with a blameless heart." Look at yourself and say, "OK, what are thirty things I need to clean up about myself?" The more you do, the stronger God will work in you. God will come to your aid. Remember, you are no longer under condemnation. You are blessed, chosen, adopted, accepted, redeemed, and forgiven; you are loved. You belong to God. Chew your food and chew on God's Word. I leave you with that. The Word of God endures forever. It is flawless. It is your life. Just as you get food into your mouth, get God's Word into your mouth. You will not have strength without it. Take one step at a time and follow the path of righteousness that He has for you.

Next week, we will discuss the chemical phase of digestion and our *true help* in time of need.

WEEK 7

CHEMICAL DIGESTION

OUR TRUE HELP IN TIME OF NEED

Welcome to week seven. If you have been implementing the action steps, you must be experiencing improvement. Keep at this. Don't give up. You are at the halfway mark of the twelve weeks. Be patient and give everything time; do not be in a hurry. Every effort you make is sure to have a beneficial impact on your entire person.

Before we jump into the week seven material about the chemical phase of digestion in the stomach, I want to spend some time reviewing the very strategic and specific information we have covered in the first six weeks of the Health through the Psalms program. Doing this should help to solidify how digestion along with the aspects of epigenetics and inflammation are related and how they influence our immediate and long-term health.

Below is a chart to outline the topic we covered each week, along with the main point and the psalm we used to make the connection to God's Word. I will briefly give a quick snapshot using short statements to remind us of the focus of the information. The first four weeks were devoted to the aspect of epigenetics. We looked at these four topics: environment, movement, mindset, and food. These four aspects of our personal situation affect our genetic expression. This is important because we are able to influence our genes, and this influences our health.

Topic	Brain	Body	Beliefs	Action Steps and Scripture
Environment	Clear clutter from brain—lies and negative thoughts.	Clear clutter from pantry, schedule, activities, people.	Clear clutter of lies, complaining, and sin.	Psalm. Live a blameless life!
Movement	Envision moving in the direction out of oppression; envision the action to take.	Begin exercising wherever it is comfortable for you.	Move out of the oppression of shame by believing that no one who hopes in the Lord will be ashamed.	Psalm 25: move out of the lie of oppression.
Mindset	Think on what you are grateful for.	Write notes to three people to thank them. Thank God for three things daily.	Have an attitude of gratitude. Bless the Lord daily. Tell the hosts of heaven to bless the Lord.	Psalm 103: realize, receive, and respond to what God has done, is doing, and will do with gratitude.
Food	Think about food that is nourishing; envision buying and eating it.	Go into the store and select three nourishing food items. Buy only them and leave the store. Refrain from buying anything in a bag or box.	Look to the Lord to satisfy you, and remember that your food comes from Him. Thank Him for satisfying you with good things.	Psalm 104: realize, receive, and respond to the good things God gives you as well as to what God wants you to eat.

Cephalic phase thinking	Think about what you are going to eat; give thanks.	Let the body get primed for digestion. Take deep breaths before eating.	Give thanks before eating anything. Pour your lament to God before approaching any table.	Psalm 5: engage the cephalic phase of digestion to get the body primed for digesting food. Think about it, relax, and give thanks.
Mechanical phase chewing	Think about food becoming smaller while chewing.	Chew each bite of food thirty times.	Chew on God's Word to gain a heart of wisdom.	Psalm 90: do thirty things to clear the clutter of the land of your heart and mind.

Week one discussed environment; the goal was to clean up the environment of our brains, bodies, and beliefs by clearing the clutter out of our lives. We want to clear the clutter from our brains. We want to clear the clutter from our pantries and schedules. We want to clear the clutter of lies and complaining and sin from our lives. We used Psalm 101 with the focus on living a blameless life.

Week two discussed movement. We want to envision ourselves moving in the direction out of oppression. The goal was to move out of ourselves, specifically to move out of any area of oppression by taking action and stepping out to effect a change. We used Psalm 25 with the focus on moving out of oppression and away from shame. We also focused on the importance of exercise in the health of our brains and bodies.

Week three discussed mindset; the goal was to develop the mindset of gratitude. We used Psalm 103 with the focus on gratitude and commanding our souls and all of heaven to praise the Lord. We wanted to focus on God's goodness and what He has done, is doing, and will do, as well as to focus on other people. We focused on acknowledging what they have done, are doing, and will do for us.

Week four discussed food; the goal was to envision and then begin selecting food that was really food, that had traveled little from garden to gut, and that was not in a bag or box. We used Psalm 104 with the focus on remembering that our food comes from God, with the purpose to satisfy us, not to increase our cravings but to satisfy and nourish us, and that the ultimate purpose is to be able to achieve optimum health to do His will. I challenged you to walk into the store and buy only three nourishing items and to avoid the junk food aisles. This would also help with financial struggles as well as to develop the habit of self-control, which will permeate to other areas of life.

The second four weeks of the program are devoted to the topic of digestion and how this impacts our health. The topics discussed so far have been the cephalic phase of digestion and chewing. In the next two weeks, we will discuss the chemical and microbial aspects of digestion.

Week five discussed the cephalic phase of digestion; the goal was to realize that digestion begins in the brain and that taking a moment to give thanks before we ingest anything is important and actually helps with digestion. Also, to think about food gets our body ready for or primed for digestion. We used Psalm 5 with the focus on presenting our lament to God about anything and before we approach any table as we wait in expectation for Him. I addressed the "table of concern" that all of us have at different times and emphasized that we are able to remind God about it while we wait in expectation for Him. I also brought up the action step of deep breathing to help with stress and with digestion.

Week six discussed the mechanical phase of digestion with chewing, both on food and on God's Word; the goal was to chew our food so that we have an easier time digesting and absorbing the nutrients from the food to optimize our nourishment, along with the goal of chewing on God's Word to strengthen our spiritual health. We used Psalm 90 with the focus on numbering our days to get a heart of wisdom along with numbering our chews to help us digest and absorb the nutrients from our food. We topped this off with the challenge to chew each bite of food thirty times before swallowing, as well as to do thirty things to improve the environment of our own land, the land of our hearts and brains, so that we truly live blameless lives. Furthermore, I emphasized that if we aren't chewing on God's Word, we are not healthy, and that our ultimate goal of health is to do His will. We need His Word for this. With the theme of thirty as a prominent number here, I challenged you to read your Bible and pray at least thirty minutes a day.

Psalm 121 and Chemical Digestion

So now let's look at the chemical phase of digestion, which takes place in our stomach, while using God's Word of Psalm 121 as our foundation for discussion.

Let me start today's presentation with a report on a timely occurrence, as it is relevant to today's discussion. This week, I received both a text and an email warning me of two possible dangers and what to do to prevent the negative effects of them or at least to be aware of them. In other words, to be in the know about something that is way beyond my scope of control. I did not solicit this information; it came to me. Again, I was a passive recipient of what came into my environment. This information could have toxified my brain; it was actually clutter, in my opinion, and was not promoting blameless living but instead was evoking man's carnality and vain imagination. It was instigating man's power and control, not God's, and it clearly had no focus on the faithful of the land. In other words, it was a bunch of environmental toxins in the form of intellectual property and conspiracy theory via words. Hitting delete is a lot easier than clearing the clutter of the pantry, but both are necessary for health.

Let me explain the foe and enemy I was supposed to get my mindset on rather than the grand mountains and the God who created them. The first was a national security type of situation that depicted a conspiracy of why something was happening and who was behind it, and then of course a call to "support" the political leader who might solve the problem. Ugh … another vile attempt to get my eyes off the faithful of the land; to get my goal off of seeking peace and pursuing it; to cause me to get angry and fret. Again, it was so easy to hit delete. God is bigger than any conspiracy. God knows the foe and the enemy. I cannot be aware of all of them. It is too big for me. I am not saying that we should live under a rock or keep our heads in the sand; I am only trying to get our focus back on God and not get caught up in matters that are not our concern or that are beyond our control.

The second anecdote was similar, another "might happen to you" type of thing. In this case, it concerned getting robbed while locking your car in a parking lot before entering a store. It offered a very ridiculous sequence to engage in just in case "someone" is watching you. Again, too big for me. I cannot be aware of a hundred different cars in a parking lot and who might be hiding in them. Yes, too big for me but not for God. Again, this does not mean that I will not walk with prudence, but it does mean that I must rely on God to have my back and be my protector from harm.

This is what I want you to see this week. Everything is too big for us, but nothing is too big for God. He knows all. He doesn't sleep. He watches over our coming and going. He is our defender, our shade, our protection from harm. We can't possibly be aware of all the enemies; it is enough to know that we do have enemies and that we are to be watchful and vigilant, that we are to live a life worthy of Christ, that we are to be careful to live a blameless life. We must break the big idea down into manageable pieces like we discussed in our study concerning chewing last week, using Psalm 90 to teach us to number our days to gain hearts of wisdom. Yes, enemies are numerous, but in truth, if God showed us all of our enemies, we could not handle it, just like we could not handle it if He showed us His glory.

However, our God can handle anything. Nothing is too hard for the Lord. This is the point I want to make this week. God is our help against all. Yes, we do our part by having a mindset on Him, by obeying Him, by chewing on His Word—in truth, by doing what is basic. We do the same with our health. We do our part by doing what is basic, not by knowing everything. We can't possibly know all of the nutrients in food, all the germs, all the possible disease-causing agents, all the possible environmental toxins or all of the different types of supplements that might be good for us. This whole of information is too much for us, but we can do all the little things that add up to the whole, one day at a time. We just do the basics … clear the clutter, eat real food, exercise, drink water, have a mindset of praise, chew our real food and God's Word well, and now, concerning this week … look to hydrochloric acid or stomach acid to be your help and my help too.

Here we go with Psalm 121.

Psalm 121

1   I lift up my eyes to the mountains—where does my help come from?

2   My help comes from the Lord, the Maker of heaven and earth.

3   He will not let your foot slip—He who watches over you will not slumber;

4   Indeed, He who watches over Israel will neither slumber nor sleep.

5   The Lord watches over you—the Lord is your shade at your right hand;

6   the sun will not harm you by day nor the moon by night.

7   The Lord will keep you from all harm—He will watch over your life.

8   The Lord will watch over your coming and going both now and forevermore.

The immediate concept that revs us up today is this: *God is our help.* No question exists about this. Nothing can stand against the Lord. It does not matter what you are up against, what challenge you have, what need you have, what frustration or desire you have. *God is your help.* Engage the cephalic phase here. Get your mindset on that attitude—that God is your help. What more do we need to say about anything that comes our way, about any table we approach, about any oppression or environment we encounter? God is our help. He knows about what we are going to experience on our path of righteousness long before we do, and He is our help. You can look to the mountains, you can look to your immediate environment, you can look to the faithful of the land; all of these may change from time to time, but the truth that God is your help will never change. It is true forever, both now and all your days, every minute.

Realize that the correlation I want to make here is this: just as God is our help—in other words, He is the main thing, both spiritually and physically—just as He is our help, we also have another huge help concerning our physical health, and this help is stomach acid. No matter what smaller helps we have in our lives, whether it is people, money, ability, or fortitude, God is still the source of this help, and He brings it forth at the proper time when we need it. So it is with stomach acid. No matter what other helps we have in our nourishment, whether it is selecting healthy food, engaging the cephalic response, eating with people, or chewing, stomach acid is the source for the ultimate strength of digesting food. If we do not have adequate stomach acid, we will not get adequate nutrient absorption, just like if we do not have adequate help from God, we will not get adequate protection or have a good spiritual life. He is the main thing, and stomach acid is also a main thing. Although the other actions on our part are important, when we eat good food and chew our food well, we still need stomach acid to optimize digestion, just like when we chew on His Word, we need God to optimize our wisdom and strength.

Let's look at similarities:

God is the strongest help we have.	Stomach acid is the strongest help to digest food.
God destroys our enemies.	Stomach acid destroys pathogens.
God does not sleep.	Stomach acid is available at all times.
God wants our mindset on Him.	Stomach acid is more plentiful when we engage our mindset.
The Lord watches over our lives.	Stomach acid, in a sense, watches over our gut life.

Again, the Lord is strong; stomach acid is strong. The Lord doesn't sleep and keeps us from harm even when we do not look to Him. Stomach acid doesn't sleep and tackles pathogens even if we don't engage our mindset on it. However, might I posit this to you—how much more the Lord will work when we ask Him. The Lord hears us when we call; the Lord knows whose hearts are fully devoted to Him; the Lord responds to our lament. In truth, He keeps in perfect peace those who are steadfast, whose minds are on Him because they trust in Him.

As we learned in the cephalic phase of digestion, when we engage our mindset on the fact that we are eating, our entire digestive system is engaged. This means that stomach acid begins to be secreted along with bile production, pancreatic enzymes, and other processes. This happens just because we are thinking about food, and even if we are only smelling the aroma of food, because digestion starts in the brain. Might this be a connection to the process of God working in our lives just because we go to Him? We look to Him. We ask Him for help. We have our mindset on Him. Yes, He indeed works when we don't go to Him, but how much more when we ask Him. He hears our cries for help; He is near the brokenhearted. We do not need to know all the details, all the foes, all the enemies, all the possibilities for disaster or hardship. We only need to know that we have enemies, but He is able to defend us. He doesn't sleep. He is our strongest defense against enemies, just like our stomach acid is our strongest defense against pathogens. He is our help.

I liken this to our bodies. We do not need to know all the details of the pathogens that are on food or that might gain entry into our bodies through our mouths. We only need to know that we have a defender given to us by God, and this defender is stomach acid. We do not even need to know all of the different nutrients we need. We only need to focus on eating real food and consider the quality, quantity, timing, and diversity of the real food we have selected; remember, real food has traveled little from garden to gut, from field to fork, and it is not in a bag or a box.

However, even if we are eating all of the right things at the right times and in the right way, if we are low on stomach acid, we will not get the added benefit of pathogen destruction, nor we will get the benefit of fully digested food. This is why we spent time on the cephalic phase of digestion, because it helps to increase stomach acid. Remember that when we think about eating, then proceed to chew our food thoroughly to break it into small pieces, the stomach is better able to have the desired effect of doing even more chemical digestion on the smaller food particles by churning it, as well as by the stomach acid breaking it down further. This is the most powerful digestion that occurs, the digestion done by the stomach acid. We do not want to decrease our stomach acid due to this important aspect of digestion.

If you remember, this is especially true for proteins, because protein digestion occurs in the stomach. This is where the protein is broken up into peptide bonds that are later broken up into amino acids. If this full breakdown of protein does not occur, a complete peptide bond or protein could cross the intestinal barrier and cause havoc in the body. This is not good, but even before we consider this, we could have poor nourishment just because we do not have adequate stomach acid to break the protein down. Either scenario means the body is depleted of a very important nutrient—protein and the amino acids it supplies.

Protein drives our metabolism and our health, especially as we age. We need protein for our bodily processes, for neurotransmitters, for hormone production, for tissue repair, and for many other functions of the body. Thinking about our food, chewing our food, and now supporting our stomach acid are three actions we can take to encourage protein breakdown and absorption.

Here are two other important nutrients to consider: iron and Vitamin B. We need adequate stomach acid to be able to digest iron and B_{12} vitamins that we get from our food. If our stomach acid is low, we will not be getting the iron absorption or B_{12} vitamin absorption that we need. We need iron for muscle development and for oxygen transport. Without it, we are weak and tired. We need B_{12} vitamins for energy and DNA synthesis and lots more. Possibly your lethargy is rooted in low stomach acid, which means your body is not getting the nutrients that you think you are supplying. It's worth attacking to make an improvement.

How could we support this aspect of digestion for improved health so that we are better able to do God's will? Just like we can support the aspect of numbering our days so that we apply our hearts to gain wisdom by chewing on God's Word, by looking to Him, by taking action like Rahab, the woman who bled for years, and Mary Magdalene, we can support our stomach's function of breaking food down so that we gain a body of health by continuing to engage the cephalic phase of digestion, but here are some other suggestions for you.

1. Drink more water. We produce about 1.5 liters of stomach acid per day. Yes, liters. This requires water. If we are dehydrated, our stomach acid will be low, and this will hinder digestion.

2. Add apple cider vinegar to your daily plan. Apple cider vinegar (or lemon juice) naturally increases the acidity of the stomach acid. This is good. This helps break food down so that we can absorb the nutrients. Just add a teaspoon or tablespoon of apple cider vinegar to a cup of water and drink it ten minutes before you eat. You could incorporate this into your deep breathing and prayer time before your meal.

3. Quit your antacids or PPIs (proton pump inhibitors). Many people think they have acid reflux or GERD (gastroesophageal reflux disease) when in reality they have low stomach acid. If our stomach acid is low, we won't digest food properly, which will lead to acid reflux or GERD. If our stomach acid is low, our lower esophageal sphincter might become weak, which will lead to acid reflux. In fact, when stomach acid increases and food digestion improves with more stomach acid, the lower esophageal sphincter has been shown to tighten up, which further decreases any acid reflux symptoms. When a person ingests an antacid or PPI, they are in fact lowering stomach acid. A PPI is a proton pump inhibitor; these are commonly prescribed by doctors to clients who complain about acid reflux. This in itself might not be a good idea due

to the fact that lower stomach acid impairs digestion, which will further perpetuate the problem. Our goal is to have adequate stomach acid so that we are able to digest our food properly while it is in the stomach. This is our most powerful help to digest the food and kill pathogens, just like God is our most powerful help to gain a heart of wisdom and to protect us against our enemies.

4. Stop your own prescribed PPIs. This is what I mean. Stop your own *preplanned inconsistencies*. Good habits can be hard to establish; bad habits can be hard to break. This takes engaging the cephalic phase of the tables you encounter. Don't plan on failure; don't plan on inconsistencies. Plan on success. Set yourself up for success. Get your environment rid of toxins or clutter that foster preplanned inconsistencies. Get your environment clear so that you see, hear, and touch what you need—like your Bible, your water, your apple cider vinegar, your time to slowly eat and chew your food, your schedule, and your time so you exercise instead of waste it on the unfaithful temptations of the land. Add this to your list of action steps: *preplanned prudence that instills*, a PPI that will not harm anyone.

Do you see the connection I want you to make so that you do not get overwhelmed in your spiritual walk or in your health walk? We can't know every step of the path of righteousness God has for us. We can't know all our years at once; one day at a time is enough. We can't know all the enemies or foes we are going to encounter. We can't know the whole. We only need to know the parts to be able to manage the whole. Rahab only looked to God and to the spies who were in front of her. She did not worry about the whole battle or if the men would remember; she did not worry about all the soldiers she would have to encounter or could encounter before the red cord was seen again by the faithful, God-fearing men. The woman who had bled for years and who just wanted to touch the hem of Jesus's garment to be healed broke through the crowd; she did not worry about how she was going to do this. She overcame the shame she could endure as she plowed through the crowd to get to Jesus. She kept her eyes on that mountain of her faith, the Lord Himself, who was her help. Mary Magdalene followed Jesus. She never denied Him out of fear—all through the crucifixion, through the agony of the days without Him, through the tears. She only knew that her Lord was behind the stone which needed to be rolled away, but she did not trouble herself with that small detail. She wanted her Lord. Think about this. She was the first person the Lord appeared to after He rose from the dead. "Oh, when will you come to me?" Remember this question from Psalm 101? Maybe the Lord will come to you and to me when we seek Him like this, like Mary Magdalene.

Could I bring up another heroine? Esther. Beautiful Esther. I have never detected worry or fear concerning her—in Mordecai, yes, but not in Esther. I have always detected peace without anger concerning her, complete surrender to her Lord; in Mordecai, I have always detected angst with anger, not surrender to anything except the mindset to take up his arms in the name of Lord and with vengeance. The strength of the palace and its kingdom, along with the king, were too great for both Mordecai and Esther. Neither had power to overcome these. Esther, as a woman, surely had no power. She had great beauty, but oh how she must have numbered her days to gain a heart of wisdom. Indeed, she spent more time chewing on God's Word than on the delicacies of her queenhood. Her masterful handling of saving the Jews showed that she realized, received, and responded to the help that came from far beyond the hills. Her help came from the Lord, the maker of heaven and earth.

I have to make some other important distinctions about God's attributes and the attributes of stomach acid. Just as we hinder God's ability, or possibly his preference or His requirement, to walk by faith and not by sight, when we do not seek Him, we also hinder the ability of stomach acid to help us digest food when we do not engage the cephalic phase of digestion. We hinder it by failing to breathe deeply and by lacking adequate water intake. This can be improved only by us. Just as in the morning we are to lay our requests before Him and wait in expectation, we are to pause before eating, give thanks, and engage our mindset on the table set before us.

Another distinction here. God's glory is too much for us to handle, too powerful for us, but in due time, we will see the glory of the Lord. However, He shows this daily through His creation. The heavens declare the glory of God. This is also true of stomach acid. We are unable to handle the very strong and powerful aspect of stomach acid outside of its intended environment of the stomach. This is why acid reflux is so uncomfortable and why people seek a solution or relief from it. However, God has given us the right protective lining in our gastric wall that is able to handle the powerful action of stomach acid. He created us this way; what glory He shows us here. This is no accident, but we are still responsible for putting action to our faith, to our belief that stomach acid is a powerful component to our whole health process, just as living a blameless life, waiting in expectation, chewing, and having a mindset of gratitude are also powerful components of our complete health.

In conclusion, let me make this very important distinction. Although we can hinder the power and action of stomach acid by what we do, what we think, how we manage stress, our lifestyle and other habits, nothing can stand against the Lord. He truly is our help. We look to the mountains, and we see where our help comes from. Our help comes from the Lord, the maker of heaven and earth. He never sleeps, and He watches over our coming and going, both now and forevermore. Hallelujah. Get the lining of your spiritual wall up so that you are able to handle the glory that our Lord is ready to show you. Breathe in the freshness of God so that all that is rancid, whether in your soul or in the soil of your body, will be clutter cleared, so that you have a blameless environment by chewing on the Word of God and absorbing His truth and true nourishment.

OK, team! Let's pull out your five-column journal. If you need one, please download it from my website, www.dynamotruth.com.

Sample Chart for Chemical Digestion—
Our True Help in Time of Need

Topic	Brain	Body	Beliefs	Scripture and Action Steps
Chemical digestion and stomach acid. Our true help in time of need.	Think about eating so that more stomach acid is produced. Envision chewing food thirty times, turning it into small particles.	Drink water with one tablespoon of apple cider vinegar in it ten minutes before each meal.	Do I really believe that my help comes from the Lord? At all times? For everything? Do I really believe stomach acid is this relevant?	Read Psalm 121 aloud daily. Memorize verse 2. Give thanks before each meal. Breathe deeply. Realize, receive, and respond to the help that God gives you for all things.

Column one is our topic, and today's topic is the chemical phase of digestion—stomach acid. Please write this: "chemical phase—stomach acid."

Column two is our brain column. In column two, let's engage our brain by thinking about eating and the aftereffect of more stomach acid being produced. Envision chewing your food into small particles and then having your stomach acid digest it even further.

Column three is our body column. Let's engage our body to action by adding apple cider vinegar (one tablespoon) to a glass of water and drinking it before each meal. This will get your water intake up as well. Both will help to increase stomach acid production.

Column four is your beliefs column. Let's write what is true according to our beliefs as we know in the law of the Lord and in the law of health. "Just as my help comes from the Lord, the Maker of heaven and earth, the One who keeps me from the harm of enemies, stomach acid is my help to keep me from the harm of pathogens." You could shorten this to say, "My help comes from the Lord *and* from stomach acid."

Column five is our action steps and scripture. Our scripture, of course, is Psalm 121. Here are the action steps I suggest:

1. Read Psalm 121 daily. Memorize verse 2: "My help comes from the Lord, the Maker of heaven and earth."
2. Before each meal, pause to give thanks. Breathe deeply and engage the cephalic phase of digestion so that stomach acid production will be enhanced.
3. Mix one tablespoon of apple cider vinegar in a glass of water; drink before each meal.
4. Breathe deeply to reduce stress before eating. Remember, stress decreases stomach acid.
5. Realize, receive, and respond to the help that God gives you to keep you from the harm of your enemies and from the harm of pathogens.
6. Pray.

Here is a sample prayer:

Lord, we will sing praise to You. We will be careful to live blameless lives. We lift our souls unto You, Lord, and we will not be ashamed. We praise Your name with all the hosts of heaven who do Your will. Lord, thank You for satisfying the desires of every living creature and for giving us the food we need. Lord, You are our help. We look to You. We lay our requests before You, and we wait in expectation. Lord, we know You do not sleep and that You watch over both our coming and going. Lord, thank You that we can hope in You and that we will not be disappointed. Lord, we will continue to gain a heart of wisdom and digest the truth You have for us. Thank You for teaching us and for helping us to have a better brain and body. We realize You are our help. We receive Your help, and we respond to Your help by putting action to our faith. Amen.

Keep at this, everyone. Every small step, every action, and every day matter. We will never be done. This is a lifestyle; it is not a project to check off your list. Everything we are talking about will help anyone.

Next week, we will discuss the microbial phase of digestion while we hang out in the small intestine.

WEEK 8

MICROBIAL DIGESTION

THE SECRET PARTS, FEARFULLY AND WONDERFULLY MADE

Welcome to week eight, everyone. Congratulations! You have done so much to get to this point. Keep at it.

This week, we will use Psalm 139 as our scripture foundation while we discuss the microbial phase of digestion in the small intestine, which contains many things we can't readily see. Psalm 139 clearly indicates that we are fearfully and wonderfully made, and this includes all systems of our bodies and how they are connected to and work with one another. However, what we think and understand about our bodies is usually related to the big things we see, such as our arms, legs, eyes, feet, and hands, as well as the big parts of our internal systems that we speak often about, such as our brains, our lungs, our hearts, and our bones. However, we do not often speak about one aspect of our fearfully and wonderfully made creation called the microbiome. This is definitely one of the hidden or secret parts that God has in His full view, even though we do not. The importance of it cannot be diminished. It has as much of an impact on our health as the aspects we readily see and know are working each second, and actually, the microbiome has an even larger impact on our health because it affects our immune system, our mental health, and our overall digestive health, which affects us on a daily basis.

Just a couple of facts about the importance of the microbiome: it contains well over forty trillion bacteria, which is about as many cells as the human body; it is larger than the liver in both its size and function, and the liver is quite necessary for health and life; finally, it is composed of five to ten million genes; this is more than our entire genetic makeup as we have only about 22,000 genes in our human genome. Think about this. You knew you were fearfully and wonderfully made without even considering your microbiome; now you know that you are even more fearfully and wonderfully made due to this aspect of your innermost being, a hidden part.

Let's read Psalm 139 together, but as we read it, I would like you to notice a couple of things:

- God has already searched this person.
- God knows his thoughts from afar and even knows his words before they are on his tongue.
- The psalmist cannot escape God's view or His presence.
- The psalmist is completely known by God, even to the innermost being.
- God Himself fearfully and wonderfully created the psalmist.
- The psalmist prays that God would search his heart.
- He makes the request to test his anxious thoughts, to see if there is any offensive way in him.
- Nothing is hidden from God's view.

Psalm 139

1 You have searched me, Lord, and you know me.

2 You know when I sit and when I rise; you perceive my thoughts from afar.

3 You discern my going out and my lying down; you are familiar with all my ways.

4 Before a word is on my tongue you, Lord, you know it completely.

5 You hem me in behind and before, and you lay your hand upon me.

6 Such knowledge is too wonderful for me, too lofty for me to attain.

7 Where can I go from your Spirit? Where can I flee from your presence?

8   If I go up to the heaven, you are there; if I make my bed in the depths, you are there.

9   If I rise on the wings of the dawn, if I settle on the far side of the sea

10   Even there your hand will guide me, your right hand will hold me fast.

11   If I say, "Surely the darkness will hide me and the light become night around me."

12   Even the darkness will not be dark to you the night will shine like the day, for darkness is as light to you.

13   For you created my inmost being; you knit together in my mothers' womb.

14   I praise you because I am fearfully and wonderfully made; your works are wonderful; I know that full well.

15   My frame was not hidden from you when I was made in the secret place, when I was woven together in the depths of the earth.

16   Your eyes saw my unformed body; all the days ordained for me were written in your book before one of them came to be.

17   How precious to me are your thoughts, O God! How vast is the sum of them!

18   Were I to count them, they would outnumber the grains of sand—when I awake, I am still with you.

19   If only you, God, would slay the wicked! Away from me, you who are bloodthirsty!

20   They speak of you with evil intent; your adversaries misuse your name.

21   Do I not hate those who hate you, Lord, and abhor those who are in rebellion against you?

22   I have nothing but hatred for them; I count them my enemies.

23   Search me, O God, and know my heart; test me and know my anxious thoughts.

24   See if there is any offensive way in me and lead me in the way everlasting.

Our pivot verses today will be the final two verses as well as verse 13. I want you to focus on these for two reasons:

1. God created our inmost being and knows it thoroughly, even though it is hidden from us.
2. He knows any offensive way in our innermost being, both physically and spiritually.

I want us to consider our innermost being as a part of the body we do not discuss too often—the small intestine. Along with this, we are going to consider the state of our hearts.

First, let's talk about the small intestine and why we need to bring this into the realm of our health discussion. The small intestine is the part of the body where food goes immediately after it leaves the stomach, and this is where most of our nutrient absorption occurs. If you put your hand right below your belly button, you will be right on top of your small intestine. You might notice this area becoming larger after you eat due to the digestion that has occurred; the digested food and liquid travel through the small intestine from the stomach. Food usually stays in the stomach for two to four hours but takes about six to eight hours to travel through the small intestine before getting to the large intestine.

Digested food is absorbed into the bloodstream by crossing the wall of the small intestine. This wall is only one cell thick. This is why we want to make sure that food is broken down adequately before getting into the small intestine. If the one-celled wall of the small intestine has any holes or weak areas, it might allow an undigested particle to pass through it. If a large molecule, such as a protein, is not broken down to its amino acids and crosses the wall of the small intestine into the bloodstream, an inflammatory response could occur. This is especially significant when we consider such food particles as gluten or a dairy protein called casein. In addition to this, the small intestine is filled with what we call the microbiota, which is the microbiome located in the small intestine; it is a normal and important part of our small intestine.

So what actually is the microbiome? The microbiome is the set of microorganisms that live in and on our body, in our tissues and on our skin, in our mouths and in our gut. This week, I want to emphasize the part of the microbiome that lives in our gut. I refer to this as the microbial aspect of digestion. If our microbiome is not healthy, we are not healthy. If our microbiome is not healthy, we may experience gas, bloating, constipation, diarrhea, inflammation, and poor nutrient uptake. If our microbiome is not healthy, our brain is not healthy. Yes, you heard me. If our microbiome is not healthy, our brain is not healthy.

The connection I want to emphasize here is the gut-brain connection. Many people experience gut issues, such as IBS, Crohn's, SIBO, gas, bloating, diarrhea, constipation, and even pain. Other people experience brain or mental impairment with such symptoms as anxiety, depression, fogginess, lethargy, ADHD, or even poor cognition or memory loss. The real truth is that these can be very much related, and most definitely, they are related. Many people who experience gut issues also experience mental health issues. This is due to the fact that the gut and brain communicate with each other. We call this bidirectional communication. We cannot dismiss this. It is a very relevant part of how we are made.

These two systems are connected by the vagus nerve, which we discussed in week five when we focused on the cephalic phase of digestion. Both the digestive system and the nervous system send and receive signals via the vagus nerve. This is how the digestive system, which is part of the enteric nervous system, communicates with the nervous system—via the vagus nerve. When a part of either of these systems is not functioning properly, the other system is impaired. This is why constipation can lead to anxiety. This is why anxiety can lead to diarrhea. This is why what we eat affects our mood or our neurotransmitter production and function. This bidirectional aspect of the gut and brain should not be ignored. If you have trouble with anxiety or depression, you must consider that your gut could be the culprit behind this. If you have trouble with your gut, such as constipation or bloating or irritable bowel syndrome, you must consider that the health of your gut is impaired and that possibly the brain has something to do with it as well.

Of course, we talked about food, and when we did, I asked you to focus on the four characteristics of food choices. These were quality, quantity, timing, and diversity. The reason for this was to encourage proper selection so that you would be ingesting the variety of nutrients that your body needs, such as protein, healthy fats, and adequate vitamins and minerals. We don't want too much or too little of anything, and this is why variety matters. We need variety in our diets to feed our microbiome. We nourish not only the parts of the body we see when we eat, but we also nourish the microorganisms we don't see that live inside of us, in the deepest parts of our bodies. This is why probiotics and prebiotics are important. The prebiotics feed the probiotics in our gut. The probiotics are the good bacteria in our gut, mainly in our small intestine. However, we must ingest these prebiotics and probiotics by eating a variety of foods; we call this eating the colors of the rainbow. When we eat berries, peppers, and green, leafy vegetables, we get many colors, and the more colorful our diet, the more variety of prebiotics and probiotics we are sure to ingest.

Remember, our microbiome is the set of microorganisms that live in and on our bodies. We call this our normal flora, and it is important for several reasons. It protects us from other pathogens that we do not want to reside in our bodies or that we must keep in check, in their proper place and in their proper amounts. It produces antibacterial agents. It helps produce vitamins such as biotin, folate, and vitamin K, which we need for proper blood clotting. It helps with digestive motility. It strengthens our immune system. It reduces chronic inflammation. It helps to heal leaky gut, a condition which can lead to other health issues as well as brain and mental challenges. By eating a diverse diet, we are strengthening these aspects of our digestion as well as our brain health.

Our small intestine has about one hundred thousand anaerobic organisms per milliliter. We need to support this microbiome on a daily basis. When we do not do this by eating a variety of foods and nutrients, such as what are present in the colors of the rainbow, the microbiome becomes impaired, and the bad bacteria can take residence in the small intestine, which will lead to intestinal and health issues. Every time we eat sugar, we are fighting the necessary bacteria because sugar feeds the bad bacteria. When we do not eat enough fiber and have poor bowel elimination, we end up with toxins and more bad bacteria in the large intestine, and this can move up into the small intestine and cause trouble, a condition called SIBO, small intestine bacterial overgrowth. When we don't support our stomach acid and possibly deal with rancid food in our small intestine, we again cause a situation where the bad bacteria can take residence and impair the function of the good bacteria, the normal flora. All of this can lead to mental health issues due to the fact that our gut is not healthy. Think about how awfully dirty our gut could become and how challenged our good bacteria could be by sugar invasion, low fiber intake, and poor bowel elimination. This is like the garbage never being taken out or like the garbage truck never picking garbage up ... rancid material that lingers and produces toxins. Think of this dirtiness in our gut, which then can affect the brain. One quick comment here: bacteria is not necessarily good or bad; if it is not in the proper location at the proper time, it is bad for us; if it is in the proper location at the proper time and in the proper amount, it is good for us; bacteria is part of our normal flora.

I want to give you a visual here. Remember, the intestinal wall is only one cell thick. Although we call this a barrier, you can easily envision that one cell thick does not seem like a strong barrier, and in fact, it does need help. This help comes in the form of the microbiome God has given us. Imagine that the cell wall is filled with guards on the wall making sure the right things cross over it, which in this case would be digested food particles, the nutrients we need to absorb. Well, these tiny guards are the microbiota that we want to consistently nourish and support so that they consistently nourish and support us in the hidden parts.

Now back to the gut-brain connection. How in the world can our brain health be related to our digestive system? Remember, the vagus nerve is the communication highway between the nervous system and the digestive system. The vagus nerve is referred to as the wandering nerve because it innervates so many different aspects of our bodies; it decreases heart rate, relaxes smooth muscle, helps with digestion, decreases stress, constricts bronchioles, and many other actions. It is a main player in our gut and mental health. Consider that over one hundred million neurons exist in our gut. Neurons are brain cells. These communicate signals to our brain, which then sends signals to other parts of our bodies. These include signals for hormone production and secretion, chemical and enzyme secretion and production, and neurotransmitter secretion and production. This is definitely a fearfully and wonderfully made type of situation.

This is not supposed to be an anatomy and physiology discussion; it is simply material given to point you to the fact that all things matter and are connected. We cannot separate our food choices, our environment, our mindset, our digestion, and how our body responds to all of these influences from the health of our brain and our overall health. All of these aspects affect our digestion, and our digestion affects our brain and body health, and these affect the health of our belief system … which pursues the goal of doing God's will. We must not forget this.

But let's just take one aspect of our person that we are usually aware of. This is the mood we may experience on a daily basis, or should I say, the low mood or the depressed mood or the anxious mood we experience all too often, even though we might be chewing on God's Word and even though we have good, encouraging connections with other people. Our mood is affected by our serotonin production; serotonin is a type of feel-good neurotransmitter. It is increased when we are happy about someone else's good news. It is increased by feelings of goodness rather than selfish ambition to feel good about ourselves or by addictive tendencies. Please notice the difference between serotonin and other neurotransmitters like dopamine, which is a reward neurotransmitter, a driving force to achieving goals as well as to addiction. Let's stay on track with serotonin here, however. Please take this fact seriously: 95 percent of serotonin production is activated in the gut. Yes, 95 percent of it. However, the brain is what needs the serotonin. Do you see the connection? If your gut is not healthy, you will not have healthy serotonin production, which can lead to mood issues, as previously mentioned. Your gut is not healthy if your microbiome is not healthy. Your microbiome is not healthy if you are not eating a diet full of color and diversity with adequate protein and healthy fats, along with good chewing and adequate stomach acid availability.

Serotonin is just one example of how the gut and brain share this bidirectional communication and how what we put into our mouths can affect the health of our brain via the gut. We cannot ignore the facts, and we cannot ignore the truth of God's Word that whatever a man sows is what he will he reap. We cannot ignore that what we sow in our bodies by the food we ingest and how we ingest it will provide consequences or benefits that we will reap. If you want another example of why the gut is important concerning your mental health or your brain health, look up information on GABA. This will show you another important connection between your gut and brain. Just a quick comment here. GABA has a calming effect on us. It helps us deal with feelings of stress as well as anxiety and fear. We need GABA, but again, these details are beyond the scope of explanation in this program. Books are written on GABA. Just realize that God has created us, and He knows all. We don't have to worry. He made our bodies able to do what they need to do. We just need to do our part, little by little, day by day.

One final important note on the microbiome and our digestive health. If we are not eliminating on a daily basis due to constipation or poor bowel habits, we are putting our bodies under stress. Bowel elimination is a major detoxifier for our bodies. When we do not rid our bodies of the fecal matter from our large intestine, we are keeping the toxic material inside, and this is not healthy for us. By improving the health of our microbiome, we are also improving our chances for healthy bowel elimination, which improves our toxin elimination, which further encourages a healthy brain and body. It all matters.

Spiritual Connection

Now let's make a spiritual connection about the innermost part of our small intestine to the innermost part of our heart. Just like we have many different bacteria that we want to reside in our small intestine, we have many emotions that we want to reside in our hearts and in our brains. The opposite is also true, however. Some emotions, at times, are toxic to us. There is a time and place for everything. Just like the wall of the small intestine is only one cell thick and could allow toxic material in, our hearts and minds could possibly have a weak barrier and let such things as thoughts or emotions in. These might be beneficial in the right time and place but could be harmful as well. Let's take one emotion such as anger. There is a time and place for anger. Jesus was angry when he addressed the money changers in the temple, turning over the tables and vehemently confronting these people because they did not consider God as holy. This was a righteous anger. We can have a righteous anger that is not at all toxic but rather very necessary. We should be angry at injustice, stealing, lying, or the weak being taken advantage of.

However, anger that is not in its proper place, just like certain proteins that are not broken down, is not good. Anger that is the result of selfishness or impatience or judgment and pride is toxic. Yes, anger is an emotion and has its proper place. If we do not get angry about injustice, we are not having the compassion we should for the victim; however, when we get angry over the little things that inconvenience us, we are feeding the bad bacteria, the bad thoughts and emotions, of our hearts and minds. Think about the toxicity of unforgiveness, of hatred, of slackness, of jealousy or unwarranted anger.

It is also important to note that even though I have called bacteria both good and bad, in reality, they are neither. Bacteria exist, and they need to be in the right place so that we do not get sick. Yes, we should wash our hands and fight germs by washing food and other items, but in our bodies, the same bacteria could do something good for us as well as something bad for us, depending on where it is. Just like the emotion of anger, which can be both righteous and sinful, bacteria can do good or cause harm. One example of this is E. coli, which I am sure you have heard of many times. E. coli naturally resides in our large intestine, and we want it there. It helps us with our vitamin K and vitamin B_{12} production. Their functions are essential for blood clotting, energy, DNA synthesis, and red blood cell formation, among another things. However, if E. coli travels back up into the small intestine from the large intestine, we could get sick and have digestive issues. It all depends on where it is and what is going on in our bodies. Again, this is why we do the basics, because we cannot manage the whole; we must break the whole down so that we can manage the parts by making daily choices that benefit our brains, bodies and beliefs.

God knows the innermost being of our small intestine and our hearts and minds. We indeed want Him to search us to see if there is any wicked way or offensive way in us. We want the wall of our small intestine to be strong so that only what is healthy for us will enter our bodies via this avenue, and we want the walls of our hearts and minds to be strong so that we are able to live lives worthy of Christ from hearts of love and purity. Nothing is hidden from God's view. He knows us; He knit us together in our mother's womb; we are fearfully and wonderfully made, but God has given us the responsibility to take care of ourselves. We also should search our hearts and our health to see if there is any offensive way in us, any weak barriers in us, any toxins that need to be removed so that we allow God to lead us in His way. He will show us what we need to know, but we do need to look to Him and be willing to realize, receive, and respond to what He wants us to chew on—and to chew on it well.

OK, team! It is time to pull out your five-column journal.

Topic	Brain	Body	Beliefs	Scripture and Action Steps
Microbial digestion— the secret parts, fearfully and wonderfully made. Small intestine: microbiome.	Think about the guards on the wall of the small intestine that need to be fed. Think about the thoughts of your mind that need to be fed.	Eat the colors of the rainbow. Quit sugar completely so I don't feed bad bacteria.	I must watch what feeds my mind and heart and body.	Read Psalm 139 daily. Memorize verses 23 and 24. Give thanks, take deep breaths, chew food thirty times, and use apple cider vinegar before each meal. Search my own heart. What bad signs of unforgiveness, anger, jealousy, or negativity are present? Do I have gas, bloating, or constipation? How is my mood doing?

Remember, column one is our topic. Please write "small intestine—microbiome" under column one.

Under column two, the brain column, please write the following: "Think about the guards on the wall of your small intestine and that they need to be fed by the healthy variety of food you eat. Think about the thoughts of your mind that need to be fed. Am I letting anything into my mind that is causing an unhealthy response, or am I feeding the bad bacteria of my mind? Am I feeding the bad thoughts of my mind?"

Under column three, the body column, please write, "I will eat the colors of the rainbow to feed my microbiota. I will quit eating sugar so that I do not feed the bad bacteria of my gut."

Under column four, the beliefs column, please write, "I must watch what I let enter my mind and heart and keep emotions in their proper place. God searches me and knows me."

These are just my suggestions. You can make your own suggestions particular to your situation, but remember, if your gut is not healthy, your brain will not be healthy, nor will your body be healthy. This means you are not going to be healthy in your decision-making, in your financial management, in your relationships, in your work performance, or in your efforts in learning. Every area of your life is affected by your gut, including how happy and content you feel.

Under column five, the action steps and scripture column, please write, "Psalm 139. Memorize verses 23 and 24."

Here are your action steps and scripture for this week:

1. Read Psalm 139 daily. Memorize verses 23 and 24.
2. Give thanks, breathe deeply, chew food thirty times, and use apple cider vinegar before each meal.
3. Increase your intake of the colors of the rainbow—green, blue, red, yellow, orange.
4. Search your own heart and the response of your small intestine. Do you see any bad signs like unforgiveness, anger, or jealousy—or gas, bloating, or constipation?

5. Assess your mood. Could this be improved? What might be causing negative moods in me even though I pray and am in God's Word, chewing thoroughly?
6. Pray!

Here is a sample prayer:

> O Lord, You have searched me, and You know me; You knit me together in my mother's womb. I am fearfully and wonderfully made, and I cannot hide from You, nor do I want to. You know all and understand every word before it is on my tongue. Lord, You know where my weak barriers are, and You are my help. You will not let me be put to shame. You establish justice for all who are oppressed, and Lord, this includes all of me, from my heart to my brain to my small intestine. Lord, please strengthen me; strengthen every part of me and use the food I eat to strengthen my inmost being, both in my gut and in my brain, so that I am nourished and healthy to do Your will with joy, with vigor, with emotions that honor You. Thank You, Lord. See if there is any offensive or weak way in me and lead me in Your way everlasting. Amen!

Just a note here. You could be doing all of the right things in your spiritual walk by reading your Bible, praying, and looking to the Lord. You could be humble, loving, forgiving and encouraging to others but still might have anxiety or stress due to gut issues. It's not your fault. You just might not have known it, so you could now be dealing with condemnation or regret. Hang in there. Do what you can from here on out. We move forward with new action.

God bless all of you. You must feel delighted that you are sticking with this and that this connection of the small intestine to our brain health is meaningful to you and that it will truly be an answer to some of the dilemmas you face, especially concerns you might have about your mood or about walking in the fruit of the Holy Spirit. The Lord is our help, and He searches us. He will teach us and guide us in His path of righteousness for His name's sake.

Next week, we will move on to our last four weeks of information and deal with the topic of inflammation. We are going to clear things up, calm things down, modulate to improvement, and enhance everything before we end our twelve weeks.

Thanks for joining me today. Bye-bye!

WEEK 9

CLEAR COMPLETELY

UNFAILING LOVE AND FULL REDEMPTION

Welcome to week nine, everyone. You are doing a great job sticking with this. Persevere.

I just have to pause and say something to you. I am most passionately diligent to get people excited about God's Word, to encourage people to chew on it, to be nourished by it, to relish it, and to allow it to transform their lives because loving God's Word means we are healthy. At least we are loving that, and this is healthy for us.

This week, we begin our four-week phase of dealing with inflammation. During the first four weeks of the twelve-week program, we discussed the aspects that affect our genes; these were the environment, mindset, movement, and food. The second four weeks, we discussed the aspects that affect our digestion; these were the cephalic phase, the mechanical phase, the chemical phase, and the microbial phase of digestion. Now we are going to discuss the third part of the program by spending time on combating inflammation. The next four weeks will be devoted to this by focusing on clearing, calming, modulating, and enhancing what we can to keep inflammation at bay. This is important because inflammation is behind illness and disease. If we back it up, we realize that keeping inflammation at bay will help to prevent disease. So how do we keep inflammation at bay? We do this by keeping our stress at bay. And how do we do this? We clear, we calm, we modulate, and we enhance what we do and what we allow to enter our bodies and minds, what we allow to influence our bodies and minds, what we allow to nourish our bodies and minds, and what we allow to benefit our bodies and minds. We clear, calm, modulate, and enhance.

An Unhappy Toddler—Clear the Clutter

We will use Psalm 130 for our scripture this week, but before we delve into this wonderful Word, I want to give you a visual. Envision a small child, possibly about age two, who is in a nursery, separated from his mother and yet attended to by others who are attempting to comfort and calm him. No matter what they do, the child will not calm down. He cries and screams and has no peace because he wants his mother. Those who are trying to help the child are actually clutter from the child's viewpoint. They represent danger, confusion, and stress. After some time, the mother finally arrives, and at once, the child appears to become less stressed and settles down but is still whimpering. After the other adults leave the presence of the child, the whimpering stops. All is almost well.

Now envision this same child in its wonderfully safe environment with his mother. He is calm, and there is no seeable clutter in his world. By clutter, I mean no other unknown individuals, no inputs that scare, no inputs that trigger stress or any feelings of distress. However, as the day progresses, the mother and father, though they care for the child greatly, indulge this child with what the child wants. This includes frequent treats and a doughnut with frosting right before bed, as well as no demand to get to bed and go to sleep. Thus, the child stays up too late and does not get adequate rest.

Let's look at what is happening to this child from the outside and from the inside. First of all, from the environmental perspective, the child is stressed and has no peace, and this does not diminish completely until the other adults leave the presence of the child. Even though the mother is present, the child continues to have fear and stress. Let's use this scenario to represent your environment. You might have many good inputs that are present in your life, but if you have the negative inputs, the stressful inputs, the toxic inputs, or what we call the inflammatory inputs, you will still have stress in your brain and body. You might not throw a tantrum or whimper like a toddler, but your body will be whimpering with silent inflammation, which leads to disease. We want to clear this clutter from our lives. This includes things that we need as well. We need certain nutrients, certain emotional supports, and certain habits like sleeping well, eating nutritiously, and exercising. If we lack these, we are actually having toxic exposure due to this omission, which causes stress, which causes inflammation, which leads to disease. Yes, even lack of sleep can lead to disease; to name a few of these, I mention increased risk of cancer and poor blood sugar regulation, which can lead to type 2 diabetes. It leads to weight gain because it hinders metabolism; it contributes to mental illness challenges, not to mention overall stress in general.

Psalm 130

1   Out of the depths I cry to you, Lord;
2   Lord, Hear my voice. Let your ears be attentive to my cry for mercy.
3   If you, Lord, kept a record of sins, Lord, who could stand?
4   But with you there is forgiveness, so that we can, with reverence serve you.
5   I wait for the Lord, my whole being waits, and in his word I put my hope.
6   I wait for the Lord more than watchmen wait for the morning, more than watchmen wait for the morning.
7   Israel, put your hope in the Lord, for with the Lord is unfailing love and with him is full redemption.
8   He himself will redeem Israel from all their sins.

Now that we have read this, I want you to think about very specific ideas that I glean from this psalm, ideas that relate to health, to your environment, to the whole world, to moving out of oppression, and to commanding others with your mouth as you take action with your faith and with your complete being, with your brain, body, and beliefs. These specific ideas are the following:

- We can cry out to God, mindset on Him, and engage the cephalic phase.
- We really can't stand before Him. We are dirty, sick, and unable, but He allows it.
- He forgives and fully redeems, and in fact, following this, we are to serve Him with reverence.
- We are to wait like watchmen.
- This is not just for you or me; it is for all of Israel, for the entire church, truly for the world.
- God has unfailing love and redeems us completely.

Clear the Clutter

Admission is a wonderful action; it sets us free immediately. So often, our problem is not the actual problem that we seemingly have, but it is the failure to admit that we have the problem. We won't speak the truth in our own hearts. We might ignore it, refuse to believe it, or, in fact, deny it completely to ourselves and to others, and even worse, to God. However, He knows all; He understands our thoughts from afar; He created our inmost being. He already knows our needs before we go to Him. Before a word is on our tongue, He knows it. He knows our struggles. He knows our history and where we have traveled and how we got to the place where we are, the successes and the failures, the joys and the sorrows, the pride and the humility. He knows it.

The psalmist opens up from a very low point; out of the depths, he cries. He is pouring out his lament like Psalm 5 tells us to do: "In the morning Lord, I pour out my lament and wait in expectation." This psalmist actually tells God to be attentive to his cry for mercy. He acknowledges that no one could stand before the Lord if the Lord kept a record of sins but that there is forgiveness. Oh what good news that is. There is forgiveness; there is a chance for healing; there is an escape, a way out. God always provides a door for us, a path of righteousness. This might be a narrow escape and a narrow road to travel, but nonetheless, it is for us, to lead us to life, to Him, to do His will.

This is not just a quick fix or a temporary phase or a partial relief. With God is full redemption, full forgiveness; in fact, I would just call it fullness or "wholeness," but it is not for our pleasure. The purpose is so that we serve Him with reverence. Remember this: you might want improvement in your life, such as getting better relationships, more financial ease, restoration of peace and mental health, more energy in your body, or relief from sickness, but the ultimate goal is to be healthy so that we can do God's will, so that we are more like Him, so that we serve not ourselves but Him with reverence.

The psalmist fully admits that he is sinful and that no one could stand before God if He kept a record of ours sins. I would like you to consider that our sinful ways mean spiritual death for us, and this should be our main concern; however, we have sinful ways that affect our brains and bodies too. I will refer to these as our habits or lifestyle choices and the toxins that affect us. Think about your overall health and the different habits that have caused you to be where you are now, those that have benefited you as well as what has harmed you. Be honest with yourself. No one else can determine this. You must do it. The psalmist does this about his sin as he cries out to God. He calls it like it is. "If you kept a record of sins, Lord, who could stand?" None of us could stand, and we know it!

We must do the same with our health goals. We must ask ourselves the same question. If our body kept a record of sins or unhealthy habits or toxins, who could stand in full health, in full strength, in full life? Who could stand before God or a doctor unashamed? Thankfully, just like God has provided a way for forgiveness and full redemption, our bodies and brains do have built-in ways to clear clutter without our conscious effort. Our liver, our kidneys, our skin, our digestive system, and our lymphatic and immune systems are actively working on our behalf to fight and clear toxins from our bodies without any command from us. We don't have to ask them to do this or tell them to do this. Even our brain clears the clutter from within itself while we sleep. It sifts through data and gets rid of a huge amount of unnecessary data accumulated during each day. Yes, the brain does this while we sleep, which is another reason why we need adequate sleep. It also sorts the information out while we sleep; this is why "sleeping on it" actually works. The brain solves problems while we sleep. Our liver also works at detoxifying our bodies at night. It is indicated that this is between 11:00 p.m. and 3:00 a.m. at night. This is another reason to refrain from eating three hours before bed; it allows the liver to work on detoxification rather than on helping the digestive system digest food. It also contributes to better sleep so that the brain is able to detoxify while we sleep.

Let's just admit that while we have sinned against God, and He has provided a way for us to have spiritual life, we have also sinned against our bodies in the health sense, and our bodies and brains are doing what they can to keep us alive. However, this does not mean we should not take seriously our responsibility and opportunity to do what we can to limit the toxins, the clutter, and the bad habits from our lives. If we are going to cry out to God for full forgiveness and admit that we have sinned and that we are willing to turn from this to serve Him with reverence, shall we not also turn to Him and to our bodies and admit that we have harmed them by the clutter we have allowed into them with our food choices, our lifestyle habits, and other toxins? Then shall we not proceed to serve our bodies, the temple of the Holy Spirit, with reverence and with what is good for it? Not just our bodies but our brains, our relationships, our attitudes, and our beliefs. It all matters.

If we go to God for forgiveness, we admit that we have sinned and need Him. So it is with everything else. If we go to Him for healing in our bodies, in our relationships, in our home life, or with whatever problem or struggle we face, we must also be willing to repent or turn from the sinful or harmful habits or inputs we have allowed that caused us to be in the condition or situations we experience. If we want full redemption, full forgiveness, full healing, and full strength, we must cry out to God with a spirit of reverence and be willing to say, "If you kept a record of everything I have done to my body, there is no way I could be healthy, but with You is full forgiveness, full redemption. Lord, You can restore my whole being." I am not promising that you are going to have the health or "feeling" of your youth or the health or "condition" of any other previous time in your life or of any other individual. I am only pointing out that God is able to make you *whole*. He knows what *your* wholeness is.

Where Are You? Be Completely Honest!

Do you really believe this? Do you really believe God can do this? Do you really believe that you are responsible and can move forward with choices that will reflect a mindset engaged in the wisdom that God has to intervene on your behalf, fully and completely, to clear your whole being of the clutter that is standing in the way of life, standing in the way of doing His will, standing in the way of your health, energy, and vigor, of your peace of mind and clarity, of your movement out of any type of oppression? Remember, as a man thinks in his heart, so is he. I want clutter gone from my life; how about you? I know I need God's help; how about you? I know I have to make some choices to put action to my faith. How about you?

I would like us to notice Psalm 130 and the situation of the complete depths of despair that the psalmist is in. We don't know exactly what is going on in his life. We do not know the depths of turmoil that anyone might be experiencing, especially if they hide it from us. These depths could include anxiety, insomnia, loneliness, addiction, anger, depression, fatigue, nausea, weight gain, poor immune health, declining health in general, financial troubles, family conflict, church upheaval, deception. We have no idea what other people are experiencing or why. We might think we know, but we really do not. Sometimes, we do not even admit it too ourselves, but remember, admission is powerful. Once we admit to God that we are in the depths of despair, and we cry out to him to pay attention and incline His ear to hear us, we have taken the first step.

So, as I said, let's use Psalm 130 as our basis for crying out. However, I don't want to focus on the concept of sin because I think we all have admitted to God that we have sinned against Him and that we have received His gift of salvation. Instead, I want to replace the concept of sin with the concept of poor habits, unhealthy choices, undisciplined lifestyle, imbalanced living, arrogant attitude, or disobedient mindset. I could go on and on. You might think that your stress or lack of energy is due to your hurried life, when in reality it is rooted in unforgiveness. You might think your trouble sleeping is due to stress, when in reality it is rooted in too much sugar, eating at the wrong times, or not having good relationships. You might think that your financial troubles are due to spending too much money, when in reality it is rooted in lack of organization or lack of satisfaction due to the fact that you are using shopping as a means to feel fulfilled.

Remember, there is no judgment here. This is between you and God as well as between you and the people you have asked to support you. Doing this without support is unwise. He who walks with the wise grows wise. We are sharpened by others who care for us, who nurture us, and who understand us. Don't build a wall that leads to destruction; allow others in to embrace you with empathy. This is powerful because it helps you to feel valued, and this is a true statement: you have value; you matter to God; others love you and want to see you healthy. No one wants to see you stuck and struggling.

So let's just call the sinful ways as noted in Psalm 130 a different word. I am going to suggest "poor habits" because this seems more inviting than *unhealthy choices* or *disobedient mindset.* It also reminds us that messing up from time to time is not the same as a daily choice to do something that is not healthy. Let's just try our best, but here is the challenge. If you go to God for complete forgiveness and redemption, you have fully admitted your need for His intervention as well as for your need to change. You have a mindset that is focused on Him and that is admitting that you did not do what you should have done. All of us understand this, and we are here daily in this position; this is why we search our own hearts and minds while we are on our bed at night. We go to God with everything and realize, receive, and respond to what He wants to show us through our obedience and disobedience, as well as through our folly and our moments of wise living.

If we go to God about the sins of the heart, let's also go to

Him about the sins of poor habits and just call it what it is. "Lord, please forgive me for these poor habits that have caused [fill in the blank]. Lord, these poor habits that have caused weight gain; these poor habits that have caused unforgiveness to run rampant in my heart; these poor habits that have caused an unruly house or toxic relationships or bad relationships at church; these poor habits that have caused me to avoid being involved with other people; these poor habits that have caused me to have a diminished desire for your Word. Lord, I want to serve You with reverence with my whole being. I know changes need to be made and that I cannot stand before a doctor, a pastor, a counselor, or any family member without their seeing my poor habits and what they have done to me and those around me. Please forgive me, Lord."

I think enough has been said here. So if you are willing to call out your poor habits just like you would call out unforgiveness, lying, stealing, profanity, malice, evil speaking, complaining, or any other sin the apostle Paul readily convinces us to throw off, then you are ready to call all of it out. I am going to give a list. Just remember you are looking at yourself, not others. You might be the picture of physical health, but your financial health is awful. You might be the picture of spiritual health, but your physical health is slowly killing you so that you won't experience a long life. You might be the picture of the perfect pastor and teacher, but you are not sleeping at all and are overeating at night due to this as you persevere to get more biblical knowledge. Possibly, this is moving you toward an addiction to fulfilling your needs and desires with what is death to you, all because you really have selfish ambition and arrogance due to your acquired knowledge, and yet you are after more.

Please understand I can relate to all of these situations, except I am not a pastor, but I seek after knowledge, and I respect those who have it, and therefore, I want the respect of others due to my regard for knowledge. Just a sidenote here. God has given me a little princess who keeps this in check. Yes, for those of you who know me, my little Mollie is the epitome of knowledge, of wisdom, of love, of all that is good, and she doesn't say a word. My little Mollie is my accountability tool because no matter what I accomplish in a day, whether it is more knowledge, an act that gets praise from men, or an accomplishment that feeds my pride, I have full admission at the end of the day and renewed realization that my greatest achievement is being Mollie's mother. This took no college education, no divinity degree, no health expertise. This is a gift from God. Remember, we are in this together. We comfort each other and encourage each other with what we have experienced. (For those who do not know me, Mollie is my daughter who is nonverbal and weighed less than two pounds at birth. She also has Down syndrome and sparks sweetness from most people when they meet her.)

So back to your full admission of the poor habits you need to lay before God and at the same time ask for His full redemption from them. You call them out! The goal is to clear the clutter.

- Name them.
- Name the consequences of them.
- Name the improvement you would have in your life if you stopped them.
- Name how this would benefit those around you—close circles and the complete world.
- Name them!

Do not be ashamed. Admit them at least to yourself and to God. Be honest about the consequences of these poor habits. Imagine the improvement in several areas of your life if you stopped these habits. Feel the joy of how this would benefit you and others.

Do not minimize how wonderful and effective just making one change could be. Remember, do not despise the small things, the part of the foundation that is never seen or heard, the unnoticed heroes, which in this case could be the smallest step forward. Remember, no one looks at the hinges of the doors and shouts ohs and ahs, but those unassuming hinges serve a great purpose and make the door functional. Without the hinges, the door falls down.

Let's just take one habit that is common to many Americans today—buying daily coffee. Remember, no judgment here. I like coffee;

my daughters like coffee; my pastors like coffee; my mother likes coffee. But just for our purposes, let's admit that this is a poor habit for many people, because it is a habit that has become a master rather than a permissible enjoyment. It masters them in the sense of spending money that would be better used elsewhere; it masters them in the sense of the time it takes to obtain the coffee; it masters them in the sense that they are seeking the caffeine not for enjoyment but for need.

Here is the admission:	I buy coffee daily.
Here are the consequences:	I am addicted to this.
	It costs too much money.
	It takes up too much time and makes me late and hurried.
Here are the possible improvements:	I would have more money to pay down debt.
	I would be able to overcome this addiction or the mastery it has over me.
	I would have more time to get to work or to do other things.
I would put fewer miles on my car because I'd stop this travel.	
	I would reduce stress due to increased time and finances.
Here are some benefits for others:	I could give more money to those in need.
	I could give back to God what He requires and requests of us.

Do you see how one small change affects several areas of your life? This choice to quit the daily coffee could lead to debt reduction, more time, and the ability to help others who are in need. It could free up money for you to join a gym and have more social connections along with a quality exercise plan, or it could free up time to spend in God's

Word or join a Bible study. One never knows what opportunities or improvements could be possible unless the action is taken to move out of the state of oppression, stress, or limitation.

Do Not Despise the Small Things

You might say to yourself that this won't work, that taking one small step to clear the clutter or to clean up your environment will be futile. Remember, don't despise the small things, the small beginnings. Think of an acorn that becomes a giant oak; think of the fertilized cell that becomes a baby; think of the twenty-six letters of the alphabet that come together to bring a visual of the spoken word.

We all have heard magnificent life-changing stories about alcoholics or drug addicts whose lives were transformed tremendously, having families restored with a new path for a hopeful future. We have heard stories of people's compete health reversals when the families and the doctors had given up. We have heard of children's overseas adoption that gave one individual at a time the blessing of having a home and a family and, therefore, a completely different life, due to one change, a change in their environment. We all know the story of Naaman, who was told to wash himself in the Jordan River seven times to be healed of his leprosy. He scorned this idea, was angry in fact, but God brought about the healing after Naaman took the action to do what God instructed. Follow his example. Take action; just take the first step. Let God show you what this is and follow His lead. No matter how small you think the step is, do not scorn the action. Realize! Receive! Respond!

I took a step this week. There is a habit that I needed to break in my life—nothing immoral, but it was not serving me well. My daughter laughed at me when I told her that I needed to quit this habit. It was not a big deal to her, but to me it was, and I can see long-term negative consequences because of this habit. I took the first step by admitting it; then I spoke my intention "to stop" to my daughter. I am currently on month seven of eliminating this poor habit from my life. Again, not a big deal to you probably, but to me, it was. I had to take action. I have to admit now that by taking this action, I have more time, and I am less stressed. It has omitted a couple of cluttery kinds of situations in my life, so the benefits have been good, especially the time factor. You can do the same. Go to God to realize, receive, and respond to what He shows and has for you. It could open up doors you didn't even know existed.

The Toddler Revisited

Let's get back to the toddler who cries for his mom when in an environment that does not feel safe to him. Although he calms down a bit when his mother returns, he might not be able to completely calm down until the other adults leave the room—in other words, until the toxins leave. Please make this connection to your body. Although you might bring in good things for your body and brain, like fish oil, vitamins, veggies, water, or sleep, you can never get your body calm until you remove toxins. In other words, you must clear the clutter. Only you know what the clutter is for you and your particular situation. Again, let God show you and do something, even the smallest step forward. Remove the financial clutter by getting rid of a couple of credit cards or opening up your mail immediately. Dealing with the bills and paying them right away could clear a lot of clutter, and you won't be moving it around the counter for a week or two. This will improve the organization of your home and give you more time. The visual improvement of a cleared counter will be a natural stress reliever.

Now think about the toddler who is with his mom and who is free from the unknown people who were causing him stress. He still has that doughnut in his system, and this doughnut triggered a blood glucose jump and put stress on his body. The toddler does not know why his body is feeling stressed. He and his mom don't know that the doughnut spiked his blood sugar very quickly, and now his blood sugar is taking a dive because insulin was secreted to manage it. This in itself is stressful, but when it gets too low, the toddler will again be stressed. However, no one sees the culprit, nor do they make the connection. Understand that the culprit or the toxins can come from the external environment, but they can also enter your emotions, your brain, or your body and become an internal toxin. Sometimes this might take a while to actually show up. We must pause and analyze; engaging the cephalic phase of this table of concern is definitely necessary. If we want God to pay attention to our cries for help, we must pay attention to what He instructs that will help us.

Now consider that after the day is done and the toddler needs to go to bed, his mother and father do not enforce this. The toddler stays up too late, getting off schedule and becoming exhausted and insecure due to the lack of sleep, which is another stressor, another toxin. Again, we can't see it, and we can't blame the environment or the grocery store. The blame is on the habit or the lack of enforcement of what is needed. You can't lie to the body. It needs safety; it needs blood sugar regulation; it needs sleep. It all matters. Failure to get what we need is a stressor; it is a toxin.

So it is with you. You need to have clutter cleared so that the calm will come. The focus of today has been to clear the clutter. Next week, we are going to discuss getting calm after the clutter has been cleared. The toddler did become calm when the toxins were removed and when the blood sugar was managed; in other words, when the clutter was cleared. However, the lack of sleep in a sense was another toxin that prevented complete calmness. Keep this in mind as you assess your own situation. What is affecting you from the outside? What is affecting you from the inside? What are the internal and external stressors? What do you need that you are not getting? Consider all of these things, go to this table and engage the cephalic phase, call upon your Lord, and wait in expectation for Him to show you your next step and to calm you.

Well, team, it is time to take out your five-column journal. You can download this from my website, www.dynamotruth.com, or make your own.

Sample Chart for Clearing Clutter Completely: Unfailing Love and Full Redemption

Topic	Brain	Body	Beliefs	Scripture and Action Steps
Clear completely. Unfailing love and full redemption.	Remove negative thoughts, lies, lustful pursuits, improper focus of goals, PPIs.	Remove sugar. Remove bags and boxes of food. Remove inflammatory items, such as gluten and dairy. Remove obstacles that impair sleep. Remove things from schedule.	Remove sins of my heart by confessing them. How are these toxins affecting me? Do I really believe that what I think in my heart affects my health? What about what I eat or do? Am I calling to God for help? Am I really living a blameless life in my own house? Am I really praying about the matters that concern me?	Read Psalm 130 aloud daily. Memorize the whole psalm. Clear the clutter from everything you can think of. Chew, drink water, exercise, and continue on with other action steps. Don't eat anything from a bag or box. Thank God for His unfailing love and His full redemption.

Remember, column one is our topic; column two is *Brain*; column three is *Body*; column four is *Beliefs*, and column five is *Scripture and Action Steps*.

Under column one, please write our topic of clear the clutter.

Under column two, the brain column, please write the clutter that needs to be cleared from your mind. These are my suggestions:

- negative thoughts
- lies
- lustful pursuits, selfish ambitions, or goals that you focus on too much or that have become imbalanced
- PPIs—preplanned inconsistencies—like leaving early to get your daily coffee that costs you, or even thinking about the PPIs or thinking about making the wrong or inconsistent choices (think about the right choices to make)

Under column three, the body column, please write these suggestions:

- Remove and limit sugar intake.
- Remove food that is in a bag or box.
- Remove inflammatory foods, such as gluten and dairy.
- Remove food from bags and boxes.
- Remove obstacles to getting good sleep—screen time and food before bed.
- Remove things from your schedule like activities, people, or imbalanced work.

Under column four, the beliefs column, please write the following:

- Remove the sins of my heart, like unforgiveness, malice, bitterness, gossip, lack of love, jealousy—oh there are so many toxins that could come into our brains and beliefs and affect our bodies, our peace, and our joy.
- What do I believe is a toxin in my life?
  o Do you really believe unforgiveness is a toxin?

- o Do you really believe sugar is a toxin?
- o Do you really believe lack of sleep is a toxin?
- o Do you really believe seed oil is a toxin?
- What do I read, see, hear, touch that interferes with blameless living? (I love Psalm 101 and the concept of blameless living.)
- Am I chewing on God's Word as one who believes His Word is what makes me strong?
  - o Think about it. This is the strength the Lord gives to us. Are you spending time on it? Remember the rule of thirty? Thirty minutes a day, thirty verses; tell the Lord thirty times a day how thankful you are for something or for thirty different things.
- Am I calling out to my helper, the Lord, the maker of heaven and earth?
  - o Are you actually calling out to Him or do you say that you do? A lot of times, we are concerned about something, and we are talking about it, but we don't actually go to God about it. Recently, I was very specific about a certain issue that was troubling me, so I prayed, "Lord, I need You; I need You to be the Lord of this situation." And today, the situation I had to encounter was so much better. Truly, I thanked the Lord, and I am going to pray about it again tomorrow because I have to enter the same situation again, but I know God is able. If He can part the Red Sea, if He can calm the waters, then He can handle any situation. I also prayed about another matter that was far beyond my control. I had no idea what to pray, so I just prayed, "God, this is too big for me. I am completely powerless to do anything about this. Lord, please handle it. It belongs to You." Never did I expect that a complete turnaround of a situation would occur. I hoped that God would make it a little better, but His intervention completely turned a situation that was going south into a situation headed to improvement. I could not have imagined such a turnaround. Nothing is too hard for the Lord.

Under column five, let's write our scripture and action steps. Our scripture is Psalm 130. Here are your action steps:

1. Read Psalm 130 daily, aloud, several times.
2. Clear the clutter: pick one thing that you think is harmful to you and clear it out. This could include activities, bad food, bad habits, messes, junk, daily expenditures, temptations, gossip, complaining, or habits that prevent sleep or healthy choices. Pick something!
3. Chew, drink water, exercise … do anything/all from our other action steps.
4. Don't eat anything from a bag or box. This will remove a lot of clutter and help your body, and it will help your recycling efforts, another chance for more time to yourself and to do God's will.
5. Thank God for His unfailing love and full redemption. Embrace this for blameless living.
6. Pray. As usual, here is a sample prayer:

Lord, out of the depths I cry to You. Please pay attention to my cry for help. Lord, my sinful ways, my unhealthy habits, are beyond the help of human hands; they are beyond the grace of people or time; yet, Lord, there is full forgiveness with You. Lord, no one can stand before You; no one can heal themselves; no one can change their habits, but with You, Lord, is full forgiveness, with You is full redemption, and with You is fullness of hope. You are able to do above and beyond what we could ask or think. You are my helper; if You are able to redeem Israel from all their troubles, You are certainly able to grant Your unfailing love and full redemption to me. Lord, this is what I ask of You, full redemption from the unhealthy consequences of my choices. I lay this request before You, Lord, and I wait in expectation more than a watchman waits for the morning. Lord, I will wait. I will not scorn the little actions I can take to walk according to the wisdom You give me. I will realize, receive, and respond to Your teaching as I wait for You and serve You with reverence. Thank You, Lord.

One final word here. Psalm 130 speaks of serving the Lord with reverence and waiting like a watchman for the morning. First of all, let me challenge you: are you living a blameless life and serving the Lord with reverence? Only you can answer that. Second of all, are you waiting like a watchman waits for the morning? Have you ever been awake in the middle of the night, unable to sleep? Do you know how brutal this is? The time goes so slowly. Consider this waiting, waiting all night like a watchman, just waiting. This is not easy. This takes a calm spirit, and this is what we are going to do next week as we talk about our next topic—*calm*. In dealing with inflammation, we first clear things up. Then we look to calm things down. Just like the toddler who needed to clear the toxins, the unfamiliar people, out of the room and who needed to get the blood sugar balanced from the doughnut, we need to clear the toxins first and then seek to calm things down. This will not happen overnight, but some immediate results are possible if you take the first step out of your oppression. Do not despise the smallest effort you decide to take. It all matters for a better brain and body. Just focus on getting rid of the toxins first. Remember, if we want God to pay attention to our cries for help, could we not just try to do one small thing, remove just one toxin or one bad habit? This is your goal this week: clear the clutter. Next week, we will work on the calm.

God bless all of you. I am so glad you have made it this far. See you next week with the calmest demeanor and with the strongest hope of sitting like a weaned child close to his mother.

WEEK 10

CALM LIKE A WEANED CHILD

COMMIT TO THE CALM

Welcome to week ten. This week, we will continue our discussion on inflammation. Last week, we began this with the goal of clearing the clutter, and now that we have done this or are trying and continuing to do this, we will move forward with the intention to calm. Our scripture foundation this week will be Psalm 131.

Psalm 131

1   My heart is not proud, Lord, my eyes are not haughty; I do not concern myself with great matters or things too wonderful for me.
2   But I have calmed and quieted myself. I am like a weaned child with its mother; like a weaned child I am content.
3   Israel, put your hope in the Lord both now and forevermore.

As we use this psalm to encourage our whole life, I want you to focus on three themes:

1. The importance of humility and acceptance
2. The concept of a weaned child as well as the concept of a maturely weaned adult
3. The commitment to now and the future—no turning back—for you and all of Israel

Humility and Acceptance

No secret exists about the importance of humility. Scripture makes it very clear that the wise are humble, but the fool is arrogant. Scripture makes it very clear that receiving instruction is the way of life, and one is not able to receive it without being humble. Scripture makes it very clear that God is close to the humble. We also know that God is far from the proud, that pride goes before the fall, and that God will bring down the proud but lift up the humble. I want you to embrace this. Embrace the ultimate importance of humility. First, we need it to receive instruction. Secondly, God is close to us when we are humble. Furthermore, God is far from us when we are not humble, when we are arrogant, when we concern ourselves with matters too great for us. In essence, there is no success if we are not humble, if we are arrogant, if we are resistant to instruction. God opposes all of this arrogance.

There is no future hope for us if we are not humble. Take this seriously. If you want answers or ideas on what to do to improve any aspect of your health—relationships, physical, emotional, mental, financial, you name it; if you want a problem or struggle to go away, you must be ready to admit, accept, and act with a movement forward to do what God shows you. Be humble enough to realize, receive, and respond to what is true. It is OK if you say, "God, I don't know; please help me. I will listen. Teach me Your ways, Lord; You are my helper. I will wait in expectation." Be humble enough to hear Him and to heed Him.

A Weaned Child

Please picture this psalm in your mind. Picture a child who is weaned from his mother yet sits on her lap content, not grabbing or demanding anything. I see peace and calm. I see no stress, no struggle, no striving. Do you see this too? We are like this weaned child when we let God hold and care for us. This weaned child is more mature than a baby, yet he still needs his mother. This weaned child is not at all capable of managing his environment and relies heavily on the mother, who of course is quite faithful to provide for his needs and most of his wants. She is his helper, even to the point of depriving herself of her own needs; she will fulfill her responsibility. She will do what she can to prevent anything from harming her child.

This is just like God. He is our helper. He doesn't slumber or sleep. He will not let harm come to us. And He longs for us to be still, like a weaned child, and not get caught up in matters too wonderful for us; in other words, too "big" for us. He longs for us to be quiet, to be still, to just *be* and *enjoy* Him. He cares for us tenderly, and yet He is powerful and mighty. Keep this picture in mind; keep it as a goal for yourself to be calm and let God, who is powerful and mighty, do the work.

All of Israel, Now and Forevermore, No Turning Back

Now the "all of Israel". Remember, our health is not just for us. It is to do God's will. It is for the benefit of our families, our church, and indeed the whole world. It is for all of Israel. It is for the past, the present, and for the future. Your personal decisions affect others, whether you realize it or not. Your poor health or struggle might be a sadness to others who love you, or it might be a stressor on those who love you or who desire to minister to you. Your poor health could be in the form of fatigue, unforgiveness, malice, bitterness, fear, worry, debt, anxiety, depression, disorganization, gossip, pride, or even procrastination. All of these descriptors represent the sickness of sin, the potential for more harm, the progress toward death.

We are to work out our salvation with fear and trembling. It is OK to admit it. In fact, this is what God wants. Turn from your wicked ways. We can't hide anything from Him. Before a word is on our tongue, He knows it. This is why we are to ask Him to search us and know our hearts to see if there is any wicked way in us. Let Him show you what He wants you to do. It is the path of righteousness He has for you. What He has for you is not what He has for others. He fashioned you and ordered your days before you were born. He has done this for all of us, and this works together for all of Israel, the whole church, not just today but in the future, for posterity.

This is not just for this moment of your life either. The admission you make right now is for tomorrow, the next day, and the rest of your life, unless God shows you differently in the future. However, I don't think He will ever direct you to bring a toxin back into your life. This is why we search our hearts daily and take heed, lest we fall. This is not a mathematical equation. It is life, and remember, life is fluid like water, never stagnant, always responding, giving, and receiving. Although God doesn't change, we change, but the purpose of this is to grow and become mature, to become more like Christ, to learn of Him, to do His will; this change is to take us through the process of becoming mature and complete. At first, our dependence is on just the milk of the Word, but then we are to grow and become like a skilled craftsmen, handling the Word of God and doing His will without complaining about it or resisting it. In essence, we are to become a maturely weaned adult. However, we are to never lose sight of our need to be like a weaned child, hoping in God, ready to be content, ready to be calm, ready to be concerned for all of Israel, not just ourselves. Along with this, we put our hand to the task at hand and never turn back. This is our Rubicon. We realize, receive, and respond to what God shows us. We admit, accept, and act with obedience, and we never turn back to the old way; we proceed with movement to blameless living to stay in the calm. Most importantly, we do this with the whole counsel of God's Word, not just the parts of it we find more delicious than others. Being calm, let His Word pierce you with His tenderness.

Creating and Committing to the Calm

Let's focus on the weaned child scenario that is mentioned in the psalm. Could we possibly describe a weaned child with the following? A weaned child ...

- is dependent on the mother;
- probably is not arrogant and is unable to understand great matters;
- does not look down on others;

- trusts in his mother;
- views his mother as the ultimate help;
- is content just to be with the mother, not grasping after her like a baby would;
- has the ability to do some things independently;
- still needs to be taught;
- receives help without question;
- believes what he is taught;
- follows the path the mother establishes;
- yearns for his mother's comfort.

We could continue to describe this weaned child, but let's stop with this and agree that a weaned child could be considered as we described, not 100 percent of the time but in general. This is how I want you to become for our purposes of creating the calm in yourself. Be like this weaned child for now. Please speak the following statements aloud to yourself and to all the hosts of heaven. Speak these attributes to yourself to create this calm. Let's do this together.

I am dependent on God.
I am not arrogant.
I cannot understand great matters without God's help.
I do not look down on others.
I trust God.
I know that God is my ultimate help.
I am content just to be with God, to enjoy His presence.
I have some abilities, but these came from God, and I still need His help.
I need to be taught by God.
I receive God's help and teaching without question.
I believe what God teaches me.
I follow the path of righteousness God has prepared for me.
I yearn for God.

Create the Calm

This is our goal each day—to create calm in our whole being with our choices, not by ourselves, of course, but with God's help. Last week, we were determined to clear the clutter. By doing this, we started the process of getting calm. We cannot become calm without clearing the clutter. So no matter what clutter you cleared, no matter what toxins you removed, you took a huge step to start this process of behaving like a weaned child, calm and content. This is what we want for our brains, bodies, and beliefs. We want calmness and contentment. We want to be still before God and content with what He has for us. We do not want to be the ones standing in the way of this by clinging to clutter and refusing to respond.

As far as dealing with inflammation (or poor habits), the first step is to clear, and the second step is to calm. So how do we calm things down? We keep doing what we started. We continue to clear clutter one thing at a time as God shows us. This is a process. Doing it all at once is too hard and can actually cause more stress on your body and brain. Take it slow and do what you can, but in the meantime, I challenge you with some actions in the area of thoughts, food, and your family and church lives.

Thoughts

Considering your thought life, assuming you cleared a lot of clutter from your brain last week, let's proceed forward with purposeful and cautious action as we continue to keep calm rather than being on the defense. In this case, let's purposely think on what is good, true, pure, lovely, godly, beneficial, or productive. Let's be in the present and be focused on what God has given to us and be content with all. Be like the weaned child, not concerning himself with matters too high for him, not arrogant and wanting more, not struggling to achieve. Be who you are now, where you are now. Realize, receive, and respond to this because this is from God, and He meets you here. Don't strive to add more things in right now. Don't strive to start the twenty-one-day fix or the ten-day reset. Just be calm and quiet. If you try to take action and do more than you can handle, you might create stress rather than calm. Just continue to clear the clutter and realize the calm and bask in it. We need this for healing and to move on to the next steps to fight inflammation, which are *to modulate* and *to enhance*. We will tackle these in the next two weeks.

Food

Concerning food, I must be honest. If you have not removed certain clutter from your pantry or your grocery list, you must understand that the effects of them are probably causing inflammation in your body and brain. The big three are gluten, dairy, and sugar. I highly suggest that you do your best to refrain from these as much as possible, if not completely. No matter who you are, no matter how healthy you are, no matter what your weight or your blood sugar or blood pressure is, your body is stressed every time you ingest these. You might think that you do not react to these, but some people definitely respond negatively to these big three. This might not be you, or you might not think it is you, but documentation exists that these affect the body and its systems and put stress on the body, and this means everyone's bodies. Yes, we might manage it, but at some point, it overloads the body, and when this is coupled with other stressors, like emotional stress or lack of sleep or a viral infection, the body could get overwhelmed to the point of being triggered and then becoming sick. Omitting this is part of creating the calm and being committed to it. Suggesting this to you is being truthful with you. Failing to point this out would not be truthful, and I am all about truth. Please consider what I am saying.

If you are up for creating even more calm, consider omitting legumes, eggs, and all grains, just for a while. This is not forever; however, it could be. The goal is to create calm, and the more stressors you remove and the more clutter you clear, the more beneficial it will be for your brain and body. Again, do what God shows you. Each change you make will benefit you. Just so you know, I really like eggs and eat them. I really like cheese but refrain. I am always open to what works or doesn't work for each individual. It is not about legalism but about what provides your body and brain with what it needs to be whole. This is why we all should look to God who satisfies us with good things.

Family

Concerning your family, again, seek to create calm. You might be the mother, but you can still behave like a weaned child in front of your children and husband. You can still express the realization that you depend on God, that He is your help, that you are going to quit striving and begin to listen to God, that you will admit, accept, and take action with what He shows you. Your humility and teachability will be a huge example to your whole family. This in itself will create a calmness. After all, how comforting to a husband that His wife is submitted to God and not concerning herself with matters that are out of her realm; how comforting to children that their mother is not striving but is calm and content with God. Let this be your theme. This will create calm in your home. Be committed to this. It will benefit everyone. For you husbands, you can do this too. Ponder the peace this would bring to your wife and family.

Finally, let God concern himself with the details of the family matters that are too great for you, matters like correcting, micromanaging, and teaching. Be calm and let it go for a while. Let God do the correcting. Let Him teach you how much to intervene as you seek to be calm instead of managing all the details. This does not mean you are shirking your responsibility. It just means you are letting God do the work. You will lay the requests before Him and wait in expectation, because you need to be committed to the calm.

Church

Concerning your church, are you telling others what you believe more than you are living it? Are you trying to teach others more than you are being taught or taking in the teaching? Are you judging and trying to make things better more than you are encouraging? Let this go for a while. Just be a calm and content brother or sister in Christ who is not concerning themselves with matters that are too great. It's OK if you just take the sermon in without analyzing it too much. Let it feed you. It's OK if you take a break from all the activities because you need to create calm. It's OK to be the recipient instead of the leader who is always giving. Your goal is to create and be committed to the calm, not to continue the race to achieve and make magnificent. Let God do this. He is able.

Remember, Rahab just waited and made sure the red cord was hanging. She did not take up a sword. Remember, God works through our weakness, not our strength. Truly, He is glorified through us, through our trust, our calm, our humility, and our acceptance. Remember, this is for all of Israel. Your action could help so many others. It is not just about your health; this is about the health of the whole church and all of Israel, putting their hope in the Lord now and forevermore. The change is not to be temporary. It is for the new path that God makes in the wilderness of poor health and stress, no turning back, no going back to Egypt, as we might say, concerning Israel. Even if you get tired or weary, refrain from grumbling and complaining and from impatience. Wait in expectation for God to answer you and to give you the help you need when you need it to keep the calm, to be about blameless living.

OK, team, let's take out our five-column journal. You can download this from my website, www.dynamotruth.com, or create your own.

Sample Chart for Calm Like a Weaned Child: Commit to the Calm

Topic	Brain	Body	Beliefs	Scripture and Action Steps
Calm like a weaned child. Commit to the calm.	What is true, good, pure, lovely, encouraging, productive, and helpful? What are good habits? Think on all of this!	Be calm; be still. I will be calm and still. I will let God do the work. I will let others act. Chair time—fifteen minutes for stillness.	I will realize, receive, and respond to what is present now. I will admit, accept, and act—be calm. I will give thanks and wait in expectation. I will believe God's perfect plan that He has ordained for me right now.	Read Psalm 131 aloud daily. Memorize it. Read only God's Word this week—nothing extra except for work. Use the internet and so on only for work and for what is mandatory in a responsible way. Think on what is present—no worry about the future, no regret about the past. Embrace the basic truths of God.

Remember, column one is our topic, column two is *Brain*, column three is *Body*, column four is *Beliefs*, and column five is *Scripture and Action Steps*.

Under column one, please write our topic, which is calm.

Under column two, the brain column, please write what you will purposely think about. This includes the following:

- what is true and good
- what is pure and lovely
- what is encouraging
- what is beneficial and productive

- what is helpful
- what are good habits

Think about doing these habits; it will strengthen them.

Under column three, the body column, please write the following:

- I will be calm; I will stop trying to do everything.
- I will let God do the work.
- I will let others solve the problems for a while.
- I will sit in a chair fifteen minutes each day to be calm and like a weaned child.

Under column four, the beliefs column, please write the following:

- I will realize, receive, and respond to what is present now, not trying to change things.
- I will admit, accept, and act according to what I need to do now—I will be calm.
- I will thank God for all of this and wait in expectation.
- I will believe that God has ordained this for me right now, to be calm and wait.

Under column five, our scripture and action steps, please write our scripture, Psalm 131.

These are the action steps I suggest this week:

1. Read Psalm 131 daily. Memorize the whole psalm. Envision being the weaned and content child with God as your Father.
2. Read only God's Word this week—no other materials, books, or studies unless you absolutely have to. This will keep you focused on the calm and not allow you to get sidetracked by seeking more knowledge or going after other less important things.
3. Stay off the internet and social media as much as you are responsibly able. Yes, you need to keep in touch with people

and possibly to do work, but definitely see if you can limit this to create more calmness.

4. Think on what is present and thank God for it; no wishing and praying for more.

5. Embrace what you know is true; go with the solid basics, nothing controversial. For instance, God answers prayer. This is solid. Don't think on anything like, "Does God do miracles?" We know He does; He does what He pleases but not what we demand.

6. Pray!

Here is a sample prayer:

> Lord, thank You for Your goodness. Lord, I bow down to You in humility, like a weaned child ready to receive what I need at the time I need it, not craving or wanting for more, not concerning myself with the how, why, when, and where of anything but entrusting it all to You because You know all, Lord, and You are able to give me what I need in Your time. Lord, I have calmed and quieted myself like a weaned and content child with his mother, fully trusting in You, fully ready to receive Your instruction and help, fully admitting that I don't know what I should do. Lord, thank You that I can put my trust in You, and even as I do this, You will work, for You do not slumber or sleep, and You watch over my coming and going. Lord, I will be calm; I will be still; I will wait for You like a watchman waits for the morning, not demanding anything of You but waiting with contentment and expectation. Thank You, Lord.

Well, everyone, I am so glad you joined me again this week. I am so glad that you are in agreement that clearing the clutter and creating the calm and committing to it will be beneficial to you and the entire church. Hang in there. Every small step of action or of obedience to what God shows you will be huge. He will use it. Remember, God multiplied the fish and the loaves. He is surely able to multiply the benefits of your willingness to work and to honor Him with each step you take. God bless all of you.

Next week, we will continue to keep inflammation at bay by discussing the aspect of *modulation*. This will go right along with clearing and calming for better brains, bodies, and beliefs.

WEEK 11

MODULATE

TRANSFORMATION TAKES TIME

Welcome to week 11. This week, we will be discussing the topic of modulating. The last two weeks, we have been dealing with the big topic of inflammation, with our focus on clearing and calming. Now it is time to modulate toward more improvement. I really hope you are starting to love God's Word more so that you learn of Him, so that you are strengthened, so that you are getting healthier, all for the purpose of doing His will and doing His will vigorously.

Let's define modulation.

Definition of Modulation

Defining the word *modulation* will be important for our discussion today. Modulation is used quite frequently in the musical sense, as it means to vary the strength, tone, or pitch of one's voice as well as one's instrument. Another definition is to regulate or adjust to a certain measure or proportion. You could also consider the aspect of "to gradually make quieter, higher or lower, or to move gradually." This is quite unlike the aspect of control or the aspect of dictating or having complete regulation. The intention of this meaning in my opinion is to actually change to make better or to diminish or increase to make better, but doing this gradually so it is unnoticed in such a way that it doesn't cause stress.

As we continue, I want you to keep this in mind with regard to our recent information on clearing and calming. The last two weeks of discussion encouraged combating inflammation with the clearing of clutter and the commitment to calm. Now that we have begun this process of dealing with inflammation, we want to modulate to strengthen, to lessen, to increase, to decrease, to tweak, or to regulate what we can to move forward for better brain, body, and beliefs. Think of it this way. When you first came to be alive in Christ, the clearing was the admission of sin, and the calming was the accepting of the Savior and the free gift of salvation. Then the modulation began and will continue forever; this is the transforming work of the Holy Spirit in your life to become more like Christ. The more you allow this and the more this is done, the more your spiritual life will be modulated to its potential, the more you will be about God's will with pleasure, with more ease, with no turning back. Next week, we will be talking about the *enhance* phase, but for now, let's stick with modulating as we have begun to clear and to calm.

Let's begin with Psalm 51. Read it with me.

Psalm 51

1   Have mercy on me, O God, according to your loving kindness; according to the multitude of your tender mercies, blot out my transgressions.

2   Wash me thoroughly from my iniquity and cleanse me from my sin.

3   For I acknowledge my transgressions, and my sin is always before me.

4   Against you, you only, have I sinned and done this is evil in your sight; so you are just when You speak, and blameless when You judge.

5   Surely I was sinful at birth, sinful from the time my mother conceived me.

6   Yet you desired faithfulness even in the womb; you taught me wisdom in that secret place.

7   Cleanse me with hyssop, and I will be clean; wash me, and I will be whiter than snow.

8   Let me hear joy and gladness; let the bones you have crushed rejoice.

9   Hide your face from my sins and blot out all my iniquity.

10   Create in me a pure heart, O God, and renew a steadfast spirit within me.

11   Do not cast me from your presence or take your Holy Spirit from me.

12   Restore unto me the joy of your salvation and grant me a willing spirit, to sustain me.

13   Then I will teach transgressors your ways, so that sinners will turn back to you.

14   Deliver me from the guilt of bloodshed, O God; you who are God my Savior, and my tongue will sing of your righteousness.

15   Open my lips, Lord, and my mouth will declare your praise.

16   You do not delight in sacrifice, or I would bring it; you do not take pleasure in burnt offerings.

17   My sacrifice, O God, is a broken spirit; a broken and contrite heart you, God, will not despise.

18   May it please you to prosper Zion, to build up the walls of Jerusalem.

19   Then you will delight in the sacrifices of the righteous, in burnt offerings offered whole; then bulls will be offered on your altar.

A Quick Bit of History Concerning David, King of the Ammonites, the Ark of the Lord, His Wife

We know that this psalm is famous for the reflection that David had after he was confronted by Nathan about his sin with Bathsheba. Let's not forget what else he did. He covered it up; he gave command to organize the death of her husband; he abused his power; he continued his kingship without repentance; he judged others, as he demonstrated when Nathan told him the story about the rich man who took the ewe lamb from the poor man; he commanded another should die. It all sounds pretty ugly, doesn't it? Aren't we all guilty of ugly sin, of bad choices, of cover-up, of secrecy? Yes, we all are guilty, but now that we are committed to blameless living, this will have no part in us. We are moving forward with a mindset of praise to chew on God's truth, to call on Him as our helper, to clear clutter from our lives, to commit to the calm, and to immediately turn back to God if we even approach a table of such traumatic magnitude.

I challenge you to have understanding in your attitude toward David and to yourself right now. God is just, but He is full of mercy and ready to give full redemption. It is His reflex to show mercy; it is His reflex to embrace. I really believe that it takes more effort on God's part to administer justice and punishment than it does to embrace us with His grace and forgiveness. Let's realize, receive, and respond to this, not just for ourselves but for others as well.

Concerning David, I want to posit this to you: David was weak due to being disheartened and challenged on other fronts. Now compare this to you. You are weak when you are disheartened and challenged on other fronts, like when you aren't sleeping enough, when your relationships are struggling, when you are lonely, when you are fighting illness, when you have clutter and inconsistencies around you (PPIs), when others don't support you or when they take you for granted, when you are self-absorbed and not concerned about others, when you are not giving thanks but instead complaining. All of these weaken you *and* me.

So what am I talking about concerning David? Prior to his sin with Bathsheba, three events occurred. The first was concerning the king of the Ammonites and his son Hanun. David decided to show kindness to Hanun because his father, the king, died. So David sent a delegation to him; however, this was not received, and the men in the delegation were seized, their beards were shaved half off, and their garments were cut at the buttocks. Thus, a battle ensued. David's effort was to bless, but instead he was judged to be obnoxious and untrustworthy. I would be disheartened at this response to my effort to do good, wouldn't you?

Prior to this, however, was an even more disheartening struggle that David endured. Yes, God was teaching him as well as all of Israel, but I see how this lesson in God's holiness could have been a very difficult time in David's life or anyone's life. Instruction is the way of life, but it is not always easy; thus, the commitment to realize, receive, and respond to what God shows you as well as to admit, accept, and act accordingly must be a habit. The incident to which I am referring is when David and his men went to Baalah in Judah to bring up the ark of God. Uzzah and Ahio were guiding the ark, which was on a cart. David and all of Israel were celebrating with all their might before the Lord. This sounds like a wonderful situation. God was not pleased, however. Uzzah was struck by the Lord because he reached out to take hold of the ark when the oxen stumbled. Here is a powerful caution about anger to encourage you to receive and to clear, commit to, and modulate anger in your life. David was angry because the Lord's wrath had broken out against Uzzah. We understand his anger. However, many times we do not understand our own anger, and even more seriously, we do not understand what God has for us to learn.

I understand his anger. His intentions were good, they were honorable, they were seemingly glorifying to God from the human perspective, but not from God's. God made it very clear how the ark was to be transported. David must have realized this because shortly thereafter, the ark again was transported, but this time it was done according to God's requirement, with men carrying it the prescribed way. Along with this, there was dancing and rejoicing and sacrifices being offered along the way.

But we are not done. A further disheartening incident occurred, which would be hard for any man to endure concerning the attitude of his wife; it would also be very hurtful for any individual to endure. This was in the form of disdain. David was dancing before the Lord with all His might. I think God was pleased; it certainly shows the depiction of a man after God's own heart. However, David's wife, Michal, despised him from her heart. Oh ... another dart to dishearten.

You can agree with me or not, but my view is that David had three severe blows to his emotional state, his inner stamina and strength.

When disappointments, hurts, and challenges like this happen, we do become weakened. God knows this, and He teaches us through this; He strengthens and comforts us through this, but we must turn to Him. We are going to have trials and tribulations throughout our whole lives, sometimes due to our own fault, sometimes due to others, and sometimes due to the events common to man. We cannot escape this, but God does provide a way of escape, and it is always through the path of righteousness He has for us, not through our own wisdom but through His truth. This is why we chew on God's Word daily, morning and night. This helps us to see our situations and experiences from God's perspective of truth and wisdom, not from our frail human perspective only. It reminds us that His loving hand is guiding all of the events for our eternal good and the eternal good of everyone.

So what do these three events have to do with Bathsheba and Psalm 51? My point is this. Just like David was weakened from these disappointments and then sinned tremendously, we too are weakened through disappointment, which can cause us to give in to sin or to decisions that are not good for us or for God's church. This is why it is important to clear clutter from our lives, so that we are not challenged by our environment or mindset. Let's talk about David's environment when he sinned with Bathsheba. Trust me, I am not at all condoning or dismissing David's behavior, nor am I making excuses for him. I am only trying to help you see how your past, both long term and very recent past, affects you and can have an effect on you that you might not realize. If you are aware of this possibility, you will be better able to handle the situations that arise and challenge you. We must learn from our experiences. Knowing how our past affects us is a tremendous asset to our current understanding and the ability to move on from it as we develop godly habits and lifestyles that foster our health and walk with God.

David's Environment and How It Weakened Him

Scripture says that David was not out to battle like the other kings. Where was he? He was on the palace balcony, looking at something that he should not have been viewing. Remember, we have more visual receptors than any other sensory receptors. Remember how powerful our sense of sight is? Remember that we are to live a blameless life? As it says in Psalm 101, "I will not look with approval on anything that is vile. I will be careful to live a blameless life. I will walk within my own house with a blameless heart." Wow! What a call to action here!

David's environment was not conducive to staying on the path of righteousness God had for him. It truly was filled with clutter he did not need; this was just one item, a woman, a woman who was married, a woman whose husband was out fighting without the command of the king who would later command this husband's death to cover up sin. Do you see how important your environment is? Don't underestimate the power of each decision you make and how it will affect you later. Think about this: what might still be in your environment that is not conducive to following your law of health based on Psalm 1? I don't mean just your pantry either; I refer to the environment of your brain, body, and beliefs, the environment of your heart, the environment of your relationships, the environment of your thought life, your internet life, your social life, or your time. Where are you "standing" right now? What balcony do you choose to inhabit? It all matters.

The point I want to make here is that when we have to make too many decisions or overcome too many temptations, we gradually become weaker, and then we might finally give in to a poor decision or a temptation that overwhelms us. This is why we set ourselves up for success and do not look with approval on anything that is vile. When we keep temptations at bay by preventing bad options in our environment, we don't have to make a decision about them, to refrain from them, to utilize self-control to resist them, or to say no to ourselves. The decision made to omit them from our environment, to clear clutter and commit to the calm by keeping them out, along with the habit of doing this, sets us up for success to walk in the path God has for us.

Compare this to David on the palace balcony. If he had been out to war, he would not have committed this great sin. It would not have been an option. The temptation would have never occurred. God would not have been dishonored. A woman would not have been sinned against. A man would not have been murdered. A baby would not have died. Do you see all the aftereffects just because of one's environment and personal choice? Yes, he may have been disheartened, but this is never an excuse to justify sin, never a reason to become slack in obedience, never a reason to sit in the seat of the scornful, and furthermore, it is never a reason to quit chewing on God's Word day and night so that you learn of Him and what He wants to teach you. Be admonished and motivated by David's example as we continue our discussion of Psalm 51 and how it can be applied to our health. And remember, if a habit is not established, we cannot stand up against the tempting choices that confront us; it takes too much energy. Eventually, these will overwhelm us, and we will give in just like David did. However, as we continue our discussion, you will see that David did in fact learn what God wanted to teach him.

David Realized, Received, and Responded

Let's just briefly summarize the encounter between David and Nathan right now. Nathan ultimately confronted David with these direct words, "You are that man!" For you, immediately rejoice if someone confronts you. Don't oppose it. Be humble, embrace it, and move forward with action. You will be free. God will be close to you. Even if it is a donkey, take the truth and chew on it for your own health, for your own decrease in stress, for your own peace, for your own right standing with God. David had ample opportunity to repent long before Nathan confronted him in secret. The husband had been killed; the baby was two years old. God is in no hurry; He is patient, and He is both merciful and just. In essence, David realized the truth. He received Nathan's rebuke and responded with repentance. In essence, he cleared, he calmed, and now he was in a position for God to modulate things for improvement.

If you look at the first nine verses of Psalm 51, you will see the focus is on repentance and forgiveness, along with the request that God blots out his transgressions. I view this as clearing the clutter and committing to the calm. This is admitting, accepting, and acting in accordance with the truth. You have done this already by clearing clutter from your pantry, your house, your brain, your heart, and your relationships. You have already done this by praying Psalm 101 and being careful to live a blameless life, starting in your own house and in your own heart, keeping your eyes on the faithful of the land and putting to silence all the wicked of the land, especially with yourself.

David's movement forward with action did not spare him from consequences of his past actions. Remember, the past, present, and future are all part of the process and are relevant. The consequences included the death of David and Bathsheba's son, despite David's plea for the child to live, despite his fasting, his sackcloth at night, despite lying on the ground. He did not wallow in this consequence, however. After the baby died, he cleaned up, he calmed down, and he ate. He moved on. The observers were quite surprised, saying, "Why are you acting this way? While the child was alive, you fasted and wept, but now that the child is dead, you get up and eat!" His outward behavior seemed to indicate the state of his heart and what he was believing his next steps might be.

He answered that he had hoped God would spare the child. He knew God was merciful, but in this situation, God did not act according to David's plea. David's acceptance of this is demonstrated by his answer to those who questioned him, as well as how he proceeded to comfort Bathsheba. Again, we see this is not just about you; what you do affects others; how you respond affects others. David's movement forward after he was cleared of sin and calmed liked a weaned child actually modulated the situation for improvement, to strengthen the situation by decreasing further continuation in the damaging state of the inflammation of sin that would have slowly killed him and all of Israel. The confrontation was unpleasant, but this is what brought movement forward for blameless living. Until David admitted, accepted, and acted, the continued lack of health not just for him but for all of Israel would have progressed further. Be thankful for full redemption.

Admission, Acceptance, Action—The Before, the Transformation, the Movement Forward

We have already looked at David's admission, his acceptance, and his action and how nourishing this is to us. This should be an inspiration for all of us to follow his example. How free we become when we admit and accept. Ignoring what is true, denying what is true, running from what is true will never work for any successful path for you or me, whether it is emotional, mental, physical, or relational; whether it is in your brain, your body, or your beliefs; whether it is unforgiveness, pride, or jealously; whether it is debt, self-absorption, or slackness. Embrace the truth like a weaned child. There is full redemption and forgiveness for you and me. This is a daily process. Think of it—full forgiveness, full redemption. If God kept a record of our sinful ways, none of us could stand, but with Him is unfailing love and full forgiveness.

He has called us to peace. Remember what Paul says in Romans, "If at all possible, live at peace with all men." Paul did not know all the scientific data on the importance of health and relationships, but God did. He established healthy relationships as part of our overall well-being. If you are not at peace in your relationships, you don't have complete health. Relationships can be one of the most stressful aspects of our entire being and, therefore, our health. Don't be afraid to be honest about them. Move forward for peace.

About the before aspect. The before includes David's sinful ways from birth. The transformation includes the depths of despair he was possibly in and the anger that he felt along with the great sin and cover-up. The movement forward was the response he chose after he was confronted by Nathan. But let's look at the psalm and piece this out.

After the confession of the first nine verses of Psalm 51, David makes this prayer, "Create in me a clean heart, O God, and renew a right spirit, a steadfast spirit within me. Cast me not away from your presence and do not take your Holy Spirit from me. Restore unto me the joy of your salvation and grant me a willing spirit, to sustain me." I want this to be your pivot verse for the focus today. This verse is powerful and is for all of us. Cleansing from the inside is a work done by God when we humbly admit all to Him. He has unfailing love for us, full redemption. Again, I want to emphasize He will never look upon you like Michal did on David, with disdain, but instead, our Lord longs to show you compassion. Believe this. Realize and receive this unabashedly, with eagerness. Respond to this with gratitude.

This is absolutely huge in the sense that we must do things in the correct order. We began our twelve weeks with a goal, then proceeded to clear the clutter and calm things down on the inside by monitoring what we put into our brains, bodies, and beliefs and by how we sustain these by chewing on what is good for us (our digestion), including the chewing of God's Word and going to Him as our ultimate help. David likewise began on the inside, with the request for God to create a clean heart and restore a right spirit within him. This should be our request too. "Create in us a clean heart, O God."

But take this action in relation to your body. Confess the sin and bad choices you have made against your body. After this, proceed to ask God to give you full redemption, but be ready to realize, receive, and respond to what He shows you. Ask for a willing spirit to sustain you in the action forward. It is the same principle for our physical and mental health as it is for our spiritual health. Confess it, turn from it, take the step forward to be cleansed, and continue with a right spirit, a right mindset for what is healthy.

Remember, this is not just about you. Verse 13 lets us know this. Hear what David said, "Then I will teach transgressors your ways so that sinners will turn back to you." After you have admitted, accepted, and acted, you are ready to share this with others, both spiritually and physically. You can share what great things God has done for you to grant salvation to you, along with your responsibility to follow the law of the Lord. You can also share the great things God does for you in the area of your health, along with your responsibility to follow your law of health. It is for the whole church. Think of the individuals who could benefit from your movement forward, from your action to clear, calm, and modulate. This would truly affect others. How could anyone ignore the transformation? Just like David's friends saw the change in him, the admission and acceptance and his action to do it God's way, you are able to make this same impact on others without saying a word. They will see it because you have a better brain and body, because you have a movement to clear, calm, and modulate relationships and other aspects of your life to peace. This is teaching transgressors about God's hope for them too. This is living a blameless life and silencing all the wicked of the land. This is not judgment; it is truth; it is behaving like a weaned child, not trying to be about the great things that are too wonderful for you but behaving like a weaned child, fully dependent on God.

Let me just interject this important concept and word for you. Personal anecdotes are powerful. Your personal testimony matters; your life story matters. Someone is going to be nourished, encouraged, and changed because of it. Others will learn to know that they are not alone in dealing with their issues. Use your story and your choices to help others. It is for all of Israel. It's for the whole church and the whole world. Don't be afraid to let others know what you have learned. You are able to teach transgressors what you have learned from Him. You have absolutely no idea how God will use your humility and your admission to bring hope and restoration to another individual. Just as He cares for you, He cares for everyone. He cares for a world that is in darkness and that opposes Him. Your humility will multiply His majesty. Think about this: *your humility will multiply His majesty.* Just like the loaves and fishes were multiplied to provide what was needed, God is able to multiple your life story for what is needed for your posterity and for others even now. Remember, this is not just about you; it is about the whole world. Everything and all of us are connected.

Before we conclude, I want to bring out another point. David repented and asked for deliverance before he decided to do something to win God's favor. He did not offer sacrifices but instead acknowledged that the real sacrifice was a broken spirit. This was the true sacrifice for God, a broken and contrite heart, which God will never despise. Only after this would a sacrifice of something else be accepted. We can't fool

God with outward action or appearance. He looks at the heart, the intention. He wants a broken spirit and a contrite heart.

Liken this to our bodies. Many people refuse to clear the clutter first. Instead, they add things in like supplements or quick fix ideas. They focus on doing one thing in hopes that it will work. Why do they do this? Or should I say, why do we do this? I think the reason is because it is easier than clearing the clutter, but it doesn't work. You can take all the fish oil and all the zinc and vitamin C and other types of supplements that might be recommended, but these will not clear you of the toxins that deprive you of full health, especially if you or I keep putting them in our bodies. I equate this to offering a sacrifice to God without confessing our sin; it's like offering a bull or giving a tithe without having a broken and contrite heart. It doesn't work. Man looks at the outside, but God looks at the heart. God cleanses from the inside out. This is true for our bodies and brains. They must be cleansed from the inside first. So stop the clutter from coming in.

Remember when we began our twelve weeks and talked about the soil. This is what a farmer does. He works the soil so the seed will grow, and therefore, that fruitfulness will come. We cannot bear fruit without abiding in the vine, and this is part of blameless living, clearing clutter, calming and modulating—being transformed by the gardener. It might be possible to bear fruit without being at optimum health, but think about it: we select fruit that is luscious, healthy, vibrant, full, and delicious. We are able to identify the good fruit from the bad fruit. Seek to produce good fruit, healthy fruit. This starts at the soil level, the hidden parts. Do *not* despise the small things, the unseen things.

Did you also notice that after David prayed for a clean heart and before he offered any sacrifice, the heart-to-mouth action occurred? "Open my lips, Lord, and my mouth will declare your praise," he announced. This is not a unique occurrence in David's life. His usual pattern was to praise God. Even if he was downcast, he praised the Lord. We see it over and over again, and even now, in his great sin, in his behavior like a weaned child who has been taught again, he praises the Lord. Remember, an attitude of gratitude is an antidote to so many problems. No matter how low you get, no matter how sinful you have been, no matter how hopeless you feel, after you have poured your lament or your confession out to God, begin to praise Him. This is movement forward both in speech and action. We ultimately believe this too; we ultimately believe that God is worthy of praise.

Furthermore, giving praise to God modulates your whole being. It increases and strengthens your faith. It increases and strengthens your relationship with your Lord. It increases and strengthens your mindset to move forward. It increases and strengthens your personal integrity because you know that giving thanks to your Lord will always be the right thing to do, will always be a sign of humility and trust, and will always be a powerful habit for your brain, body, and beliefs. It modulates you to better health overall. This is backed up by research, which has shown that gratitude improves sleep, encourages physical health, decreases inflammation, and lessens fatigue. On top of this, it has been shown to encourage the development of patience, humility, and wisdom. Wow! God's Word instructs us to praise the Lord, and this is our life. God's Word is backed by science. It is not fluff. So much of it is blatantly obvious that we should wonder why it would ever be questioned. Trust His Word. Trust Him. Trust the process of admission, acceptance, and action. Just like instruction is the way to life, so is this, constantly admitting and accepting and then moving forward with action. Be a doer of the Word. Be a doer of what is true. Be a doer of what God shows you.

Let this be your Rubicon that no matter what happens, you will give thanks to your Lord, and you will not turn back to the old manner, to complaining, to hopelessness, to a balcony that beckons you to bad behavior that hinders you from blameless living. Cross over, modulate to the clear and calm, and stay there.

Well, team, with this focus on gratitude to help modulate us to better overall health, let's pull out our five-column journal. You can download this from my website or make your own.

Sample Chart for Modulate: Transformation Takes Time

Topic	Brain	Body	Beliefs	Scripture and Action Steps
Modulate. Transformation takes time.	Complete forgiveness. What would Nathan say to me? Focus on full forgiveness.	Remove myself from locations that are not good for me … all balconies.	How do I view Nathan's role with David? What about a Nathan for me? Is this rebuke good? What do I really believe about the consequences of my sin concerning others?	Read Psalm 51 aloud daily. Memorize verses 10–13. Be your own Nathan and get another one to confront you. Be ready with full admission and acceptance. Purposely leave locations that have little benefit for you or that challenge your blameless living.

Remember, column one is our topic, column two is *Brain*, column three is *Body*, column four is *Beliefs*, and column five is *Scripture and Action Steps*.

Under column one, please write our topic of modulate.

Under column two, our brain column, let's write the following: Focus on the complete forgiveness or possibilities for improvement that are potentially within your realm right now. Imagine that you had a Nathan in your life. What might he confront you about? Be honest.

This is between you and God. Don't just focus on the Nathan either, but focus on the full forgiveness of God and the purpose of the Nathan.

Under column three, the body column, let's write the following: Choose to physically remove yourself from a location that is not good for you right now. (Think about the money and time you might save as well as the regret you will avoid.) Just as David should not have been on the balcony, where might you find yourself that is leading or could lead you to trouble? Is it a coffee shop where you spend money, keep your caffeine up, waste time with meaningless conversations, or gossip? Is it the gym where you are feeding your pride by developing muscles that aren't really necessary or by connecting with others who might lead you to steroid use or bad relationships or unhealthy goals? Is it your computer chair, which allows you to visit any location on earth at any time for any purpose? Is it the chip aisle in the grocery store? Is it the sports store where you are buying too many pairs of shoes or other clothing just based on their appearance, not based on your need?

The location that I am trying to leave or avoid is the kitchen, due to my constant temptation to snack. This is hard for me because I am the one responsible for preparing the food for my family and for cleaning up the mess. Look, we don't need Bathsheba or a balcony to go down a wrong path. We only need a pair of eyes and a heart that can so easily be tempted by what we see and, therefore, entice us to disregard the law of the Lord.

Under column four, our beliefs column, please write this: How do I view Nathan's confrontation of David? Do I believe it was God's intervention for His glory, for the health of David's life, for the rest of Israel? Would I readily receive this in my own life or would I refuse it? Do rebuke and confrontation come from God or just others who judge too much? Would I rather someone speak the truth to me or just ignore it like those in David's life who knew but said nothing, those who knew about the plan and did nothing to stop it? Do I applaud Nathan and rejoice in the truth enduring, despite the pain and hardship that came as a result? Do I see the greater good of turning from behaviors that are not in accordance with blameless living? Do the weak areas of my life and the failure to live blamelessly really affect others, including the church and the world?

These are good questions. They even confront me now as I look at them again. Remember, we are never done with blameless living.

Under column five, our scripture and action steps, please write our scripture of Psalm 51. Here are your action steps:

1. Read Psalm 51 daily. Memorize verses 10–13 or whatever verses really speak to you at this time.

2. Be your own Nathan and ask someone to be a Nathan to you; envision what they might say to you or about what they might confront you. Envision responding like David, with complete admission, acceptance, and action. Also, don't focus on the Nathan; focus on the purpose of the Nathan, no matter who or what it is. The message God has for you is important no matter where it comes from.

3. Purposely leave as many locations this week that you know are not serving you well or could lead to trouble. Do this as much as possible, even if it means leaving a quick conversation that you deem to be a waste of time or that is taking you from your real responsibility, even if it means leaving a drive-up window or a parking lot; even if it means turning the other way because you see someone coming that you know you should not be involved with or who might cause you to talk about something you should not discuss.

4. Ask yourself again what you really believe. Is this Nathan experience needed in my life, even with the smallest detail? Consider the most insignificant detail in your life to determine if it is harming you, your family, or your church. This could simply be that you don't stay for even two minutes of fellowship after church to build connections. It could mean you don't reach out to anyone to pray for or with them. It could mean that you never say thank you to your pastor or those in your family for the little things they do for you. Find something. It could mean you procrastinate and don't pick up clutter when you see it, and the accumulation causes stress. Just the smallest detail. What could you confront yourself about?

5. Pray! Here is a sample prayer:

Lord, You are holy, and when we sin, we ultimately sin against You. Lord, sin is doing what we know we should not do; it is not doing what we know we should do. Lord, help us to see the balconies in our lives and deal with them before they lead to more trouble. Lord, may we not cover up anything but instead fully confess our transgressions to You with the full expectation that You grant full forgiveness and full redemption. Lord, create in us a clean heart and renew a right spirit in us, a steadfast spirit to do Your will; to declare Your praise. Lord, I stand before You like a weaned child with a contrite spirit and a broken heart. I stand before You with the confession of the clutter I have allowed in my life, and I receive the calmness You grant. I respond to what You are doing to change me, to modulate me, to strengthen me. Lord, I will endure. I will daily meditate and chew on Your Word, day and night, so that I will be constantly reminded of what a blameless life is. Lord, I realize my sin and my poor habits; I receive Your rebuke; I respond right now with a mouth that praises You and moves forward with action so that I do not turn back. I will progress forward for my health and for the health of the whole church and for the whole world, to do Your will, the ultimate reason for good health. Thank You, Lord, my ultimate help. Amen!

Well, team, I am cheering for you. Keep at it. Keep clear of the clutter, keep the calm, and continue to let God modulate your whole being with how you respond with action to what is true. Next week is our last week of the twelve-week Health through the Psalms program. We will discuss enhancing our lives with our choices and strategic actions. Have a great week.

WEEK 12

ENHANCE FOR EVERYONE
FOR ETERNITY

YOU, YOUR CHURCH, THE WHOLE WORLD

Welcome to week twelve. Congratulations on making it to our last week. Just reading and doing your best with all of this information took a commitment and a choice on your part, and continuing on after today will take a commitment and a choice. Also, our topic this week is to enhance everything that we have been trying to do these past twelve weeks by pressing on forever. Don't give up. With the Lord is unfailing love and full redemption. Transformation takes time. Decluttering is a constant process. Your determination to continue to move out of oppression from anything by setting all of your concerns at the table of the Almighty will bring peace. The mindset of gratitude will keep your focus on Him who is faithful to complete the work He has begun in you. He knows everything, secret and hidden, challenging and stressful, bitter and sweet—yes, even the smallest detail, which even He does not despise, is known to Him.

To preface today's discussion, I want you to hear the overall message, which is this: *Keep at it. Don't give up.* In essence, I could stop here and say goodbye, but I won't. I still have more to say, but hear me loud and clear. *Keep at it. Don't give up.* This is exactly what the apostle Paul would say to you. He would say, "Run the race. Press on." And Jesus Himself said, "He who endures to the end will be saved." So agree with me now that it is a good message to keep at it. Believe with me now that giving up is not an option. You can do it.

Let's jump right in to Psalm 141 for our last week together.

Psalm 141

1   I call to you, Lord, come quickly to me; hear me when I call to you.

2   May my prayer be set before you like incense; may the lifting up of my hands be like the evening sacrifice.

3   Set a guard over my mouth, Lord; keep watch over the door of my lips.

4   Do not let my heart be drawn to what is evil so that I take part in wicked deeds along with those who are evildoers; do not let me eat their delicacies.

5   Let a righteous man strike me—that is a kindness; let him rebuke me—that is oil on my head. My head will not refuse it, for my prayer will still be against the deeds of evildoers.

6   Their rulers will be thrown down from the cliffs, and the wicked will learn that my words were well spoken.

7   They will say, "As one plows and breaks up the earth, so our bones have been scattered at the mouth of the grave."

8   But my eyes are fixed on you, Sovereign Lord; in you I take refuge—do not give me over to death.

9   Keep me safe from the traps set by evildoers, from the snares they have laid for me.

10   Let the wicked fall into their own nets, while I pass by in safety.

Let's look at the definition of *enhance*. It means to "intensify, increase, or further improve the quality, value, or extent of." Combine this definition with what we have been doing these last eleven weeks and especially the last three weeks. We have been clearing, calming, and modulating this entire time, whether you realized it or not. Even though the last three weeks were definitely focused on clearing, calming, and modulating, we have been attempting to do this from the beginning when we stated our goal of health and then moved on with strategic action. We started with our environment; we began moving, we chewed on what was good for us, we engaged our cephalic abilities by focusing on what table we were approaching so that we set ourselves up for success, we called on God and stomach acid to aid in our daily efforts and to aid in our digestion, we called in the guards of our microbiome to do further work for us, and then we proceeded to really tackle inflammation by clearing, calming, and modulating. Now we want to enhance all of this. We do this not just for today but for all of eternity and for the benefit of the whole church, the whole body of Christ. So we enhance for eternity, for the eternal good of everyone.

Be Patient—It Takes Time

Consider and accept this: to enhance takes time. Think about all of the other actions, habits, decisions, and life processes we experience or choose to develop that take time with focused attention and effort. We think nothing of waiting for a baby to grow and develop for forty weeks in the mother's womb. We accept the many semesters of pursuit it requires to obtain a college degree. We readily commit to the daily requirement to practice or study to acquire a new skill or new information. When we do these things, we have cleared time for ourselves to do it, we have calmed ourselves to accept that this is what is necessary, and we have modulated our schedules and our efforts to actually do them. Furthermore, we have enhanced who we are as we accumulate these skills or achievements, and the longer we do all of this, the more enhancement and transformation we will see in our person. So why would we think that we will have a quick fix to our health struggle when it took us years to get to where we are? We think nothing of taking our children to school, athletic practices and music practices, and other activities for several hours on a daily basis because we know that this is necessary for the end result, the goal, the achievement—to be winners, or should we say to do the will of the coach or the teacher. Could we not realize this same truth to make the effort to improve our brains, bodies, and beliefs to be winners and learners, or should we say to do the will of the Lord.

Remember, concerning David, God waited more than two years before He allowed Nathan to confront him. Could you give your efforts here more time? Could you give it two years to become healthier, to develop good habits, to commit to the clear, calm, modulating, and enhancing. I ask you again. Could you give it two years? Could you not make the commitment to two years of your life to enhance for all of eternity, for the entire body of Christ, for everyone? Think of the impact you could make if you committed to two years of better brain, body, and beliefs. We readily support a missionary who commits his or her life for the work of the Lord. Look at all of the effort they put in. They raise money, they leave their homes and other comforts, they learn a new language, they say goodbye to loved ones. In essence, they deprive themselves of what they want, what is easy, and they clear out what has to go in order to continue the movement forward to do God's will. The rest of us support them with financial donations and prayer which I think is far easier. Let's mimic their efforts.

If you can't commit to two years, could you commit to fifty-two days? This is the time it took Nehemiah and his fellow cohorts to rebuild the wall of Jerusalem, which had been in shambles for years. They had great opposition. You might have opposition too. This might come from your own body, your own brain, your own false beliefs, your own family and friends, your own usual patterns and habits. Determine now to face the difficulties with your ultimate help, the Lord your maker, who has a plan for you, a path of righteousness for you, and better health for you so that you can do His will. In the meantime, let's continue to use God's Word to strengthen and guide us daily.

Psalm 141 and the Application—Continuation of Prayer for Help

It is a scriptural principle that we go to God for everything. It all matters. He knows and understands us. He has a path of righteousness for you, and this is filled with the microdetails of His perfect will. Some pastors refer to the divine appointments that the Lord orchestrates.

We know this is true. Engaging the cephalic phase of the table of our day so that we continue to enhance our lives with all of the actions we have discussed these last twelve weeks is still important. Do not turn back from what you know is true. Continue to call on God for help. Just because you might have a new realization or desire to implement action does not mean you will be successful. We need His help. The psalmist does this in verses 1 and 2. He actually implores the Lord to come quickly, to hear his call. He is specific about this. He asks God to consider his prayer as an evening sacrifice, which I am sure the Lord always does. After all, a broken and contrite heart is a sacrifice to God. The psalmist also asks the Lord to keep the door of his lips, to set a guard over his mouth, to keep his heart from being drawn to evil. We need this help for everything. *We* need this help, too, not just the psalmist, not just David on a balcony. We need it. We need this help to be healthy in our spiritual lives and our physical lives and in our thought lives. We need God's help, and we need constant oversight by a tender overseer, by the Holy Spirit. We are like a child who needs to be watched or guarded and protected. It is OK. This is the way God made us. He is our Father, and He will do this.

Today, I dealt with some of this, this human condition of challenges and need for help; I needed this help to refrain from complaining and gossip, two very damaging toxins. I participated in a conversation that was somewhat less godly than what I would prefer; I will call it gossip and criticism; it was sin. I admit it. Every day brings challenges, and every day brings a chance to admit, accept, and act according to what God shows us so that we will learn, do His Word, and be ready for the next situation.

Why do we need this daily and continuous help? We need this because we constantly face enticements to draw us away from the thoughts and purposes of God, from the healthy habits of life, from all that is good. We need this constant help to refrain from bad choices, from unforgiveness, from slackness, from indulgence, from malice, from selfish ambition, from judgment, and from any sinful behavior. Enticement is all around us. It is so easy to be deceived and fooled, so easy to be lured away. So many things look safe on the package or with the person, but snares are set up for us by the enemy to get us to return to the former way of life, to carnality, to what was our usual pattern before the crossing of our personal Rubicon to a better brain, body, and belief. Let's again consider God's Word and our words as we move forward.

Our Words Matter—Chew on the Right Words

This is why your words matter and your mindset of praise matters. Just like the psalmist will lift his hands in prayer as an evening sacrifice and continue to praise the Lord, and just as he prays that God would keep a guard over his mouth, we also need to pray this. We need to praise daily, we need to watch our words, and we need to call for His help. We need to do this because our hearts can so easily be drawn to what is evil, to what is not healthy for us. If you consider that all that is unhealthy is an evil to you, you will readily see that you are surrounded by it. Just like we are in the world but not of this world, we also need to separate ourselves from the way many people view health as well as how to optimize it. You will be on a narrow path here, which is all the more reason to surround yourself with people who support and understand you, people who are committed to blameless living.

Along with this, continue to welcome the Nathans in your life. Verse 5 states it like this: "Let a righteous man strike me—that is a kindness; let him rebuke me—that is oil on my head. My head will not refuse it." Yes, take all the rebukes that come your way. Take all the challenges that spark you to stay on this road to recovery of stronger living so that you are able to do God's will. Instruction is the way of life, but so often, we know what to do and don't do it. This is where our Nathans come in. They hold us accountable so that we will keep our eyes fixed on God and what He has for us. It is a kindness to be confronted if we try to cross back to the clutter. Keep your eyes fixed on God, just like the psalmist continues to do in verse 6: "But my eyes are fixed on you, Sovereign Lord; in you I take refuge—do not give me over to death."

Consider that the more Nathans you encounter, the more enhancing that will occur. After all, a gardener prunes his garden. In a way, the gardener is a Nathan to the plant so that it will bear fruit. Jesus said, "I am the true vine, and my Father is the gardener. He cuts off every branch in me that bears no fruit, while every branch that does bear fruit he prunes so that it will be even more fruitful." Rejoice and be glad when the gardener sends a Nathan your way because this is his action to get you to admit and accept, to steer you away from the bad balconies. Realize it, receive it, and respond with clear and concise cooperation. It is a kindness to you. It is God's kindness to you even if it hurts. It's OK to say, "Ouchie," as you hold your hands to heaven like a weaned child waiting to be solaced. Pruning is a process; it is a passive position allowing the pruner, the loving expert, your heavenly Father, to handle you with care. It is a kindness.

Not only do our words matter, but remember, God's Word matters. Remember, we need to be chewing on God's Word daily. Can you keep thirty minutes of Bible reading and meditation in your daily routine? Can you keep thirty verses a day as a focus? Can you keep thirty statements of gratitude going? Yes, God's Word matters, and it is in your life. Be careful to do what it says. It is what will transform you through the power of the Holy Spirit. Along with this, remember to have the other very important stuff to chew on—real food. Just like God's Word is not in the form of another book or in the form of all the media that comes at you daily, real food is not in the form of a bag or box. Keep the focus on God and on the food He made. Chew on the real Word of God and chew on real food. Don't worry about adding more books to your reading schedule, and don't worry about adding more supplements right now. Do the basics: clear the clutter and commit to the calm with God's Word and the food He gives to satisfy you, to satisfy the longing of every living creature.

Secure Safety

The last two verses of psalm 141 address the fact that we will have temptations, snares, and opportunities to turn from the path God has for us. The psalmist prays, "Keep me safe from the traps set by evildoers, from the snare they have laid for me. Let the wicked fall into their own nets, while I pass by in safety." Consider that we live in a society with an overwhelming abundance of unsafe options. Just accept the fact that you are going to be surrounded by these, that they are unhealthy and might be evil, that they are not part of a blameless life, and that they might come from places and people who mean no harm. Remember what Jesus said to Peter when Peter opposed the idea of the Lord's death and complete sacrifice. Jesus said, "Get behind me, Satan." You might have to do some of this too. This did not mean that Peter was evil, just as it doesn't mean that your friends, family, coworkers, or church buddies are evil when they put temptations in front of you, temptations that include bags, boxes, sugar, inflammatory foods, or ideas questioning you about how you have decided to move forward with action to be healthier to do God's Word, or with temptations to gossip or talk about things you shouldn't, or even to complain or be envious or ungrateful. These are temptations that any of us can fall into. It doesn't mean they (or you) are mean and evil; it just means they don't understand and believe, or they are being tempted themselves, for if they did understand completely and believe, they would not try to talk you out of a mindset determined to build your own wall of Jerusalem, of health, or to flee your own balcony of bad behavior.

This is why you prepare in advance for success. Get your PPIs ready—your preplanned prudence that instills. Don't be ashamed of this either. It is your life. Just like Moses gave the Israelites the law of the Lord and instilled in them the truth that they must be careful to follow it, to not even bring what is evil into their homes, we also have decided to diligently follow our interventions to keep clutter cleared from the homes of our brains, bodies, and beliefs. Truly, we won't even bring it into our homes because bringing anything into our homes that is clearly from the other side of the Rubicon is like building our own little balcony, which will require Nathan to show up. Remember, admit, accept, and act according to what you believe, and now, you believe that bags, boxes, and balconies, along with stress, sugar, and lack of sleep, among other inputs and toxins, are not part of the path of righteousness God has for you. It is not part of His will for you.

Neither is complaining, grumbling, or arguing; neither is unforgiveness or malice or hatred.

Love one another. Forgive. Pass on the goodness that has been given to you to others. Freely you have been given; freely give; make sure you pass it on. Pass on the knowledge and your personal story if an opportunity presents itself. In a way, this could be a "gentle Nathan experience" for the other individual. Your effort to give in sharing with honesty is a gift to others who are hungry for the truth. It is more blessed to give than to receive. This is all to do His will. He will replenish you. Don't worry. God is faithful, and He is able to do more than we could ask or think.

And with this, I leave you to focus on the same truth that the psalmist did in his last verse of Psalm 141. "Let the wicked fall into their own nets, while I pass by in safety." Indeed, passing by safely is true for you. You have cleared, calmed, and committed to this even though others have not. You have realized, received, and responded to your Lord. Many others have not even considered this as an option, just like at one time many Israelites did not know about the law of the Lord. However, when this was found and read to Josiah the king in 2 Kings 22, he tore his robes and proceeded to spread the Word. Major changes took place. Major health improved, all because of the Word and this man who heeded it. Do not underestimate the influence you also may have with heeded-to words you have realized, received, and responded to. Remember, the goal of your health is to do God's will, not just you but everyone. It is for you, your circles, your church, and the whole world. Enhance for everyone for all of eternity. All of this is for the eternal benefit of everyone. It is all to steer people to the Lord. If we have a better brain, body, and beliefs (our stronger faith based on God's Word and instruction), we can humbly direct people to the Lord because we will be vigorous to do His will.

OK, team, let's pull out our five-column journal. Remember, you can download this from my website, www.dynamotruth.com.

Sample Chart for Enhance for Everyone for Eternity—You, Your Church, the Whole World

Topic	Brain	Body	Beliefs	Scripture and Action Steps
Enhance for everyone for eternity—you, your church, the whole world.	Focus on long-term goal with gradual improvement. Think about daily improvement in clearing, calming, modulating, and enhancing.	Remove more and more clutter from your home, brain, body, beliefs, schedule, car, pantry, fridge, garage, and so on.	I will continue to be my own Nathan. I will welcome all Nathans God puts in my life. Get off the balconies that prevent me from doing God's will or that aren't part of blameless living.	Read Psalm 141 aloud daily. Pray the psalm from your heart. Realize snares, traps, lack of support, and anything that is an obstacle and avoid it. Get a Nathan!

Column one is our topic, column two is *Brain*, column three is *Body*, column four is *Beliefs*, and column five is *Scripture and Action Steps*.

In column one, please write our topic, which is to enhance.

In column two, our brain column, please write the following: Focus on the long-term goal and what I will see, hear, and feel as long as there is gradual improvement. Think about the fact that each day I implement the clearing, calming, and modulating, I will continue to enhance. Think about the fact that every day you do this, the habits will become stronger with the implementation of your action steps. This will help you to do what is good for your health because you won't actually be making a decision, due to the fact that the habit will automatically cause you to move in the right direction. In other words, the habit will allow for automatic behavior.

In column three, our body column, please write the following: I will remove more clutter from my home and from what I am putting in my body and from what I am putting in my brain. Remove clutter from my billfold, from my car. Whatever your goal is for health, you are going to remove more and more clutter from all areas of your life to fine-tune the clearing and calming you have established by removing clutter and implementing other healthy actions and habits.

Let me share a quick story with you. Although my son is still in college, he has established a car-detailing business. His focus is on clearing clutter, cleaning carefully down to the detail. It is so interesting to notice how much cleaning and decluttering needs to be done on the inside of the car. It is easy to wash the outside of the car (except for the details), but the inside detailing takes a tremendous effort. The end product is so wonderful and impressive, however. It truly makes a difference in the beauty and value of the car, not to mention the satisfaction for the owner. It is the same with you; it will take time, but you were bought with a price, so honor God with your body, brain, and beliefs. Your body is the temple of the Holy Spirit. Your body means all of you. So commit to this personal detailing. Enhance for eternity for everyone!

In column four, our beliefs column, please write the following: I will be my own Nathan and will welcome any rebuke I get from any other Nathan God brings into my life. We want Nathans in our lives. Do not oppose the Nathans in your life because if you do, you are opposing God! Even if it is a donkey, you take it; you take what the Nathan tells you. Get off the balcony that Nathan confronts you about; throw the bag or box away. (So what if it costs you money; it isn't in line with your goals!). The message from the Nathan could even be a look from someone that causes you to realize you must continue to call on God for help, chew on His Word, and remember that He will allow you to pass by in safety from the traps that surround you. A Nathan in your life is God saying to you, "I love you, and I will continue to redeem you from all."

In column five, our scripture and action steps, please write our scripture of Psalm 141. Here are your action steps:

1. Read Psalm 141 daily. Pray this whole psalm from your heart. This is about continuing on, calling on God for help again and again, and passing by in safety.

2. Realize that you are going to encounter traps, snares, lack of support, evil/unhealthy suggestions, or temptations that might be a step in the wrong direction. Anticipate this, prepare for this, and acknowledge how you might be weak. Try to avoid these challenging encounters and put a plan in place to resist them. For instance, a friend might invite you to an event that is not a good location for you; it could be a balcony that beckons you to what you know is not healthy or godly. It could be a restaurant, a party, a social gathering with people who lead you astray to wrong ideas. Call upon the Lord now. Go to His Word now. Determine if you should avoid it and not even consider it as an option. Go to God. Call upon him like the psalmist did in Psalm 141; this calling upon the Lord will never stop; it will always be a part of your daily walk.

3. If you don't have a Nathan, get one. Let a righteous man strike you; it will be a kindness. Actually count the number of reproofs or corrections you get this week; take these with humility and thank God for them. Hope that you get thirty and give thanks for each one. There is my theme of thirty again.

4. Pray! A sample prayer is below. We must always pray. We have to ask God for help and be willing to admit to Him that we are struggling. Situations that cause you a lack of peace will always present themselves, but our Lord is greater than any situation, and nothing is too difficult for Him. We cannot calm the storm ourselves; we cannot make the wind and the waves obey us, but our Lord can, and He can make the wind and the waves and the storm of your body and brain calm. He can do this. Thank Him for what you have, for the "two fish and the loaves" that you have, and see what He will do with them. I don't care what it is. It's amazing what the master can do. It is amazing!

Lord, how I praise You. Lord, I lift my hands up to You; I lift my prayer up to You like a sacrifice because it is acknowledging that You are God and that You are my help. Lord, keep my eyes fixed on You and keep the words of my mouth full of Your words, full of the law of the Lord because, Lord, this is what truly nourishes and strengthens me. It keeps me on the path of righteousness that You have for me. Lord, it is life. Lord, do not let my heart be drawn to what is evil, to what is unhealthy, to what is a danger to me or to others. Lord, please put righteous and wise people in my life to confront, rebuke, and strike me so that I turn from what is harmful. Lord, this is Your kindness. Lord, I know You are with me, and no matter what snares or traps I encounter, You are able to guide me in safety. Lord, I will fix my gaze on You, and I will trust You as I continue to realize, receive, and respond to Your constant help and guidance to do Your will. Thank You, Lord.

Well, team, I am so glad you joined me through this whole process. This wraps up week twelve of my Health through the Psalms twelve-week program. I have absolutely loved being transformed by this and look forward to more calming, clearing, modulating, and enhancing in my brain, body, and beliefs so that I can do God's will with vigor and love. I invite you to go to my YouTube channel (Dynamo Truth Health and Wellness) to watch recent videos, to be encouraged, and to know that you are not alone but are surrounded by the goodness of God. Please look for more handouts on my website. But most importantly, please go to God and His Word. Please look to Him. Realize again and again what He shows you. Receive again and again what He teaches you. Respond again and again to His truth. Admit, accept, and act according to this so that you do His will and do it well, with vigor. This will truly be for you, your family, your church, and the whole world— for everyone for eternity.

CONCLUSION

Please receive this concluding word from me. I want to summarize the twelve main points of the program, the spiritual and physical connections, the scriptures that were used, and the quick liners that might be a good reminder and stimulus for you when you encounter struggles or when you just want to brush up on the truth as it pertains to your life. I also want to share with you how these last twelve weeks have impacted me. As usual, none of this is medical advice. This is my effort to do good, to seek peace, and to pursue it using scripture, God's Word, and sound information.

I am so glad you have come this far. I am passionately diligent to help people get healthy, no matter in what areas of their lives they have concerns, whether it is financial, relational, or emotional, whether it is in dealing with anxiety, spiritual setbacks, weight gain and illness, or learning and cognitive challenges. I also want people to see the spiritual connections and the whole well-being of their person because it all matters. It is all connected, and when something in your life or mine is not healthy, it causes stress, and stress makes us unhealthy. God wants us to have peace. So let's move forward with this truth in mind, that God wants us to have peace, and this peace comes from Him and His truth.

I must share the impetus of this program, however. In the beginning of 2022, my pastor wanted a focus on the psalms during our worship time. So each Sunday, between worship songs, our worship leader would read a psalm or part of a psalm as part of our worship. It's been a good part of hearing God's Word. His spoken word is so powerful. Because of my pastor's focus and because I knew that there was a powerful connection of the psalms to our health (as all of God's Word is), I decided to go with his lead and create a twelve-week program based on the twelve main health points that I would use with anyone for their health, whether for weight loss, type 2 diabetes, cardiac issues, fatigue, anxiety, poor sleep, or blood sugar regulation, but I would specifically use the psalms as the scripture for the program. I have absolutely loved this experience. In fact, I never thought it would have an impact on me like it has. I am so challenged by what God has shown me and very thankful for this challenge. This in itself is an accountability tool for me. So I thank my pastor, and I thank God for this new realization that is in my life and how it has nourished me.

I have loved the psalms my whole life and have probably spent far too much time in them compared to other parts of scripture, but the emotional outpouring, the hope, the admission of shame, regret, disappointment, guilt, agony, thankfulness, concern, fear, strength, despair, and so many other emotions are linked to our health. The hope that Psalms gives shows us how we can have hope because God is our strength; He is our hope; He is our everything, including our health.

The Before

I first want to share with you that my original goal with this twelve-week program was to implement the psalms and make a connection between these and our health. The specific connections I wanted to make were incorporated into three phases. The first phase discussed how our genes can be influenced by our choices and included the topics of environment, movement, mindset, and food. The second phase emphasized that our digestion can be improved and included the topics of the cephalic, the mechanical, the digestive, and the microbial phases. The final phase acknowledged that inflammation was behind disease and that we can combat this by clearing, calming, modulating, and enhancing all that we have been doing. (These well-devised topics were based on the work of other practitioners, such as my mentor in the Functional Nutrition Alliance, where I have become certified as a functional nutrition and lifestyle practitioner.)

My goal was to instruct you, not to challenge me, but I have to be honest here. I have been so challenged. I, of course, wanted to keep myself accountable to what I believe, but I never expected to be so challenged by the truth. I also did not expect to have so many struggles and so much stress while I was developing this twelve-week psalm-based program. I did not deal with all of this stress with complete success either. However, I will move forward and not look back. Just like I have emphasized with you that this is a daily process, so it is with me, and it is with everybody. We can't live on the successes or obedience or good choices of yesterday; each day, we proceed forward and do it all again. We must look to the Lord first and proceed on the path He has for us, with the mindset of gratitude. We don't need to dwell on the past failures of yesterday either. Every day, His faithfulness is new; every morning are new mercies.

The Transformation in Me

As I said, my goal was to instruct, but what I did not anticipate was that I would realize, receive, and respond to the overall theme of the twelve-week program, which was this: the ultimate goal of health is to do God's will. I had compartmentalized health to fulfill the desire all of us have to be happy and feel good and stay clear of disease. I wanted everyone to get peace in their brains, bodies, and beliefs and to have good relationships and contentment. However, as the weeks proceeded, my realization was that none of this means anything if we do not believe that our agenda should be about God's agenda, to do His will, not just for our personal benefit but for the whole church and the whole world.

We all are connected to one another, and whether we realize it or not, we affect one another. The apostle Paul laid this out clearly in Romans 12 when he instructed us about the different parts of the body and the different gifts we each have. If we are not healthy, the whole church is not healthy. If we are not doing God's will, the whole church is not doing God's will. This is not just about our personal goals or our personal health. It is about a greater goal, a greater good, and this is for eternity, for everyone.

We actually have a responsibility to seek peace and pursue it in our brains, bodies, and beliefs. If we do not have peace, the whole church does not have peace because we are part of the church. It is like the chain on a bicycle. If one link is broken, the whole chain is broken and won't fulfill its purpose. It is the same with the body of Christ. Our position in the body of Christ is for the whole church. We all are a part of the body of Christ. If one part of our physical body is injured, we know we need to seek treatment and take action for healing so that we can function according to how we were created and for the purpose we were created. How much more do we need to have peace in our brains, bodies, and beliefs so that we function within the body of Christ the way God intends for us.

So the *before* here is that I had not even arrived at this epiphany, this realization that the goal of health is to do God's will. I had never formulated this in my own heart and mind. But this is the goal of our health—to do God's will. We can never make a mistake with this mindset and intention, and I am very glad for this transformation because it's really given me a new focus on God's will and is a daily prayer. For years, I have prayed that I would remain in God's will, that my husband and I would do His will, and that our children would be in His will. Even though I already had that mindset, I have a new realization that for everything we want, we need to see how it plays into God's will, into His path of righteousness for us—not our path but His path.

The After

I guess you could say that I have crossed another Rubicon in my life. To be honest, achieving health has always been a selfish ambition on my part; it was all about me and feeling good, strong, better, happy, and energetic. It was about looking good and doing the right thing or the good thing, being prudent and conscientious. Now I strongly believe that none of this matters if I am not focused on God's will. Yes, I wanted to do God's will before, but now I see the huge connection between my health and doing God's will. I want to be healthy for this; I want to be healthy to do God's will. I have realized it and received it, and now I will proceed by responding daily to this truth, to this goal. I hope you will too. I will be thrilled to hear that you have achieved better health following all of this instruction, but if you are not using this for the benefit of doing God's will and seeking this out, you are missing the whole intention. Let's move forward together and be committed to doing His will by making choices that promote a better brain, body, and belief.

The other realization that I have had is that it is not just about me or you or one little group of people. It is not just about getting smarter, stronger, or healthier for your or my personal aspirations or goals. It is not even so that we live a long life. It is about living for God's purpose while we are alive. It is about the whole body of Christ and the whole world for all of eternity. Jesus said to go into all the world and preach the gospel. What more important purpose could any of us realize than that getting stronger and healthier better equips us to go into all the world to preach the gospel? What more loving example could we portray to everyone that the reason for our actions to be healthy is really embedded in our mindset, our belief, and our acceptance that it is about everyone else, not just ourselves? Isn't this love in action?

I am not saying that you should not or will never get sick or will be free from health issues, but when you do, or if you do, having the mindset that you are abounding in the work of the Lord and that He has a path of righteousness for you, a path of peace, must be a part of your focus. The Lord is able to use everything for good. He is always with you, and how you feel or how healthy you are is not just for you; it is for everyone. It is not just about you. As Jesus said before raising someone from the dead, "This sickness is not unto death but for the glory of God." Jesus knew that He was always about doing the will of the Father. This is love in action, doing God's will. Always remember, however, that when health challenges come, you have a set of tools here that will always be relevant and useful. Do not disregard them. Again, even if you have health challenges, the material in this twelve-week program is relevant in dealing with the challenges. Even if you do not have health challenges, this material is relevant; it is relevant for all of us. It is sound information and based on what is true.

Remember that even though your or my choice here is about the whole world, you do not have to go across the ocean for this; you do not have to forsake your loved ones for this. The whole world includes little children, nursing homes, people with disabilities, the depressed and forsaken, the recluses, the coworker who mistreats you, the boss that takes you for granted, the people in your church body who have hurt you, and everyone else you see each day. Move out of yourself and move forward with action to effect changes in the environments of these people. You have no idea what God is able to do with just one small effort on your part. Leave the details to Him. The fish and the loaves are enough to remind us that God is able to do above and beyond what we could ask or think. The little boy shared his food with the crowd, and God multiplied his kindness, his giving, to be a huge blessing for so many. Indeed, He satisfied them with good things.

We move forward with this intention and realization, that although we certainly want to feel good, the greater purpose is about everyone, not just us. After all, think about the other blessings you have in your life: strong finances, musical skills, compassionate personalities, extra time on your hands. We think nothing of using these for the benefit of others. If we have strong finances, we probably give more money to the church and those in need. If we have certain skills, we probably use these for the benefit of the whole church and for others. Why does it have to be different with our good health? Making the decision to improve your health, no matter what area of your health, puts you in a position for God to use you in a way that you may have never even considered. You might meet new people who have some of the same health challenges you have. You might meet others who need some advice on personal matters. You might meet others who need guidance that could be inspired by your skills and abilities. You never know what door God will open.

Definitely, God can bring you out into a spacious place to be a light and encouragement to others, and remember, I am not just talking about physical health. I am talking about mental health, spiritual health, financial health, organizational health, relationship health. These all affect your total being and your total health. If you have poor relationships, there's probably a spiritual connection involved here, and this is definitely going to impact your physical health. If you have poor financial health and you are stressed, you indeed are going to experience more mental and physical health challenges and possibly belief challenges. Possibly you are not trusting God like you would hope to because you are encompassed by disorganization with your finances or you are in disobedience with your finances.

Who knows? You could be in rebellion because you choose to hold resentment toward someone. All of these things matter, and they affect your body. What you think matters. What you feel affects your body. We must strive to have God's Word as our focus. We need comfort from the psalms. All of this matters, and so if you have wrong thinking, and then on top of that, you throw in toxins like sugar and gluten or perfumes that you are reacting to, or even if your life is disorganized and dirty, your complete health will be affected. All of this is going to affect your body. Move forward with action. Ask God to show you what you need to do that will help. One small change could be a huge needle mover for your life. Health and healing are up to God, but He works with us. He works with our decisions to say, "Yes, Lord!" Be like the little boy with the loaves and the fish. He shared, and God multiplied. Turn to Him and just put your hands up and open to Him. Be ready to receive what He shows you; realize it and then respond. Trust Him.

At this time, I would like to provide brevity to our twelve weeks. Below is a chart that gives a reminder of the particular physical topic we covered, along with the spiritual analogy and a quick statement to make it simple. Here it is:

Topic	Spiritual Connection	Statement	Scripture
Week 1 Environment	Blameless life.	Clear the clutter.	Psalm 101
Week 2 Movement	Move out of spiritual oppression; spacious place.	Movement out of physical oppression. Exercise.	Psalm 25
Week 3 Mindset	Attitude of gratitude.	Your psychology dictates your biology; what you think matters.	Psalm 103

Week 4 Food	God's Word is spiritual food.	Food is medicine. Not in a bag or box.	Psalm 104
Week 5 Cephalic Phase	Table of concern; wait in expectation.	Digestion begins in the brain.	Psalm 5
Week 6 Mechanical Phase	Chew on God's Word.	Chew each bite thirty times.	Psalm 90
Week 7 Chemical Phase	God is our help.	Stomach acid is our most powerful help for digestion.	Psalm 121
Week 8 Microbial Phase	Do not despise the small things.	Gut-brain connection.	Psalm 139
Week 9 Clear	Clear the spiritual clutter of your heart.	Clear the clutter of brain, body, and beliefs completely.	Psalm 130
Week 10 Calm	Like a weaned child.	Calm down; reduce stress.	Psalm 131
Week 11 Modulate	Create in me a clean heart.	Health starts on the inside.	Psalm 51
Week 12 Enhance	Enhance for everyone for eternity.	Keep at it! Don't give up!	Psalm 141

I hope that chart makes sense to you. Let me do some explaining. The chart, as I said, is to be a quick reminder of the particular physical topic we covered, along with the spiritual analogy and a quick statement to make it simple.

During week one, we talked about the environment. We used Psalm 101, and the spiritual connection was living a blameless life. Our other connection was to clear the clutter.

Week two focused on movement, and we used Psalm 25. The spiritual connection was to move out of spiritual oppression into a spacious place. God does that for us. The statement for our physical health was movement out of physical oppression. Exercise, exercise, exercise.

During week three, we focused on mindset and used Psalm 103. It was about the attitude of gratitude—the antidote for everything in my opinion. Our statement for physical health and mental health was "Our psychology dictates our biology." What you think matters. It affects you and me. So think on what is true, pure, lovely, just, of good report, and what is praiseworthy. Think upon these things, and the God of peace will be with you. The psalms are full of things to think on that will bring you great peace.

During week four, we focused on Psalm 104. The spiritual connection was "God's Word is spiritual food." We finally got to the topic of food during week four, and believe me, food affects how you and I think and how we respond to God's Word, which is going to affect our academic performance, how we make decisions, and how we spend our time and money. It's going to affect our hunger pains. Do not dismiss this as though it doesn't matter. The statement for this is "Food is medicine. It's not in a bag or a box."

During week five, we focused on the cephalic phase of digestion, which, as you hopefully remember, starts in your head, in your brain, even before you sit down to eat. We used Psalm 5 to remind us to lay our requests before the Lord and wait in expectation. We talked about the table of concern and all the different tables we will encounter. The statement for physical health is "Digestion begins in the brain."

During week six, we focused on the mechanical phase of digestion and used Psalm 90 to remind ourselves to chew on God's Word. Our statement was, "Chew, chew, chew!" Chew each bite thirty times. It helps digestion.

During week seven, we used Psalm 121 to talk about the chemical phase of digestion. The statement for our spiritual connection was "God is our help," and our statement for our physical connection was "Stomach acid is our most powerful help for digestion." Get rid of those PPIs, which decrease stomach acid.

During week eight, we focused on the microbial phase of digestion and used Psalm 139. I love this spiritual connection. Kudos to my pastor because he has taught me also to "not despise the small things." The statement is simply "The gut-brain connection," and that these small things matter. They add up. Every grain of sand, every drop in the ocean, every little seed we plant; they add up. If you want something to grow, get planting the seeds. So do not despise the small things.

During week nine, we used Psalm 130 and focused on clearing up the spiritual clutter of our hearts. We were talking about the sins of the heart: lust, greed, unforgiveness, bitterness, wrath, anger, and other challenging emotions. Oh, please clear it. Get free; confess it to the Lord. Our statement for physical health was "Clear the clutter completely." This is just fine-tuning. The toxins you put into your body, which affect your brain and your spiritual life, are important to remove. When we feel cruddy or we feel tired, lethargic, or fatigued, we don't feel like doing God's will. We don't feel like studying His Word. We don't feel like forgiving. So clear clutter completely.

During week ten, we used Psalm 131, and our spiritual connection was "Like a weaned child." Oh, just let the Lord hold you. The physical connection was to "calm down, reduce stress." Let God handle it. He's got this! Thank the Lord. He is able to do above and beyond what we could ask or think.

During week eleven, we used Psalm 51 to focus on *modulate*. The spiritual connection was to pray as David did, "Create in me a clean heart, O God." The physical connection was that "health starts on the inside." If you are not healthy on the inside, which no one can see, you are not healthy. We can't see it. You might think you look healthy because your weight might be in an acceptable range or your skin doesn't show intolerances, but you could have a volcano inside of you ready to erupt. This would not be healthy. This inside health takes time to show up on the outside. It takes time to get healthy too, so don't give up.

During week twelve, our last week, we used Psalm 141. Our spiritual connection was to "enhance for everyone for eternity." It's not just about you. It's about the whole body of Christ, your whole community, your circles, and the whole world. The statement was to "keep at it; don't give up."

I hope this chart helps you. Just a quick glance could be encouraging to you and remind you of what is important. This is to help all of us do God's will and remind us that His Word is powerful, prayer is powerful, and reminders and goals are powerful. I don't want to forget these tidbits of helpful information. Remember, the whole focus has changed me too. Although I know I want this in my life, I need constant reminders. It is so easy to forget and get slack. It is easy to know and not do. It is easy to be a hearer only and not a doer. Usually, we know what to do. It's doing it that is hard. Take a small step in the direction of doing.

This is why we emphasized from the beginning, with Psalm 1 as our guide, that we must meditate on God's Word day and night. We are human. We forget. We get slack. We disregard. We talk ourselves out of things. We talk ourselves out of good things because we are fighting our carnal nature. Our carnal nature and our flesh fight against our spiritual goal to do God's will. Iron sharpens iron, so one man sharpens another. The man, the woman, the mentor, the confidant, or the encourager does not need to be right beside you to sharpen you, although that is helpful. But truly, we are able to sharpen one another through prayer, through a word of encouragement via a phone or text or email, and of course, praying diligently for people and being with them in person. Those are powerful, but even the words on the page will sharpen you. This is why we look at God's Word daily, to be sharpened so that we know Him and become better equipped to do His will. It's all about doing God's will, and this means peace and love. Love one another; obey Him. "When I obeyed you, then I understood your law." Obey Him; move forward with a step of obedience to bring peace, to bring love to people. This helps your health; it helps you to be abounding in the work of the Lord; it helps you to do His will. When you don't know what to do, just take a step forward with the action you know you are supposed to do. Don't be hesitant; don't be oppressed or stifled. Move forward with God as your focus.

In conclusion, let me just reiterate my overall goal for all things based on God's Word: to seek peace and pursue it. This is God's will for everyone. When we have peace, we have health. Peace promotes mental health, physical health, and spiritual health. The ultimate reason to be healthy is not just so we can feel good about ourselves; it isn't so we look good and feel good; it isn't so that we have energy to achieve career success or to impress others. The ultimate reason for health is to do God's will, to enhance the eternal benefit for everyone—for you, your family, your church, your circles, and the whole world. Admit, accept, and take action on what God shows you to do. Realize it, receive it, and respond to it so that you have a better brain and body, to believe what is true by keeping your law of health to guide you, but more importantly by keeping the law of the Lord as a day and night focus. It is your life!

Seek peace and pursue it forever!

I love you all and pray for you; we are in this together, and God is able. Nothing is too hard for the Lord.

ABOUT THE AUTHOR

Maureen Greer is both a teacher and a nurse. She holds three undergraduate degrees in education, nursing, and music and a master's in educational psychology and has devoted her life to the training and teaching of her six children. When her sixth child was born with Down syndrome, she began researching the brain/body connection and the impact that diet and lifestyle have on the development of the whole person. Her purpose is to seek peace and pursue it. She seeks to encourage others by guiding them to make strategic choices that will help them act with truth by replacing the misinformation they might believe with what is actually true. Her hope is to inspire others to rely on God for their strength and truth and to see that their faith and obedience to God, along with their knowledge of His Word, are foundational in their overall health for their whole life span.

Printed in the United States
by Baker & Taylor Publisher Services